The History of América
by William Robertson (D.D.)

Address:
HardPress
8345 NW 66TH ST #2561
MIAMI FL 33166-2626
USA
Email: info@hardpress.net

THE

HISTORY

OF

AMERICA.

VOL. III.

THE

HISTORY

OF

AMERICA.

By *WILLIAM ROBERTSON, D. D.*

PRINCIPAL OF THE UNIVERSITY OF EDINBURGH,

HISTORIOGRAPHER TO HIS MAJESTY FOR SCOTLAND,

AND MEMBER OF THE ROYAL ACADEMY OF HISTORY AT MADRID.

IN THREE VOLUMES.

VOL. III.

EDINBURGH:

PRINTED BY J. ROBERTSON, FOR THE BOOKSELLERS.

M,DCCC,V.

THE
HISTORY
OF
AMERICA.

BOOK VI.

Continued.

BUT, among the Peruvians, this unbounded power of their monarchs seems to have been uniformly accompanied with attention to the good of their subjects. It was not the rage of conquest, if we may believe the accounts of their countrymen, that prompted the Incas to extend their dominions, but the desire of diffusing the blessings of civilization, and the knowledge of the arts which they possessed, among the barbarous people whom they reduced. During a succession of twelve monarchs, it is said that not one deviated from this beneficent character *.

When the Spaniards first visited the coast of Peru, in the year one thousand five hundred and twenty-six, Huana Capac, the twelfth mo-

* Cieca de Leon, Chron. c. 44. Herrera, dec. 3. lib. x. c. 4. dec. 5. lib. iii. c. 17.

narch from the founder of the state, was seated
on the throne.   He is represented as a prince
distinguished not only for the pacific virtues
peculiar to the race, but eminent for his martial talents.   By his victorious arms the kingdom of Quito was subjected, a conquest of
such extent and importance as almost doubled
the power of the Peruvian empire.   He was
fond of residing in the capital of that valuable
province which he had added to his dominions; and, notwithstanding the ancient and
fundamental law of the monarchy against pol-
luting the royal blood by any foreign alliance,
he married the daughter of the vanquished
monarch of Quito.   She bore him a son
named Atahualpa, whom, on his death at Quito, which seems to have happened about the
year one thousand five hundred and twenty-
nine, he appointed his successor in that kingdom, leaving the rest of his dominions to Huascar, his eldest son, by a mother of the royal race.   Greatly as the Peruvians revered
the memory of a monarch who had reigned
with greater reputation and splendour than
any of his predecessors, the destination of
Huana Capac concerning the succession, appeared so repugnant to a maxim coeval with
the empire, and founded on authority deemed
sacred, that it was no sooner known at Cuzco
than it excited general disgust.   Encouraged
by those sentiments of his subjects, Huascar
required his brother to renounce the government of Quito, and to acknowledge him as
his lawful superior.   But it had been the first
care of Atahualpa to gain a large body of

troops which had accompanied his father to Quito. These were the flower of the Peruvian warriors, to whose valour Huana Capac had been indebted for all his victories. Relying on their support, Atahualpa first eluded his brother's demand, and then marched against him in hostile array.

Thus the ambition of two young men, the title of the one founded on ancient usage, and that of the other asserted by the veteran troops, involved Peru in civil war, a calamity to which, under a succession of virtuous princes, it had hitherto been a stranger. In such a contest the issue was obvious. The force of arms triumphed over the authority of laws. Atahualpa remained victorious, and made a cruel use of his victory. Conscious of the defect in his own title to the crown, he attempted to exterminate the royal race, by putting to death all the children of the Sun descended from Manco Capac, whom he could seize either by force or stratagem. From a political motive, the life of his unfortunate rival Huascar, who had been taken prisoner in a battle which decided the fate of the empire, was prolonged for some time, that, by issuing orders in his name, the usurper might more easily establish his own authority *.

When Pizarro landed in the bay of St. Matthew, this civil war raged between the two brothers in its greatest fury. Had he made any hostile attempt in his former visit to Peru, in the year one thousand five hundred and twenty-

* Zarate, lib. i. c. 15.   Vega, 1. lib. ix. c. 11. and 32—40.   Herrera, dec. 5. lib. i. c. 2. lib. iii. c. 17.

seven, he must then have encountered the force of a powerful state, united under a monarch, possessed of capacity as well as courage, and unembarrassed with any care that could divert him from opposing his progress. But at this time, the two competitors, though they received early accounts of the arrival and violent proceedings of the Spaniards, were so intent upon the operations of a war which they deemed more interesting, that they paid no attention to the motions of an enemy, too inconsiderable in number to excite any great alarm, and to whom it would be easy, as they imagined, to give a check when more at leisure.

By this fortunate coincidence of events, whereof Pizarro could have no foresight, and of which, from his defective mode of intercourse with the people of the country, he remained long ignorant, he was permitted to carry on his operations unmolested, and advanced to the centre of a great empire before one effort of its power was exerted to stop his career. During their progress, the Spaniards had acquired some imperfect knowledge of this struggle between the two contending factions. The first complete information with respect to it, they received from messengers whom Huascar sent to Pizarro, in order to solicit his aid against Atahualpa, whom he represented as a rebel and an usurper *. Pizarro perceived at once the importance of this intelligence, and foresaw so clearly all the advantages which might be derived from this divided state of the kingdom which he had invaded, that, without waiting for the reinforcement

* Zarate, lib. ii. c. 3.

which he expected from Panama, he determined to push forward, while intestine discord put it out of the power of the Peruvians to attack him with their whole force, and while, by taking part, as circumstances should incline him, with one of the competitors, he might be enabled with greater ease to crush both. Enterprising as the Spaniards of that age were in all their operations against Americans, and distinguished as Pizarro was among his countrymen for daring courage, we can hardly suppose, that after having proceeded hitherto slowly, and with much caution, he would have changed at once his system of operation, and have ventured upon a measure so hazardous, without some new motive or prospect to justify it.

As he was obliged to divide his troops, in order to leave a garrison in St. Michael, sufficient to defend a station of equal importance as a place of retreat, in case of any disaster, and as a port for receiving any supplies which should come from Panama, he began his march with a very slender and ill-accoutred train of followers. They consisted of sixty-two horsemen *, and a hundred and two foot-soldiers, of whom twenty were armed with cross-bows, and three with muskets. He directed his course towards Caxamalca, a small town at the distance of twelve days march from St. Michael, where Atahualpa was encamped with a considerable body of troops. Before he had proceeded far, an officer dispatched by the Inca met him with a valuable present from that prince, accompanied with a proffer of

* See Note CXXVIII.

his alliance, and assurances of a friendly reception at Caxamalca.   Pizarro, according to the
usual artifice of his countrymen in America,
pretended to come as the ambassador of a very
powerful monarch, and declared that he was now
advancing with an intention to offer Atahualpa
his aid against those enemies who disputed his
title to the throne *.

As the object of the Spaniards in entering
their country was altogether incomprehensible to
the Peruvians, they had formed various conjectures concerning it, without being able to decide
whether they should consider their new guests as
beings of a superior nature, who had visited them
from some beneficent motive, or as formidable
avengers of their crimes, and enemies to their
repose and liberty.   The continual professions of
the Spaniards, that they came to enlighten them
with the knowledge of truth, and lead them in
the way of happiness, favoured the former opinion ; the outrages which they committed, their
rapaciousness and cruelty, were awful confirma-
tions of the latter.   While in this state of uncertainty, Pizarro's declaration of his pacific intentions so far removed all the the Inca's fears, that
he determined to give him a friendly reception.   In
consequence of this resolution, the Spaniards were
allowed to march in tranquillity across the sandy
desert between St. Michael and Motupè, where
the most feeble effort of an enemy, added to the
unavoidable distresses which they suffered in passing through that comfortless region, must have
proved fatal to them †.   From Montupè they

* Herrera, dec. 5. lib. i. c. 3.   Xerez, p. 189.
† See Note CXXIX.

advanced towards the mountains which encom‡
passed the low country of Peru, and passed
through a defile so narrow and inaccessible, that
a few men might have defended it against a numerous army. But here likewise, from the same
inconsiderate credulity of the Inca, the Spaniards met with no opposition, and took quiet
possession of a fort erected for the security of
that important station. As they now approached
near to Caxamalca, Atahualpa renewed his professions of friendship; and as an evidence of
their sincerity, sent them presents of greater
value than the former.

On entering Caxamalca, Pizarro took possession of a large court, on one side of which was
a house which the Spanish historians call a palace
of the Inca, and on the other a temple of the
Sun, the whole surrounded with a strong ram-
part or wall of earth. When he had posted his
troops in this advantageous station, he dispatched
his brother Ferdinand and Hernando Soto to the
camp of Atahualpa, which was about a league
distant from the town. He instructed them to
confirm the declaration which he had formerly
made of his pacific disposition, and to desire
an interview with the Inca, that he might explain more fully the intention of the Spaniards in
visiting his country. They were treated with
all the respectful hospitality usual among the
Peruvians in the reception of their most cordial
friends, and Atahualpa promised to visit the
Spanish commander next day in his quarters.
The decent deportment of the Peruvian monarch,
the order of his court, and the reverence with
which his subjects approached his person and

obeyed his commands, astonished those Spaniards, who had never met in America with any thing more dignified than the petty cazique of a barbarous tribe. But their eyes were still more powerfully attracted by the vast profusion of wealth which they observed in the Inca's camp. The rich ornaments worn by him and his attendants, the vessels of gold and silver in which the repast offered to them was served up, the multitude of utensils of every kind formed of those precious metals, opened prospects far exceeding any idea of opulence that a European of the sixteenth century could form.

On their return to Caxamalca, while their minds were yet warm with admiration and desire of the wealth which they had beheld, they gave such a description of it to their countrymen, as confirmed Pizarro in a resolution which he had already taken. From his own observation of American manners during his long service in the New World, as well as from the advantages which Cortes had derived from seizing Montezuma, he knew of what consequence it was to have the Inca in his power. For this purpose, he formed a plan as daring as it was perfidious. Notwithstanding the character that he had assumed of an ambassador from a powerful monarch, who courted an alliance with the Inca, and in violation of the repeated offers which he had made to him of his own friendship and assistance, he determined to avail himself of the unsuspicious simplicity with which Atahualpa relied on his professions, and to seize the person of the Inca during the interview to which he had invited him. He prepared for the execution of his scheme with the same deliberate arrangement, and with as little compunction, as if it had reflected no disgrace on himself or his country. He divided his cavalry into three small squadrons, under the command of his brother Ferdinand, Soto, and Benalcazar; his infantry were formed in one body, except twenty of most tried courage, whom he kept near his own person to support him in the dangerous service which he reserved for himself; the artillery, consisting of two field-pieces * and the cross bowmen, were placed opposite to the avenue by which Atahualpa was to approach. All were commanded to keep within the square, and not to move until the signal for action was given.

Early in the morning [Nov. 16] the Peruvian camp was all in motion. But as Atahualpa was solicitous to appear with the greatest splendour and magnificence in his first interview with the strangers, the preparations for this were so tedious, that the day was far advanced before he began his march. Even then, lest the order of the procession should be deranged, he moved so slowly, that the Spaniards became impatient, and apprehensive that some suspicion of their intention might be the cause of this delay. In order to remove this, Pizarro dispatched one of his officers with fresh assurances of his friendly disposition. At length the Inca approached. First of all appeared four hundred men, in an uniform dress, as harbingers to clear the way before him. He himself sitting on a throne or couch, adorned with plumes of various colours,

* Xerez, p. 194.

and almost covered with plates of gold and silver enriched with precious stones, was carried on the shoulders of his principal attendants. Behind him came some chief officers of his court, carried in the same manner. Several bands of singers and dancers accompanied this cavalcade ; and the whole plain was covered with troops, a-mounting to more than thirty thousand men.

As the Inca drew near the Spanish quarters, father Vincent Valverde, chaplain to the expe-dition, advanced with a crucifix in one hand, and a breviary in the other, and in a long discourse explained to him the doctrine of the creation, the fall of Adam, the incarnation, the sufferings, and resurrection of Jesus Christ, the appointment of St. Peter as God's vicegerent on earth, the transmission of his apostolic power by succession to the popes, the donation made to the king of Castile by pope Alexander of all the regions in the New World. In consequence of all this, he required Atahualpa to embrace the Christian faith, to acknowledge the supreme jurisdiction of the pope, and to submit to the king of Castile as his lawful sovereign ; promising, if he complied instantly with this requisition, that the Castilian monarch would protect his dominions, and per-mit him to continue in the exercise of his royal authority ; but if he should impiously refuse to obey this summons, he denounced war against him in his master's name, and threatened him with the most dreadful effects of his ven-geance.

This strange harangue, unfolding deep myste-ries, and alluding to unknown facts, of which no power of eloquence could have conveyed at once a distinct idea to an American, was so lamely translated by an unskilful interpreter, little acquainted with the idiom of the Spanish tongue, and incapable of expressing himself with propriety in the language of the Inca, that its general tenor was altogether incomprehensible to Atabualpa. Some parts in it, of more obvious meaning, filled him with astonishment and indignation. His reply, however, was temperate. He began with observing, that he was lord of the dominions over which he reigned by hereditary succession; and added, that he could not conceive how a foreign priest should pretend to dispose of territories which did not belong to him; that if such a preposterous grant had been made, he, who was the rightful possessor, refused to confirm it; that he had no inclination to renounce the religious institutions established by his ancestors; nor would he forsake the service of the Sun, the immortal divinity whom he and his people revered, in order to worship the God of the Spaniards, who was subject to death; that with respect to other matters contained in his discourse, as he had never heard of them before, and did not now understand their meaning, he desired to know where the priest had learned things so extraordinary. "In this book," answered Valverde, reaching out to him his breviary. The Inca opened it eagerly, and turning over the leaves, lifted it to his ear: "This," says he, "is silent; it tells me nothing;" and threw it with disdain to the ground. The enraged monk, running towards his countrymen, cried out, "To arms, Christians, to arms; the word of God is insulted; avenge this profanation on those impious dogs *."

Pizarro, who, during this long conference, had with difficulty restrained his soldiers, eager to seize the rich spoils of which they had now so near a view, immediately gave the signal of assault. At once the martial music struck up, the cannon and muskets began to fire, the horse sallied out fiercely to the charge, the infantry rushed on sword in hand. The Peruvians, astonished at the suddenness of an attack which they did not expect, and dismayed with the destructive effect of the fire-arms, and the irresistible impression of the cavalry, fled with universal consternation on every side, without attempting either to annoy the enemy, or to defend themselves. Pizarro, at the head of his chosen band, advanced directly towards the Inca; and though his nobles crowded around him with officious zeal, and fell in numbers at his feet, while they vied one with another in sacrificing their own lives, that they might cover the sacred person of their sovereign, the Spaniards soon penetrated to the royal seat; and Pizarro seizing the Inca by the arm, dragged him to the ground, and carried him as a prisoner to his quarters. The fate of the monarch increased the precipitate flight of his followers. The Spaniards pursued them towards every quarter, and with deliberate and unrelenting barbarity continued to slaughter wretched fugitives, who never once offered to resist. The carnage did not cease until the close of day. Above four thousand Peruvians were killed. Not a single Spaniard fell, nor was one

* See Note CXXX.

wounded but Pizarro himself, whose hand was slightly hurt by one of his own soldiers, while struggling eagerly to lay hold on the Inca *.

The plunder of the field was rich beyond any idea which the Spaniards had yet formed concerning the wealth of Peru; and they were so transported with the value of the acquisition, as well as the greatness of their success, that they passed the night in the extravagant exultation natural to indigent adventurers on such an extraordinary change of fortune.

At first the captive monarch could hardly believe a calamity which he so little expected to be real. But he soon felt all the misery of his fate, and the dejection into which he sunk was in proportion to the height of grandeur from which he had fallen. Pizarro, afraid of losing all the advantages which he hoped to derive from the possession of such a prisoner, laboured to console him with professions of kindness and respect that corresponded ill with his actions. By residing among the Spaniards, the Inca quickly discovered their ruling passion, which, indeed, they were nowise solicitous to conceal, and by applying to that, made an attempt to recover his liberty. He offered as a ransom what astonished the Spaniards, even after all they now knew concerning the opulence of his kingdom. The apartment in which he was confined was twenty-two feet in length and sixteen in breadth; he undertook to fill it with vessels of gold as high as he could reach. Pizarro closed eagerly with this tempting proposal, and a line

* See Note CXXXI.

was drawn upon the walls of the chamber, to mark the stipulated height to which the treasure was to rise.

Atahualpa, transported with having obtained some prospect of liberty, took measures instantly for fulfilling his part of the agreement, by sending messengers to Cuzco, Quito, and other places, where gold had been amassed in largest quantities, either for adorning the temples of the gods, or the houses of the Inca, to bring what was necessary for completing his ransom directly to Caxamalca. Though Atahualpa was now in the custody of his enemies, yet so much were the Peruvians accustomed to respect every mandate issued by their sovereign, that his orders were executed with the greatest alacrity. Soothed with hopes of recovering his liberty by this means, the subjects of the Inca were afraid of endangering his life by forming any other scheme for his relief : and though the force of the empire was still entire, no preparations were made, and no army assembled, to avenge their own wrongs or those of their monarch *. The Spaniards remained in Caxamalca tranquil and unmolested. Small detachments of their number marched into remote provinces of the empire, and, instead of meeting with any opposition, were everywhere received with marks of the most submissive respect †.

Inconsiderable as those parties were, and desirous as Pizarro might be to obtain some knowledge of the interior state of the country, he could not have ventured upon any diminution

* Xerez, 205.   † See Note CXXXII.

of his main body, if he had not about this time received an account of Almagro's having landed at St. Michael with such a reinforcement as would almost double the number of his followers [*]. The arrival of this long-expected succour was not more agreeable to the Spaniards, than alarming to the Inca. He saw the power of his enemies increase; and as he knew neither the source whence they derived their supplies, nor the means by which they were conveyed to Peru, he could not foresee to what a height the inundation that poured in upon his dominions might rise. [1533.] While disquieted with such apprehensions, he learned that some Spaniards, in their way to Cuzco, had visited his brother Huasca in the place where he kept him confined, and that the captive prince had represented to them the justice of his own cause, and as an inducement to espouse it, had promised them a quantity of treasure greatly beyond that which Atahualpa had engaged to pay for his ransom. If the Spaniards should listen to this proposal, Atahualpa perceived his own destruction to be inevitable; and suspecting that their insatiable thirst for gold would tempt them to lend a favourable ear to it, he determined to sacrifice his brother's life, that he might save his own; and his orders for this purpose were executed, like all his other commands, with scrupulous punctuality [†].

Meanwhile, Indians daily arrived at Caxamalca from different parts of the kingdom, loaded

---

[*] Xerez, 204. Herrera, dec. 5. lib. iii. cap. 1. 2.
[†] Zarate, lib. ii. c. 6. Gomara, Hist. c. 115. Herrera, dec. 5. lib. iii. c. 2.

C 2

with treasure. A great part of the stipulated
quantity was now amassed, and Atahualpa assured the Spaniards, that the only thing which
prevented the whole from being brought in, was
the remoteness of the provinces where it was
deposited. But such vast piles of gold presented
continually to the view of needy soldiers, had
so inflamed their avarice that it was impossible
any longer to restrain their impatience to obtain
possession of this rich booty. Orders were
given for melting down the whole, except some
pieces of curious fabric, reserved as a present for
the emperor. After setting apart the fifth due
to the crown, and a hundred thousand pesos
as a donative to the soldiers which arrived
with Almagro, there remained one million five
hundred and twenty-eight thousand five hundred pesos to Pizarro and his followers. The
festival of St. James [July 25], the patron saint
of Spain, was the day chosen for the partition
of this enormous sum, and the manner of conducting it strongly marks the strange alliance of
fanaticism with avarice, which I have more than
once had occasion to point out as a striking
feature in the character of the conquerors of the
New World. Though assembled to divide the
spoils of an innocent people, procured by deceit,
extortion, and cruelty, the transaction began
with a solemn invocation of the name of God *,
as if they could have expected the guidance of
Heaven in distributing those wages of iniquity.
In this division above eight thousand pesos, at
that time not inferior in effective value to as
many pounds sterling in the present century, fell

* Herrera, dec. 5. lib. iii. c. 3.

to the share of each horseman, and half that sum to each foot soldier. Pizarro himself, and his officers, received dividends in proportion to the dignity of their rank

There is no example in history of such a sudden acquisition of wealth by military service, nor was ever a sum so great divided among so small a number of soldiers. Many of them having received a recompence for their services far beyond their most sanguine hopes, were so impatient to retire from fatigue and danger, in order to spend the remainder of their days in their native country, in ease and opulence, that they demanded their discharge with clamorous importunity. Pizarro, sensible that from such men he could expect neither enterprise in action nor fortitude in suffering, and persuaded that wherever they went, the display of their riches would allure adventurers, less opulent but more hardy, to his standard, granted their suit without reluctance, and permitted above sixty of them to accompany his brother Ferdinand, whom he sent to Spain with an account of his success, and the present destined for the emperor *.

The Spaniards having divided among them the treasure amassed for the Inca's ransom, he insisted with them to fulfil their promise of setting him at liberty. But nothing was farther from Pizarro's thoughts. During his long service in the New World, he had imbibed those ideas and maxims of his fellow-soldiers, which led them to consider its inhabitants as an inferior race, neither worthy of the name, nor entitled to the rights of men. In his compact with Ata-

* Herrera, dec. 5. lib. iii. c. 4. Vega, p. 2. lib. i. c. 98.

C 2

hualpa, he had no other object than to amuse his captive with such a prospect of recovering his liberty, as might induce him to lend all the aid of his authority towards collecting the wealth of his kingdom.   Having now accomplished this, he no longer regarded his plighted faith; and at the very time when the credulous prince hoped to be replaced on his throne, he had secretly resolved to bereave him of life.   Many circumstances seem to have concurred in prompting him to this action, the most criminal and atrocious that stains the Spanish name, amidst all the deeds of violence committed in carrying on the conquest of the New World.

Though Pizarro had seized the Inca, in imitation of Cortes's conduct towards the Mexican monarch, he did not possess talents for carrying on the same artful plan of policy.   Destitute of the temper and address requisite for gaining the confidence of his prisoner, he never reaped all the advantages which might have been derived from being master of his person and authority. Atahualpa was, indeed, a prince of greater abilities and discernment than Montezuma, and seems to have penetrated more thoroughly into the character and intentions of the Spaniards. Mutual suspicion and distrust accordingly took place between them.   The strict attention with which it was necessary to guard a captive of such importance, greatly increased the fatigue of military duty.   The utility of keeping him appeared inconsiderable; and Pizarro felt him as an incumbrance, from which he wished to be delivered *.

* Herrera, dec. 5. lib. iii. c. 4.

Almagro and his followers had made a demand of an equal share in the Inca's ransom; and though Pizarro had bestowed upon the private men the large gratuity which I have mentioned, and endeavoured to scoth their leader by presents of great value, they still continued dissatisfied. They were apprehensive, that as long as Atahualpa remained a prisoner, Pizarro's soldiers would apply whatever treasure should be acquired, to make up what was wanting of the quantity stipulated for his ransom, and under that pretext exclude them from any part of it. They insisted eagerly on putting the Inca to death, that all the adventurers in Peru might thereafter be on an equal footing *.

Pizarro himself began to be alarmed with accounts of forces assembling in the remote provinces of the empire, and suspected Atahualpa of having issued orders for that purpose. These fears and suspicions were artfully increased by Philippillo, one of the Indians whom Pizarro had carried off from Tumbez in the year one thousand five hundred and twenty-seven, and whom he employed as an interpreter. The function which he performed admitting this man to familiar intercourse with the captive monarch, he presumed, notwithstanding the meanness of his birth, to raise his affections to a *Coya*, or descendant of the Sun, one of Atahualpa's wives; and seeing no prospect of gratifying that passion during the life of the monarch, he endeavoured to fill the ears of the Spaniards with such accounts of the Inca's secret designs and prepara-

* Zarate. lib. ii. c. 7. Vega, p. 2. lib. i. c. 7. Herrera, dec. 5. lib. iii. c. 4.

tions, as might, awaken their jealousy, and incite them to cut him off.

While Almagro and his followers openly demanded the life of the Inca, and Philippillo laboured to ruin him by private machinations, that unhappy prince inadvertently contributed to hasten his own fate. During his confinement he had attached himself with peculiar affection to Ferdinand Pizarro and Hernando Soto; who, as they were persons of birth and education superior to the rough adventurers with whom they served, were accustomed to behave with more decency and attention to the captive monarch. Soothed with this respect from persons of such high rank, he delighted in their society. But in the presence of the governor he was always uneasy and overawed. This dread soon came to be mingled with contempt. Among all the European arts, what he admired most was that of reading and writing; and he long deliberated with himself, whether he should regard it as a natural or acquired talent. In order to determine this, he desired one of the soldiers who guarded him, to write the name of God on the nail of his thumb. This he shewed successively to several Spaniards, asking its meaning; and to his amazement, they all, without hesitation, returned the same answer. At length Pizarro entered; and on presenting it to him, he blushed, and with some confusion was obliged to acknowledge his ignorance. From that moment, Atahualpa considered him as a mean person, less instructed than his own soldiers; and he had not address enough to conceal the sentiments with which this discovery inspired him.

To be the object of a barbarian's scorn, not only mortified the pride of Pizarro, but excited such resentment in his breast, as added force to all the other considerations which prompted him to put the Inca to death *.

But in order to give some colour of justice to this violent action, and that he himself might be exempted from standing singly responsible for the commission of it, Pizarro resolved to try the Inca with all the formalities observed in the criminal courts of Spain. Pizarro himself, and Almagro, with two assistants, were appointed judges, with full power to acquit or to condemn; an attorney-general was named to carry on the prosecution in the king's name; counsellors were chosen to assist the prisoner in his defence; and clerks were ordained to record the proceedings of court. Before this strange tribunal, a charge was exhibited still more amazing. It consisted of various articles; that Atahualpa, though a bastard, had dispossessed the rightful owner of the throne, and usurped the regal power; that he had put his brother and lawful sovereign to death; that he was an idolater, and had not only permitted, but commanded the offering of human sacrifices; that he had a great number of concubines; that since his imprisonment he had wasted and embezzled the royal treasures, which now belonged of right to the conquerors; that he had incited his subjects to take arms against the Spaniards. On these heads of accusation, some of which are so ludicrous, others so absurd, that the effrontery of Pizarro,

* Herrera, dec. 5. lib. iii. c. 4. Vega, p. ii. lib. .
t 3º.

in making them the foundation of a serious procedure, is not less surprising than his injustice, did this strange court go on to try the sovereign of a great empire, over whom it had no jurisdiction. With respect to each of the articles, witnesses were examined; but as they delivered their evidence in their native tongue, Philippillo had it in his power to give their words whatever turn best suited his malevolent intentions. To judges predetermined in their opinion, this evidence appeared sufficient. They pronounced Atahualpa guilty, and condemned him to be burnt alive. Friar Valverde prostituted the authority of his sacred function to confirm this sentence, and by his signature warranted it to be just. Astonished at his fate, Atahualpa endeavoured to avert it by tears, by promises, and by entreaties, that he might be sent to Spain, where a monarch would be the arbiter of his lot. But pity never touched the unfeeling heart of Pizarro. He ordered him to be led instantly to execution; and, what added to the bitterness of his last moments, the same monk who had just ratified his doom, offered to console, and attempted to convert him. The most powerful argument Valverde employed to prevail with him to embrace the Christian faith, was a promise of mitigation in his punishment. The dread of a cruel death extorted from the trembling victim a desire of receiving baptism. The ceremony was performed; and Atahualpa, instead of being burnt, was strangled at the stake *.

* Zarate, lib. ii. c. 7. Xerez, p. 233. Vega, p. ii. dib. i. c. 36, 37. Gomara, Hist. c. 117. Herrera, dec. 5. lib. iii. c. 4.

Happily for the credit of the Spanish nation, even among the profligate adventurers which it sent forth to conquer and desolate the New World, there were persons who retained some tincture of the Castilian generosity and honour. Though, before the trial of Atahualpa, Ferdinand Pizarro had set out for Spain, and Soto was sent on a separate command at a distance from Caxamalca, this odious transaction was not carried on without censure and opposition. Several officers, and among those some of the greatest reputation and most respectable families in the service, not only remonstrated, but protested against this measure of their general, as disgraceful to their country, as repugnant to every maxim of equity, as a violation of public faith, and an usurpation of jurisdiction over an independent monarch, to which they had no title. But their laudable endeavours were vain. Numbers, and the opinion of such as held every thing to be lawful which they deemed advantageous, prevailed. History, however, records even the unsuccessful exertions of virtue with applause; and the Spanish writers, in relating events where the valour of their nation is more conspicuous than its humanity, have not failed to preserve the names of those who made this laudable effort to save their country from the infamy of having perpetrated such a crime *.

On the death of Atahualpa, Pizarro invested one of his sons with the ensigns of royalty, hoping that a young man without experience

---

* Vega. p. 11. lib. i. c. 37. Xerez, . 235. Herrera, dec. 5. lit. iii. c. 5.

might prove a more passive instrument in his hands than an ambitious monarch, who had been accustomed to independent command. The people of Cuzco and the adjacent country acknowledged Manco Capac, a brother of Huascar, as Inca *. But neither possessed the authority which belonged to a sovereign of Peru. The violent convulsions into which the empire had been thrown, first by the civil war between the two brothers, and then by the invasion of the Spaniards, had not only deranged the order of the Peruvian government, but almost dissolved its frame. When they beheld their monarch a captive in the power of strangers, and at last suffering an ignominious death, the people in several provinces, as if they had been set free from every restraint of law and decency, broke out into the most licentious excesses †. So many descendants of the Sun, after being treated with the utmost indignity, had been cut off by Atahualpa, that not only their influence in the state diminished with their number, but the accustomed reverence for that sacred race sensibly decreased. In consequence of this state of things, ambitious men in different parts of the empire aspired to independent authority, and usurped jurisdiction to which they had no title. The general who commanded for Atahualpa in Quito, seized the brother and children of his master, put them to a cruel death, and disclaiming any connection with either Inca, endeavoured to establish a separate kingdom for himself ‡.

---

* Vega, p. 11. lib. ii. c. 7. lib. ii. c. 12. lib. iii. c. 5. Vega, p. 11. lib. ii. c. 3, 4.

† Herrera, dec. 5.

‡ Zarate, lib. ii. c. 8.

The Spaniards, with pleasure, beheld the spirit of discord diffusing itself, and the vigour of government relaxing among the Peruvians. They considered those disorders as symptoms of a state hastening towards its dissolution. Pizarro no longer hesitated to advance towards Cuzco, and he had received such considerable reinforcements, that he could venture, with little danger, to penetrate so far into the interior part of the country. The account of the wealth acquired at Caxamalca operated as he had foreseen. No sooner did his brother Ferdinand, with the officers and soldiers to whom he had given their discharge after the partition of the Inca's ransom, arrive at Panama, and display their riches in the view of their astonished countrymen, than fame spread the account with such exaggeration through all the Spanish settlements on the South Sea, that the governors of Guatimala, Panama, and Nicaragua, could hardly restrain the people under their jurisdiction, from abandoning their possessions, and crowding to that inexhaustible source of wealth which seemed to be opened in Peru *. In spite of every check and regulation, such numbers resorted thither, that Pizarro began his march at the head of five hundred men, after leaving a considerable garrison in St. Michael, under the command of Benalcazar. The Peruvians had assembled some large bodies of troops to oppose his progress. Several fierce encounters happened. But they terminated like all the actions in America; a few Spaniards were killed or wounded; the natives

* Gomara, Hist. c. 125. Vega, p. 11. lib. ii. c. 1. Herrera, dec. 5. lib. iii c. 5.

were put to flight with incredible slaughter. At length Pizarro forced his way to Cuzco, and took quiet possession of that capital. The riches found there, even after all that the natives had carried off and concealed, either from a superstitious veneration for the ornaments of their temples, or out of hatred to their rapacious conquerors, exceeded in value what had been received as Atahualpa's ransom. But as the Spaniards were now accustomed to the wealth of the country, and it came to be parcelled out among a greater number of adventurers, this dividend did not excite the same surprise, either from novelty, or the largeness of the sum that fell to the share of each individual *.

During the march to Cuzco, that son of Atahualpa whom Pizarro treated as Inca, died; and as the Spaniards substituted no person in his place, the title of Manco Capac seems to have been universally recognized †.

While his fellow-soldiers were thus employed, Benalcazar, governor of St. Michael, an able and enterprising officer, was ashamed of remaining inactive, and impatient to have his name distinguished among the discoverers and conquerors of the New World. The seasonable arrival of a fresh body of recruits from Panama and Nicaragua, put it in his power to gratify this passion. Leaving a sufficient force to protect the infant settlement entrusted to his care, he placed himself at the head of the rest, and set out to attempt the reduction of Quito, where, according to the report of the natives, Atahualpa had left the greatest part of his treasure.

* See Note CXXXIII.   † Herrera, dec. 5. lib. v. c. 2.

Notwithstanding the distance of that city from
St. Michael, the difficulty of marching through
a mountainous country covered with woods, and
the frequent and fierce attacks of the best troops
in Peru, commanded by a skilful leader, the valour, good conduct, and perseverance of Benalcazar surmounted every obstacle, and he entered
Quito with his victorious troops.   But they met
with a cruel mortification there.   The natives,
now acquainted, to their sorrow, with the predominant passion of their invaders, and knowing
how to disappoint it, had carried off all those
treasures, the prospect of which had prompted
them to undertake this arduous expedition, and
had supported them under all the dangers and
hardships wherewith they had to struggle in carrying it on *.

Benalcazar was not the only Spanish leader
who attacked the kingdom of Quito.   The
fame of its riches attracted a more powerful enemy.   Pedro de Alvarado, who had distinguished
himself so eminently in the conquest of Mexico,
having obtained the government of Guatimala as
a recompence for his valour, soon became disgusted with a life of uniform tranquillity, and
longed to be again engaged in the bustle of military service.   The glory and wealth acquired by
the conquerors of Peru heightened this passion,
and gave it a determined direction.   Believing,
or pretending to believe, that the kingdom of
Quito did not lie within the limits of the province allotted to Pizarro, he resolved to invade
it.   The high reputation of the commander al-

* Zarate, lib. ii. c. 9.   Vega, p. 11. lib. ii. c. 9.   Herrera, dec. 5. lib. iv. c. 11, 12. lib. v. c. 2, 3. lib. vi. c. 3.

                                    D 2

lured volunteers from every quarter. He embarked with five hundred men, of whom above two hundred were of such distinction as to serve on horseback. He landed at Puerto Viejo, and without sufficient knowledge of the country, or proper guides to conduct him, attempted to march directly to Quito, by following the course of the river Guayaquil, and crossing the ridge of the Andes towards its head. But in this route, one of the most impracticable in all America, his troops endured such fatigue in forcing their way through forests and marshes on the low grounds, and suffered so much from excessive cold when they began to ascend the mountains, that before they reached the plain of Quito, a fifth part of the men and half of their horses died, and the rest were so much dispirited and worn out, as to be almost unfit for service *. There they met with a body, not of Indians, but of Spaniards, drawn up in hostile array against them. Pizarro having received an account of Alvarado's armament, had detached Almagro with some troops to oppose this formidable invader of his jurisdiction; and these were joined by Benalcazar and his victorious party. Alvarado, though surprised at the sight of enemies whom he did not expect, advanced boldly to the charge. But by the interposition of some moderate men in each party, an amicable accommodation took place; and the fatal period, when Spaniards suspended their conquests to embrue their hands in the blood of their countrymen, was postponed a few years. Alvarado engaged to return to his government upon Almagro's

* See Note CXXXIV.

paying him a hundred thousand pesos to defray the expence of his armament. Most of his followers remained in the country; and an expedition, which threatened Pizarro and his colony with ruin, contributed to augment its strength *.

1534.] By this time Ferdinand Pizarro had landed in Spain. The immense quantities of gold and silver which he imported †, filled the kingdom with no less astonishment than they had excited in Panama and the adjacent provinces. Pizarro was received by the emperor with the attention due to the bearer of a present so rich, as to exceed any idea which the Spaniards had formed concerning the value of their acquisitions in America, even after they had been ten years masters of Mexico. In recompence of his brother's services, his authority was confirmed with new powers and privileges, and the addition of seventy leagues, extending along the coast, to the southward of the territory granted in his former patent. Almagro received the honours which he had so long desired. The title of Adelantado, or governor, was conferred upon him, with jurisdiction over two hundred leagues of country, stretching beyond the southern limits of the province allotted to Pizarro. Ferdinand himself did not go unrewarded. He was admitted into the military order of St. Jago, a distinction always acceptable to a Spanish gentleman, and soon set out on his return to Peru,

* Zarate, lib. ii. c. 10—13. Vega, p. 11. lib. ii. c. 1, 2. 9, &c. Gomara, Hist. c. 126, &c. Remesal, Hist. Guatimal. lib. iii. c. 6. Herrera, dec. 5. lib vi. c. 1, 2. 7, 8.   † See Note CXXXV.

accompanied by many persons of higher rank than had yet served in that country *.

Some account of his negotiations reached Peru before he arrived there himself. Almagro no sooner learned that he had obtained the royal grant of an independent government, than, pretending that Cuzco, the imperial residence of the Incas, lay within its boundaries, he attempted to render himself master of that important station. Juan and Gonza'ez Pizarro prepared to oppose him. Each of the contending parties was supported by powerful adherents, and the dispute was on the point of being terminated by the sword, when Francis Pizarro arrived in the capital. The reconciliation between him and Almagro had never been cordial. The treachery of Pizarro in engrossing to himself all the honours and emoluments which ought to have been divided with his associate, was always present in both their thoughts. The former, conscious of his own perfidy, did not expect forgiveness ; the latter, feeling that he had been deceived, was impatient to be avenged ; and though avarice and ambition had induced them not only to dissemble their sentiments, but even to act in concert while in pursuit of wealth and power, no sooner did they obtain possession of these, than the same passions which had formed this temporary union, gave rise to jealousy and discord. To each of them was attached a small band of interested dependents, who, with the malicious art peculiar to such men, heightened their suspicions, and magnified every appearance of of-

* Zarate, lib. iii. c. 3. Vega, p. 11. lib. ii. c. 19 Herrera, dec. 5. lib. vi. c. 13.

fence.   But with all those seeds of enmity in
their minds, and thus assiduously cherished,
each was so thoroughly acquainted with the
abilities and courage of his rival, that they
equally dreaded the consequences of an open
rupture.   The fortunate arrival of Pizarro at
Cuzco, and the address mingled with firmness
which he manifested in his expostulations with
Almagro and his partisans, averted that evil for
the present.   A new reconciliation took place;
the chief article of which was, that Almagro
should attempt the conquest of Chili; and if he
did not find in that province an establishment
adequate to his merit and expectations, Pizarro,
by way of indemnification, should yield up to
him a part of Peru.   This new agreement,
though confirmed [June 12] with the same sacred solemnities as their first contract, was observed with as little fidelity *.

Soon after he concluded this important transaction, Pizarro marched back to the countries
on the sea-coast, and as he now enjoyed an interval of tranquillity, undisturbed by any enemy,
either Spanish or Indian, he applied himself, with
that persevering ardour which distinguishes his
character, to introduce a form of regular government into the extensive provinces subject to his
authority.   Though ill qualified by his education
to enter into any disquisition concerning the
principles of civil policy, and little accustomed
by his former habits of life to attend to its arrangements, his natural sagacity supplied the
want both of science and experience.   He distributed the country into various districts, he

* Zarate, lib. ii. c. 13. Vega, p. 1t. lib. ii. c. 19.
Benzo, lib. iii. c. 6. Herrera, dec. 5. lib. vii. c. 8.

appointed proper magistrates to preside in each ;
and established regulations concerning the administration of justice, the collection of the royal
revenue, the working of the mines, and the
treatment of the Indians, extremely simple, but
well calculated to promote the public prosperity.
But though, for the present, he adapted his
plan to the infant state of his colony, his aspiring mind looked forward to its future grandeur.
He considered himself as laying the foundation
of a great empire, and deliberated long, and
with much solicitude, in what place he should
fix the seat of government. Cuzco, the Imperial city of the Incas, was situated in a corner of the empire, above four hundred miles
from the sea, and much farther from Quito,
a province of whose value he had formed an
high idea.   No other settlement of the Peruvians
was so considerable as to merit the name of a
town, or to allure the Spaniards to fix their
residence in it.   But, in marching through the
country, Pizarro had been struck with the
beauty and fertility of the valley of Rimac, one
of the most extensive and best cultivated in Peru.
There, on the banks of a small river, of the
same name with the vale which it waters and
enriches, at the distance of six miles from Callao,
the most commodious harbour in the Pacific
Ocean, he founded a city which he destined to
be the capital of his government. He gave it
the name of Ciudad de los Reyes, either from
the circumstance of having laid the first stone
[Jan. 18, 1535], at that season when the
church celebrates the festival of the Three
Kings, or, as is more probable, in honour of
Juana and Charles, the joint sovereigns of

Castile.   This name it still retains among the
Spaniards, in all legal and formal deeds; but
it is better known to foreigners by that of *Lima*,
a corruption of the ancient appellation of the
valley in which it is situated.   Under his inspection, the buildings advanced with such rapidity, that it soon assumed the form of a city,
which, by a magnificent palace that he erected
for himself, and by the stately houses built by
several of his officers, gave, even in its infancy,
some indication of its subsequent grandeur *.

In consequence of what had been agreed with
Pizarro, Almagro began his march towards
Chili; and as he possessed in an eminent degree
the virtues most admired by soldiers, boundless
liberality and fearless courage, his standard was
followed by five hundred and seventy men, the
greatest body of Europeans that had hitherto
been assembled in Peru.   From impatience to
finish the expedition, or from that contempt of
hardship and danger acquired by all the Spaniards
who had served long in America, Almagro, instead of advancing along the level country on the
coast, chose to march across the mountains by
a route that was shorter indeed, but almost impracticable.   In this attempt his troops were
exposed to every calamity which men can suffer,
from fatigue, from famine, and from the rigour
of the climate in those elevated regions of the
torrid zone, where the degree of cold is hardly
inferior to what is felt within the polar circle.
Many of them perished; and the survivors, when
they descended into the fertile plains of Chili,
had new difficulties to encounter.   They found

* Herrera, dec. 5. lib. vi. c. 12. lib. vii c. 13. Calancho
Cornica, lib. i. c 37.   Barneuvo, Lima fundata, ll. 294.

there a race of men very different from the
people of Peru. intrepid, hardy, independent,
and in their bodily constitution, as well as vigour of spirit, nearly resembling the warlike
tribes in North America. Though filled with
wonder at the first appearance of the Spaniards,
and still more astonished at the operations of their
cavalry and the effects of their fire-arms, the Chilese soon recovered so far from their surprise, as
not only to defend themselves with obstinacy, but
to attack their new enemies with more determined fierceness than any American nation had
hitherto discovered. The Spaniards, however,
continued to penetrate into the country, and
collected some considerable quantities of gold ;
but were so far from thinking of making any settlement amisdt such formidable neighbours, that,
in spite of all the experience and valour of their
leader, the final issue of the expedition still remained extremely dubious, when they were re-
called from it by an unexpected revolution in
Peru *. The causes of this important event I
shall endeavour to trace to their source.

So many adventurers had flocked to Peru
from every Spanish colony in America, and all
with such high expectations of accumulating independent fortunes at once, that, to men possessed with notions so extravagant, any mention
of acquiring wealth gradually, and by schemes
of patient industry, would have been not only a
disappointment, but an insult. In order to find
occupation for men who could not with safety
be allowed to remain inactive, Pizarro encou-

* Zarate, lib. iii. c. 1. Gomara Hist. c. 131. Vega, p. 2.
lib. ii. c. 25. Ovalle, Hist. de Chile, lib. iv. c. 15. &c.
Herrera, dec. 5. lib. vi. c. 9. lib. x. c. 1, &c.

raged some of the most distinguished officers who had lately joined him, to invade different provinces of the empire, which the Spaniards had not hitherto visited. Several large bodies were formed for this purpose; and about the time that Almagro set out for Chili, they marched into remote districts of the country. No sooner did Manco Capac, the Inca, observe the inconsiderate security of the Spaniards in thus dispersing their troops, and that only a handful of soldiers remained in Cuzco, under Juan and Gonzalez Pizarro, than he thought that the happy period was at length come for vindicating his own rights, for avenging the wrongs of his country, and extirpating its oppressors. Though strictly watched by the Spaniards, who allowed him to reside in the palace of his ancestors at Cuzco, he found means of communicating his scheme to the persons who were to be entrusted with the execution of it. Among people accustomed to revere their sovereign as a divinity, every hint of his will carries the authority of a command; and they themselves were now convinced, by the daily increase in the number of their invaders, that the fond hopes which they had long entertained of their voluntary departure were altogether vain. All perceived that a vigorous effort of the whole nation was requisite to expel them, and the preparations for it were carried on with the secrecy and silence peculiar to Americans.

After some unsuccessful attempts of the Inca to make his escape, Ferdinand Pizarro happening to arrive at that time in Cuzco [1536], he obtained permission from him to attend a great

festival which was to be celebrated a few leagues
from the capital. Under pretext of that solemnity, the great men of the empire were assembled. As soon as the Inca joined them,
the standard of war was erected; and in a short
time all the fighting men, from the confines of
Quito to the frontier of Chili, were in arms.
Many Spaniards, living securely on the settlements allotted them, were massacred. Several
detachments, as they marched carelessly through
a country which seemed to be tamely submissive to their dominion, were cut off to a man.
An army amounting (if we may believe the
Spanish writers) to two hundred thousand men,
attacked Cuzco, which the three brothers endeavoured to defend with only one hundred and
seventy Spaniards. Another formidable body
invested Lima, and kept the governor closely
shut up. There was no longer any communication between the two cities; the numerous
forces of the Peruvians spreading over the country, intercepted every messenger; and as the
parties in Cuzco and Lima were equally unacquainted with the fate of their countrymen, each
boded the worst concerning the other, and
imagined that they themselves were the only
persons who had survived the general extinction
of the Spanish name in Peru *.

It was at Cuzco, where the Inca commanded
in person, that the Peruvians made their chief
effort. During nine months they carried on the

* Vega, p. 11. lib. ii. c 28. Zarate, lib. iii. c. 3.
Circa de Leon, c. 82. Gomara, Hist. c. 135. Herrera,
dec 5 lib. viii. c. 5.

siege with incessant ardour, and in various forms; and though they displayed not the same undaunted ferocity as the Mexican warriors, they conducted some of their operations in a manner which discovered greater sagacity, and a genius more susceptible of improvement in the military art. They not only observed the advantages which the Spaniards derived from their discipline and their weapons, but they endeavoured to imitate the former, and turn the latter against them. They armed a considerable body of their bravest warriors with the swords, the spears, and bucklers, which they had taken from the Spanish soldiers whom they had cut off in different parts of the country. These they endeavoured to marshal in that regular compact order, to which experience had taught them that the Spaniards were indebted for their irresistible force in action. Some appeared in the field with Spanish muskets, and had acquired skill and resolution enough to use them. A few of the boldest, among whom was the Inca himself, were mounted on the horses which they had taken, and advanced briskly to the charge like Spanish cavaliers, with their lances in the rest. It was more by their numbers, however, than by those imperfect essays to imitate European arts and to employ European arms, that the Peruvians annoyed the Spaniards *. In spite of the valour, heightened by despair, with which the three brothers defended Cuzco, Manco Capac recovered possession of one half of his capital; and in their various efforts to drive him out of it, the Spaniards lost Juan Pizarro, the

* See Note CXXXVI.

best beloved of all the brothers, together with some other persons of note. Worn out with the fatigue of incessant duty, distressed with want of provisions, and despairing of being able any longer to resist an enemy whose numbers daily increased, the soldiers became impatient to abandon Cuzco, in hopes either of joining their countrymen, if any of them yet survived, or of forcing their way to the sea, and finding some means of escaping from a country which had been so fatal to the Spanish name*. While they were brooding over those desponding thoughts, which their officers laboured in vain to dispel, Almagro appeared suddenly in the neighbourhood of Cuzco.

The accounts transmitted to Almagro concerning the general insurrection of the Peruvians, were such as would have induced him, without hesitation, to relinquish the conquest of Chili, and hasten to the aid of his countrymen. But in this resolution he was confirmed by a motive less generous, but more interesting. By the same messenger who brought him intelligence of the Inca's revolt, he received the royal patent creating him governor of Chili, and defining the limits of his jurisdiction. Upon considering the tenor of it, he deemed it manifest beyond contradiction, that Cuzco lay within the boundaries of his government, and he was equally solicitous to prevent the Peruvians from recovering possession of their capital, and to wrest it out of the hands of the Pizarros. From impatience to accomplish both, he ventured to return by a new route; and in marching through the sandy plains on the coast, he suffered, from

* Herrera, dec. 5. lib. viii. c. 4.

beat and drought, calamities of a new species, hardly inferior to those in which he had been involved by cold and famine on the summits of the Andes.

His arrival at Cuzco [1537] was in a critical moment. The Spaniards and Peruvians fixed their eyes upon him with equal solicitude. The former, as he did not study to conceal his pretensions, were at a loss whether to welcome him as a deliverer, or to take precautions against him as an enemy. The latter, knowing the points in contest between him and his countrymen, flattered themselves that they had more to hope than to dread from his operations. Almagro himself, unacquainted with the detail of the events which had happened in his absence, and solicitous to learn the precise posture of affairs, advanced towards the capital slowly, and with great circumspection. Various negotiations with both parties were set on foot. The Inca conducted them on his part with much address. At first he endeavoured to gain the friendship of Almagro; and after many fruitless overtures, despairing of any cordial union with a Spaniard, he attacked him by surprise with a numerous body of chosen troops. But the Spanish discipline and valour maintained their wonted superiority. The Peruvians were repulsed with such slaughter, that a great part of their army dispersed, and Almagro proceeded to the gates of Cuzco without interruption.

The Pizarros, as they had no longer to make head against the Peruvians, directed all their attention towards their new enemy, and took measures to obstruct his entry into the capital.

E 2

Prudence, however, restrained both parties for some time from turning their arms against one another, while surrounded by common enemies, who would rejoice in the mutual slaughter. Different schemes of accommodation were proposed. Each endeavoured to deceive the other, or to corrupt his followers. The generous, open, affable temper of Almagro gained many adherents of the Pizarros, who were disgusted with their harsh domineering manners. Encouraged by this defection, he advanced towards the city by night, surprised the centinels, or was admitted by them, and investing the house where the two brothers resided, compelled them, after an obstinate defence, to surrender at discretion. Almagro's claim of jurisdiction over Cuzco was universally acknowledged, and a form of administration established in his name *.

Two or three persons only were killed in this first act of civil hostility; but it was soon followed by scenes more bloody. Francis Pizarro having dispersed the Peruvians who had invested Lima, and received some considerable reinforcements from Hispaniola and Nicaragua, ordered five hundred men, under the command of Alonso de Alvarado, to march to Cuzco, in hopes of relieving his brothers, if they and their garrison were not already cut off by the Peruvians. This body, which, at that period of the Spanish power in America, must be deemed a considerable force, advanced near to the capital before they knew that they had any enemy more formidable than Indians to encounter.

* Zarate. lib. iii. c 4. Vega, p. 11. lib. ii. c. 29. 31. Gomara, Hist. c. 134. Herrera, dec. 6. lib. ii. c. 1—5.

It was with astonishment that they beheld their countrymen posted on the banks of the river Abancay to oppose their progress. Almagro, however, wished rather to gain than to conquer them, and by bribes and promises endeavoured to seduce their leader. The fidelity of Alvarado remained unshaken; but his talents for war were not equal to his virtue. Almagro amused him with various movements, of which he did not comprehend the meaning, while a large detachment of chosen soldiers passed the river by night [July 12], fell upon his camp by surprise, broke his troops before they had time to form, and took him prisoner, together with his principal officers *.

By the sudden rout of this body, the contest between the two rivals must have been decided, if Almagro had known as well how to improve as how to gain a victory. Rodrigo Orgognez, an officer of great abilities, who having served under the constable Bourbon, when he led the Imperial army to Rome, had been accustomed to bold and decisive measures, advised him instantly to issue orders for putting to death Ferdinand and Gonzalo Pizarros, Alvarado, and a few other persons whom he could not hope to gain, and to march directly with his victorious troops to Lima, before the governor had time to prepare for his defence. But Almagro, though he discerned at once the utility of the counsel, and though he had courage to have carried it into execution, suffered himself to be influenced by sentiments unlike those of a soldier

* Zarate, lib. iii. c. 6. Gom. Hist. c. 138. Vega, p. ii. lib. ii. c. 32. 34. Herrera, dec. 6. lib. ii. c. 9.

E 3

of fortune grown old in service, and by scruples
which suited not the chief of a party who had
drawn his sword in civil war. Feelings of humanity restrained him from shedding the blood
of his opponents; and the dread of being deemed a rebel, deterred him from entering a province which the king had allotted to another,
Though he knew that arms must terminate the
dispute between him and Pizarro, and resolved
not to shun that mode of decision, yet with a timid delicacy, preposterous at such a juncture,
he was so solicitous that his rival should be considered as the aggressor, that he marched quietly
back to Cuzco, to wait his approach *.

Pizarro was still unacquainted with all the
interesting events which had happened near
Cuzco. Accounts of Almagro's return, of the
loss of the capital, of the death of one brother,
of the imprisonment of the other two, and of the
defeat of Alvarado, were brought to him at once.
Such a tide of misfortunes almost overwhelmed a
spirit which had continued firm and erect under
the rudest shocks of adversity. But the necessity of attending to his own safety, as well as
the desire of revenge, preserved him from sinking under it. He took measures for both with
his wonted sagacity. As he had the command
of the sea-coast, and expected considerable supplies both of men and military stores, it was
no less his interest to gain time, and to avoid
action, than it was that of Almagro to precipitate operations, and bring the contest to a
speedy issue. He had recourse to arts which he
had formerly practised with success, and Alma-

* Herrera, dec. 6. lib. ii. c. 10, 11.

gro was again weak enough to suffer himself to be amused with a prospect of terminating their differences by some amicable accommodation. By varying his overtures, and shifting his ground as often as it suited his purpose, sometimes seeming to yield every thing which his rival could desire, and then retracting all that he had granted, Pizarro dexterously protracted the negotiation to such a length, that though every day was precious to Almagro, several months elapsed without coming to any final agreement. While the attention of Almagro, and of the officers with whom he consulted, was occupied in detecting and eluding the fraudulent intentions of the governor, Gonzalo Pizarro and Alvarado found means to corrupt the soldiers to whose custody they were committed, and not only made their escape themselves, but persuaded sixty of the men who formerly guarded them to accompany their flight *. Fortune having thus delivered one of his brothers, the governor scrupled not at one act of perfidy more to procure the release of the other. He proposed, that every point in controversy between Almagro and himself should be submitted to the decision of their sovereign; that until his award was known, each should retain undisturbed possession of whatever part of the country he now occupied; that Ferdinand Pizarro should be set at liberty, and return instantly to Spain, together with the officers, whom Almagro proposed to send thither to represent the justice of his claims. Obvious as the design of Pizarro was in those propositions, and familiar as his artifices might now have been

* Zarate, lib. iii. c. 8. Herrera, dec. 6. lib. ii. c. 14.

to his opponent, Almagro, with a credulity approaching to infatuation, relied on his sincerity, and concluded an agreement on these terms *.

The moment that Ferdinand Pizarro recovered his liberty, the governor, no longer fettered in his operations by anxiety about his brother's life, threw off every disguise which his concern for it had obliged him to assume. The treaty was forgotten ; pacific and conciliating measures were no more mentioned ; it was in the field he openly declared, and not in the cabinet ; by arms, and not by negotiation, that it must now be determined who should be master of Peru. The rapidity of his preparations suited such a decisive resolution. Seven hundred men were soon ready to march towards Cuzco. [1538] The command of these was given to his two brothers, in whom he could perfectly confide for the execution of his most violent schemes, as they were urged on, not only by the enmity flowing from the rivalship between their family and Almagro, but animated with the desire of vengeance, excited by recollection of their own recent disgrace and sufferings. After an unsuccessful attempt to cross the mountains in the direct road between Lima and Cuzco, they marched towards the south along the coast as far as Nasca, and then turning to the left, penetrated through the defiles in that branch of the Andes which lay between them and the capital. Almagro, instead of hearkening to some of his officers, who advised him to attempt the defence of those difficult passes, waited the approach of the enemy in the

* Herrera. dec. 6. lib. iii. c. 9. Zarate, lib. iii. c. 9. Gomara, Hist. c. 140. Vega, p. 11. lib. ii. c. 35.

plain of Cuzco. Two reasons seem to have induced him to take this resolution. His followers amounted hardly to five hundred, and he was afraid of weakening such a feeble body by sending any detachment towards the mountains. His cavalry far exceeded that of the adverse party, both in number and discipline, and it was only in an open country that he could avail himself of that advantage.

The Pizarros advanced without any obstruction, but what arose from the nature of the desert and horrid regions through which they marched. As soon as they reached the plain, both factions were equally impatient to bring this long-protracted contest to an issue. Though countrymen and friends, the subjects of the same sovereign, and each with the royal standard displayed; and though they beheld the mountains that surrounded the plain in which they were drawn up, covered with a vast multitude of Indians, assembled to enjoy the spectacle of their mutual carnage, and prepared to attack whatever party remained master of the field; so fell and implacable was the rancour which had taken possession of every breast, that not one pacific counsel, not a single overture towards accommodation proceeded from either side. Unfortunately for Almagro, he was so worn out with the fatigues of service, to which his advanced age was unequal, that, at this crisis of his fate, he could not exert his wonted activity; and he was obliged to commit the leading of his troops to Orgognez, who, though an officer of great merit, did not possess the same ascendant either over the spirit or affections of the soldiers, as the chief whom they had long been accustomed to follow and revere.

The conflict was fierce, and maintained by each party with equal courage [April 26.] On the side of Almagro were more veteran soldiers, and a larger proportion of cavalry ; but these were counterbalanced by Pizarro's superiority in numbers, and by two companies of well disciplined musketeers, which, on receiving an account of the insurrection of the Indians, the emperor had sent from Spain *. As the use of fire-arms was not frequent among the adventurers in America †, hastily equipped for service, at their own expence, this small band of soldiers, regularly trained and armed, was a novelty in Peru, and decided the fate of the day. Wherever it advanced, the weight of a heavy and well-sustained fire bore down horse and foot before it ; and Orgognez, while he endeavoured to rally and animate his troops, having received a dangerous wound, the rout became general. The barbarity of the conquerors stained the glory which they acquired by this complete victory. The violence of civil rage hurried on some to slaughter their countrymen with indiscriminate cruelty ; the meanness of private revenge instigated others to single out individuals as the objects of their vengeance. Orgognez and several officers of distinction were massacred in cold blood ; above a hundred and forty soldiers fell in the field ; a large proportion, where the number of combatants were few, and the heat of the contest soon over. Almagro, though so feeble that he

* Herrera, dec 6. lib. iii. c. 8.
† Zarate, lib. iii. c. 8.

could not bear the motion of a horse, had insisted on being carried in a litter to an eminence
which overlooked the field of battle. From
thence, in the utmost agitation of mind, he viewed the various movements of both parties, and at
last beheld the total defeat of his own troops,
with all the passionate indignation of a veteran
leader long accustomed to victory. He endeavoured to save himself by flight, but was taken
prisoner, and guarded with the strictest vigilance *.

The Indians, instead of executing the resolution which they had formed, retired quietly after
the battle was over; and in the history of the
New World, there is not a more striking instance
of the wonderful ascendant which the Spaniards
had acquired over its inhabitants, than that after
seeing one of the contending parties ruined and
dispersed, and the other weakened and fatigued,
they had not courage to fall upon their enemies,
when fortune presented an opportunity of attack-
ing them with such advantage †.

Cuzco was pillaged by the victorious troops,
who found there a considerable booty, consisting
partly of the gleanings of the Indian treasures,
and partly of the wealth amassed by their an-
tagonists from the spoils of Peru and Chili. But
so far did this, and whatever the bounty of their
leader could add to it, fall below the high ideas
of the recompence which they conceived to be
due to their merit, that Ferdinand Pizarro, unable to gratify such extravagant expectations, had

* Zarate, lib. iii. c. 11, 12. Vega, p. 11. lib. ii. c. 36.
38. Herrera, dec. 6. lib. iii. c. 10—12. lib. iv. c. 1—6.
† Zarate, lib. iii. c. 14. Vega, p. 11. lib. ii. c. 38.

recourse to the same expedient which his brother
had employed on a similar occasion, and endeavoured to find occupation for this turbulent
assuming spirit, in order to prevent it from
breaking out into open mutiny. With this view,
he encouraged his most active officers to attempt
the discov.ry and reduction of various provinces
which had not hitherto submitted to the Spaniards. To every standard erected by the leaders who undertook any of those new expeditions,
volunteers resorted with the ardour and hope
peculiar to the age. Several of Almagro's soldiers joined them, and thus Pizarro had the satisfaction of being delivered both from the importunity of his discontented friends, and the
dread of his ancient enemies *.

Almagro himself remained for several months
in custody, under all the anguish of suspense.
For although his doom was determined by the
Pizarros from the moment that he fell into their
hands, prudence constrained them to defer gratifying their vengeance, until the soldiers who
had served under him, as well as several of their
own followers in whom they could not perfectly
confide, had left Cuzco. As soon as they set
out upon their different expeditions, Almagro
was impeached of treason, formally tried, and
condemned to die. The sentence astonished him;
and though he had often braved death with undaunted spirit in the field, its approach under
this ignominious form appalled him so much,
that he had recourse to abject supplications, unworthy of his former fame. He besought the

* Zarate, lib. iii. c. 12. Gomara, Hist. c. 141. Herrera, dec. 6. lib. iv. c. 7.

Pizarros to remember the ancient friendship between their brother and him, and how much he had contributed to the prosperity of their family; he reminded them of the humanity with which, in opposition to the repeated remonstrances of his own most attached friends, he had spared their lives when he had them in his power; he conjured them to pity his age and infirmities, and to suffer him to pass the wretched remainder of his days in bewailing his crimes, and in making his peace with Heaven. The entreaties, says a Spanish historian, of a man so much beloved, touched many an unfeeling heart, and drew tears from many a stern eye. But the brothers remained inflexible. As soon as Almagro knew his fate to be inevitable, he met it with the dignity and fortitude of a veteran. He was strangled in prison, and afterwards publicly beheaded. He suffered in the seventy-fifth year of his age, and left one son by an Indian woman of Panama, whom, though at that time a prisoner in Lima, he named as successor to his government, pursuant to a power which the emperor had granted him [*].

1539.] As, during the civil dissensions in Peru, all intercourse with Spain was suspended, the detail of the extraordinary transactions there did not soon reach the court. Unfortunately for the victorious faction, the first intelligence was brought thither by some of Almagro's officers, who left the country upon the ruin of their cause; and they related what had happened, with

* Zarate, lib. iii. c. 12. Gomara, Hist. c. 141. Vega, p. 11. lib. ii. c. 39. Herrera, dec. 6. lib. iv. c. 9. lib. v. c. 1.

every circumstance unfavourable to Pizarro and his brothers. Their ambition, their breach of the most solemn engagements, their violence and cruelty, were painted with all the malignity and exaggeration of party-hatred. Ferdinand Pizarro, who arrived soon after, and appeared in court with extraordinary splendour, endeavoured to efface the impression which their accusations had made; and to justify his brother and himself, by representing Almagro as the aggressor. The emperor and his ministers, though they could not pronounce which of the contending factions was most criminal, clearly discerned the fatal tendency of their dissensions. It was obvious, that while the leaders entrusted with the conduct of two infant colonies, employed the arms which should have been turned against the common enemy in destroying one another, all attention to the public good must cease, and there was reason to dread that the Indians might improve the advantage which the disunion of the Spaniards presented to them, and extirpate both the victors and vanquished. But the evil was more apparent than the remedy. Where the information which had been received was so defective and suspicious, and the scene of action so remote, it was almost impossible to chalk out the line of conduct that ought to be followed; and before any plan that should be approved of in Spain could be carried into execution, the situation of the parties, and the circumstances of affairs, might alter so entirely as to render its effects extremely pernicious.

Nothing therefore remained but to send a person to Peru, vested with extensive and discre-

tionary power, who, after viewing deliberately
the posture of affairs with his own eyes, and
enquiring upon the spot into the conduct of the
different leaders, should be authorised to establish
the government in that form which he deemed
most conducive to the interest of the parent state,
and the welfare of the colony.   The man se-
lected for this important charge was Christoval
Vaca de Castro, a judge in the court of royal
audience at Valladolid; and his abilities, integrity, and firmness, justified the choice.   His
instructions, though ample, were not such as to
fetter him in his operations.   According to the
different aspect of affairs, he had power to take
upon him different characters.   If he found the
governor still alive, he was to assume only the
title of judge, to maintain the appearance of
acting in concert with him, and to guard against
giving any just cause of offence to a man who
had merited so highly of his country.   But if
Pizarro were dead, he was entrusted with a
commission that he might then produce, by which
he was appointed his successor in the government of Peru.   This attention to Pizarro, however, seems to have flowed rather from dread of
his power, than from any approbation of his
measures; for at the very time that the court
seemed so solicitous not to irritate him, his brother Ferdinand was arrested at Madrid, and
confined to a prison, where he remained above
twenty years *.

1540.] While Vaca de Castro was preparing
for his voyage, events of great moment happened

* Gomara, Hist. c. 142.   Vega, p. 11. lib. ii. c. 40.
Herrera, dec. 6. lib. viii. c. 10, 11. lib. x. c. 1.

in Peru. The governor, considering himself, upon the death of Almagro, as the unrivalled possessor of that vast empire, proceeded to parcel out its territories among the conquerors; and had this division been made with any degree of impartiality, the extent of country which he had to bestow, was sufficient to have gratified his friends, and to have gained his enemies. But Pizarro conducted this transaction, not with the equity and candour of a judge attentive to discover and to reward merit, but with the illiberal spirit of a party-leader. Large districts, in parts of the country most cultivated and populous, were set apart as his own property, or granted to his brothers, his adherents, and favourites. To others, lots less valuable and inviting were assigned. The followers of Almagro, amongst whom were many of the original adventurers to whose valour and perseverance Pizarro was indebted for his success, were totally excluded from any portion in those lands, towards the acquisition of which they had contributed so largely. As the vanity of every individual set an immoderate value upon his own services, and the idea of each concerning the recompence due to them rose gradually to a more exorbitant height in proportion as their conquests extended, all who were disappointed in their expectations exclaimed loudly against the rapaciousness and partiality of the governor. The partisans of Almagro murmured in secret, and meditated revenge *.

* Vega, p. 1, lib. iii. c. 2.   Herrera, dec. 6. lib. viii. c. 5.

Rapid as the progress of the Spaniards in South America had been since Pizarro landed in Peru, their avidity of dominion was not yet satisfied. The officers to whom Ferdinand Pizarro gave the command of different detachments, penetrated into several new provinces; and though some of them were exposed to great hardships in the cold and barren regions of the Andes, and others suffered distress not inferior amidst the woods and marshes of the plains, they made discoveries and conquests which not only extended their knowledge of the country, but added considerably to the territories of Spain in the New World. Pedro de Valdivia reassumed Almagro's scheme of invading Chili, and notwithstanding the fortitude of the natives in defending their possessions, made such progress in the conquest of the country, that he founded the city of St. Jago, and gave a beginning to the establishment of the Spanish dominion in that province *. But of all the enterprises undertaken about this period, that of Gonzalo Pizarro was the most remarkable. The governor, who seems to have resolved that no person in Peru should possess any station of distinguished eminence or authority but those of his own family, had deprived Benalcazar, the conqueror of Quito, of his command in that kingdom, and appointed his brother Gonzalo to take the government of it. He instructed him to attempt the discovery and conquest of the country to the east of the Andes, which, according to the information of the Indians, abounded with cinnamon and other valuable spices. Gonzalo, not inferior to any

* Zarate, lib. iii. c. 13. Ovalle, lib. ii. c. 1, &c.

of his brothers in courage, and no less ambitious of acquiring distinction, eagerly engaged in this difficult service. He set out from Quito at the head of three hundred and forty soldiers, near one half of whom were horsemen, with four thousand Indians to carry their provisions. In forcing their way through the defiles, or over the ridges of the Andes, excess of cold and fatigue, to neither of which they were accustomed, proved fatal to the greater part of their wretched attendants. The Spaniards, though more robust, and inured to a variety of climates, suffered considerably, and lost some men; but when they descended into the low country their distress increased. During two months it rained incessantly, without any interval of fair weather long enough to dry their clothes *. The immense plains upon which they were now entering, either altogether without inhabitants, or occupied by the rudest and least industrious tribes in the New World, yielded little subsistence. They could not advance a step but as they cut a road through woods, or made it through marshes. Such incessant toil, and continual scarcity of food, seemed more than sufficient to have exhausted and dispirited any troops. But the fortitude and perseverance of the Spaniards in the sixteenth century were insuperable. Allured by frequent but false accounts of rich countries before them, they persisted in struggling on, until they reached the banks of the Coca or Napo, one of the large rivers whose waters pour into the Maragnon, and contribute to its grandeur. There, with infinite labour, they built

* Zarate, lib. iv. c. 2.

a bark, which they expected would prove of great utility, in conveying them over rivers, in procuring provisions, and in exploring the country. This was manned with fifty soldiers, under the command of Francis Orellana, the officer next in rank to Pizarro. The stream carried them down with such rapidity, that they were soon far a-head of their countrymen, who followed slowly and with difficulty by land.

At this distance from his commander, Orellana, a young man of an aspiring mind, began to fancy himself independent, and transported with the predominant passion of the age, he formed the scheme of distinguishing himself as a discoverer by following the course of the Maragnon, until it joined the ocean, and by surveying the vast regions through which it flows. This scheme of Orellana's was as bold as it was treacherous. For, if he be chargeable with the guilt of having violated his duty to his commander, and with having abandoned his fellow-soldiers in a pathless desert, where they had hardly any hopes of success, or even of safety, but what were founded on the service which they expected from the bark; his crime is, in some measure, balanced by the glory of having ventured upon a navigation of near two thousand leagues, through unknown nations, in a vessel hastily constructed, with green timber, and by very unskilful hands, without provisions, without a compass, or a pilot. But his courage and alacrity supplied every defect. Committing himself fearlessly to the guidance of the stream, the Napo bore him along to the south, until he reached the great channel of the Maragnon. Turning with it towards the

coast, he held on his course in that direction.
He made frequent descents on both sides of the
river, sometimes seizing by force of arms the provisions of the fierce savages seated on its banks;
and sometimes procuring a supply of food by a
friendly intercourse with more gentle tribes.
After a long series of dangers, which he encountered with amazing fortitude, and of distresses which he supported with no less magna-
nimity, he reached the ocean *, where new perils
awaited him.   These he likewise surmounted,
and got safe to the Spanish settlement in the
island Cubagua; from thence he sailed to Spain.
The vanity natural to travellers who visit regions
unknown to the rest of mankind, and the art of an
adventurer, solicitous to magnify his own merit,
concurred in prompting him to mingle an extraordinary proportion of the marvellous in the
narrative of his voyage.   He pretended to have
discovered nations so rich, that the roofs of their
temples were covered with plates of gold; and
described a republic of women so warlike and
powerful, as to have extended their dominion over
a considerable track of the fertile plains which
he had visited. Extravagant as those tales were,
they gave rise to an opinion that a region abound-
ing with gold, distinguished by the name of *El
Dorado*, and a community of Amazons, were to
be found in this part of the New World; and
such is the propensity of mankind to believe
what is wonderful, that it has been slowly, and
with difficulty, that reason and observation have
exploded those fables. The voyage, however,
even when stripped of every romantic embellish-

* See Note CXXXVII.

ment, deserves to be recorded, not only as one
of the most memorable occurrences in that adventurous age, but as the first event which led
to any certain knowledge of the extensive countries that stretch eastward from the Andes to
the ocean *.

No words can describe the consternation of
Pizarro, when he did not find the bark at the
confluence of the Napo and Maragnon, where he
had ordered Orellana to wait for him. He
would not allow himself to suspect that a man,
whom he had entrusted with such an important
command, could be so base and so unfeeling as
to desert him at such a juncture. But imputing
his absence from the place of rendezvous to some
unknown accident, he advanced above fifty
leagues along the banks of the Maragnon, expecting every moment to see the bark appear
with a supply of provisions. [1541] At length
he came up with an officer whom Orellana had
left to perish in the desert, because he had the
courage to remonstrate against his perfidy. From
him he learned the extent of Orellana's crime,
and his followers perceived at once their own
desperate situation, when deprived of their only
resource. The spirit of the stoutest hearted
veteran sunk within him, and all demanded to be
led back instantly. Pizarro, though he assumed
an appearance of tranquillity, did not oppose
their inclination. But he was now twelve hundred miles from Quito; and in that long march
the Spaniards encountered hardships greater

* Zarate, lib. iv. c. 4. Gomara, Hist. c. 86. Vega,
p. 11. lib. iii. c. 4. Herrera, dec. 6. lib. ix. c. 2—4.
Rodriguez El Maragnon y Amazonas, lib. i. o. 3.

than those which they had endured in their progress outward, without the alluring hopes which then soothed and animated them under their sufferings. Hunger compelled them to feed on roots and berries, to eat all their dogs and horses, to devour the most loathsome reptiles, and even to gnaw the leather of their saddles and sword-belts. Four thousand Indians, and two hundred and ten Spaniards, perished in this wild disastrous expedition, which continued near two years: and, as fifty men were aboard the bark with Orellana, only fourscore got back to Quito. These were naked like savages, and so emaciated with famine, or worn out with fatigue, that they had more the appearance of spectres than of men *.

But, instead of returning to enjoy the repose which his condition required, Pizarro, on entering Quito, received accounts of a fatal event that threatened calamities more dreadful to him than those through which he had passed. From the time that his brother made that partial division of his conquests which has been mentioned, the adherents of Almagro, considering themselves as proscribed by the party in power, no longer entertained any hope of bettering their condition. Great numbers in despair resorted to Lima, where the house of young Almagro was always open to them, and the slender portion of his father's fortune which the governor allowed him to enjoy, was spent in affording them subsistence. The warm attachment with which every person

* Zarate, lib. iv. c. 2—5. Vega. p. II. lib. iii. c. 3, 4. 5. 14. Herrera, dec. 6. lib. viii. c. 7, 8. lib. ix. c. 2—5. dec. 7. lib. iii. c. 14. Pizar. Varones, Illustr. 349, &c.

who had served under the elder Almagro devoted himself to his interest, was quickly transferred to his son, who was now grown up to
the age of manhood, and possessed all the qualities which captivate the affections of soldiers.
Of a graceful appearance, dexterous at all martial
exercises, bold, open, generous, he seemed to be
formed for command ; and as his father, conscious
of his own inferiority, from the total want of
education, had been extremely attentive to have
him instructed in every science becoming a gentleman ; the accomplishments which he had acquired heightened the respect of his followers, as
they gave him distinction and eminence among
illiterate adventurers. In this young man the
Almagrians found a point of union which they
wanted, and looking up to him as their head,
were ready to undertake any thing for his ad-
vancement. Nor was affection for Almagro their
only incitement ; they were urged on by their
own distresses. Many of them, destitute of common necessaries *, and weary of loitering away
life, a burden to their chief, or to such of their
associates as had saved some remnant of their fortune from pillage and confiscation, longed im-
patiently for an occasion to exert their activity and
courage, and began to deliberate how they might
be avenged on the author of all their misery.
Their frequent cabals did not pass unobserved ;
and the governor was warned to be on his guard
against men who meditated some desperate deed,
and had resolution to execute it. But, either from
the native intrepidity of his mind, or from contempt of persons whose poverty seemed to render

* See Note CXXXVIII.

their machinations of little consequence, he disregarded the admonitions of his friends. " Be in no pain," said he carelessly, " about my life ; it is perfectly safe, as long as every man in Peru knows that I can in a moment cut off any head which dares to harbour a thought against it." This security gave the Almagrians full leisure to digest and ripen every part of their scheme; and Juan de Herrada, an officer of great abilities, who had the charge of Almagro's education, took the direction of their consultations, with all the zeal which this connection inspired, and with all the authority which the ascendant that he was known to have over the mind of his pupil gave him.

On Sunday the twenty-sixth of June, at midday, the season of tranquillity and repose in all sultry climates, Herrada, at the head of eighteen of the most determined conspirators, sallied out of Almagro's house in complete armour ; and drawing their swords as they advanced hastily towards the governor's palace, cried out, " Long live the king, but let the tyrant die !" Their associates, warned of their motions by a signal, were in arms at different stations ready to support them. Though Pizarro was usually surrounded by such a numerous train of attendants as suited the magnificence of the most opulent subject of the age in which he lived, yet as he was just risen from table, and most of his domestics had retired to their own apartments, the conspirators passed through the two outer courts of the palace unobserved. They were at the bottom of the stair-case, before a page in-waiting could give the alarm to his master, who was conversing with a few friends in a large hall. The governor, whose steady mind no form of danger could appal, starting up, called for arms, and commanded Francisco de Chaves to make fast the door. But that officer, who did not retain so much presence of mind as to obey this prudent order, running to the top of the stair-case, wildly asked the conspirators what they meant, and whither they were going ? Instead of answering, they stabbed him to the heart, and burst into the hall. Some of the persons who were there threw themselves from the windows; others attempted to fly; and a few drawing their swords, followed their leader into an inner apartment. The conspirators, animated with having the object of their vengeance now in view, rushed forward after them. Pizarro, with no other arms than his sword and buckler, defended the entry, and, supported by his half brother Alcantara, and his little knot of friends, he maintained the unequal contest with intrepidity worthy of his past exploits, and with the vigour of a youthful combatant. " Courage!" cried he, " companions, we are yet enow to make those traitors repent of their audacity !" But the armour of the conspirators protected them, while every thrust they made took effect. Alcantara fell dead at his brother's feet; his other defenders were mortally wounded. The governor, so weary that he could hardly wield his sword, and no longer able to parry the many weapons furiously aimed at him, received a deadly thrust full in his throat, sunk to the ground, and expired.

Vol. III. G

As soon as he was slain, the assassins ran out into the streets, and waving their bloody swords, proclaimed the death of the tyrant. Above two hundred of their associates having joined them, they conducted young Almagro in solemn procession through the city, and assembling the magistrates and principal citizens, compelled them to acknowledge him as lawful successor to his father in his government. The palace of Pizarro, together with the houses of several of his adherents, were pillaged by the soldiers, who had the satisfaction at once of being avenged on their enemies, and of enriching themselves by the spoils of those through whose hands all the wealth of Péru had passed *.

The boldness and success of the conspiracy, as well as the name and popular qualities of Almagro, drew many soldiers to his standard. Every adventurer of desperate fortune, all who were dissatisfied with Pizarro, and from the rapaciousness of his government in the latter years of his life, the number of malecontents was considerable, declared without hesitation in favour of Almagro, and he was soon at the head of eight hundred of the most gallant veterans in Peru. As his youth and inexperience disqualified him from taking the command of them himself, he appointed Herrada to act as general. But though Almagro speedily collected such a respectable force, the acquiescence in his government was far from being general.

* Zarate, lib. iv. c. 6—8.   Gomara Hist. c. 144, 145. Vega, p. 11. lib. iii. c. 5—7. Herrera, dec. 6. lib. x. c. 4— 7. Pizarro Var. Illust. p. 183.

Pizarro had left many friends to whom his memory was dear; the barbarous assassination of a man to whom his country was so highly indebted, filled every impartial person with horror. The ignominious birth of Almagro, as well as the doubtful title on which he founded his pretensions, led others to consider him as an usurper. The officers who commanded in some provinces refused to recognise his authority, until it was confirmed by the emperor. In others, particularly at Cuzco, the royal standard was erected, and preparations were begun in order to revenge the murder of their ancient leader.

Those seeds of discord, which could not have lain long dormant, acquired great vigour and activity, when the arrival of Vaca de Castro was known. After a long and disastrous voyage, he was driven by stress of weather into a small harbour in the province of Popayan; and proceeding from thence by land, after a journey no less tedious than difficult, he reached Quito. In his way he received accounts of Pizarro's death, and of the events which followed upon it. He immediately produced the royal commission appointing him governor of Peru, with the same privileges and authority; and his jurisdiction was acknowledged without hesitation by Benalcazar, adelantado, or lieutenant-general, for the emperor in Popayan, and by Pedro de Puelles, who, in the absence of Gonzalo Pizarro, had the command of the troops left in Quito. Vaca de Castro not only assumed the supreme authority, but shewed that he possessed the talents which the exercise of it at that juncture required. By his influence and address he soon

G 2

assembled such a body of troops, as not only set him above all fear of being exposed to any insult from the adverse party, but enabled him to advance from Quito with the dignity that became his character. By dispatching persons of confidence to the different settlements in Peru, with a formal notification of his arrival and of his commission, he communicated to his countrymen the royal pleasure with respect to the government of the country. By private emissaries, he excited such officers as had discovered their disapprobation of Almagro's proceedings, to manifest their duty to their sovereign by supporting the person honoured with his commission. Those measures were productive of great effects. Encouraged by the approach of the new governor, or prepared by his machinations, the loyal were confirmed in their principles, and avowed them with greater boldness ; the timid ventured to declare their sentiments ; the neutral and wavering, finding it necessary to choose a side, began to lean to that which now appeared to be the safest, as well as the most just *.

Almagro observed the rapid progress of this spirit of disaffection to his cause, and in order to give an effectual check to it before the arrival of Vaca de Castro, he set out at the head of his troops for Cuzco [1542], where the most considerable body of opponents had erected the royal standard, under the command of Pedro Alvarez Holguin. During his march thither, Herrada, the skilful guide of his youth and of his counsels, died ; and from that time his mea-

* Benzon, lib. iii. c. 9. Zarate. lib. iv. c. 11. Gomara, c. 146, 147. Herrera, dec. 6. lib. x. c. 1, 2, 3 7, &c.

sures were conspicuous for their violence, but concerted with little sagacity, and executed with no address. Holguin, who, with forces far inferior to those of the opposite party, was descending towards the coast at the very time that Almagro was on his way to Cuzco, deceived his unexperienced adversary by a very simple stratagem, avoided an engagement, and effected a junction with Alvarado, an officer of note, who had been the first to declare against Almagro as an usurper.

Soon after, Vaca de Castro entered their camp with the troops which he brought from Quito, and erecting the royal standard before his own tent, he declared, that, as governor, he would discharge in person all the functions of general of their combined forces. Though formed by the tenour of his past life to the habits of a sedentary and pacific profession, he at once assumed the activity and discovered the decision of an officer long accustomed to command. Knowing his strength to be now far superior to that of the enemy, he was impatient to terminate the contest by a battle. Nor did the followers of Almagro, who had no hopes of obtaining a pardon for a crime so atrocious as the murder of the governor, decline that mode of decision. They met at Chupaz [Sept. 16], about two hundred miles from Cuzco, and fought with all the fierce animosity inspired by the violence of civil rage, the rancour of private enmity, the eagerness of revenge, and the last efforts of despair. Victory, after remaining long doubtful, declared at last for Vaca de Castro. The superior number of his troops, his own intrepidity, and the martial

G 3

talents of Francisco de Carvajal, a veteran officer formed under the great captain in the wars
of Italy, and who on that day laid the foundation of his future fame in Peru, triumphed over
the bravery of his opponents, though led on by
young Almagro with a gallant spirit, worthy of
a better cause, and deserving another fate. The
carnage was great in proportion to the number
of the combatants. Many of the vanquished,
especially such as were conscious that they might
be charged with being accessory to the assassination of Pizarro, rushing on the swords of the
enemy, chose to fall like soldiers, rather than
wait an ignominious doom. Of fourteen hundred men, the total amount of combatants on
both sides, five hundred lay dead on the field,
and the number of the wounded was still
greater *.

If the military talents displayed by Vaca de
Castro, both in the council and in the field, surprised the adventurers in Peru, they were still
more astonished at his conduct after the victory.
As he was by nature a rigid dispenser of justice,
and persuaded that it required examples of extraordinary severity to restrain the licentious spirit of soldiers so far removed from the seat of
government, he proceeded directly to try his
prisoners as rebels. Forty were condemned to
suffer the death of traitors, others were banished
from Peru. Their leader, who made his escape
from the battle, being betrayed by some of his
officers, was publicly beheaded in Cuzco; and

* Zarate, lib. iv. c. 12—19. Gomara, c. 148. Vega,
p. 11. lib. iii. c. 11—18. Herrera, dec. 7. lib. i. c. 1, 2, 3.
lib. iii. c. 1—11.

in him the name of Almagro, and the spirit of the party, was extinct *.

During those violent convulsions in Peru, the emperor and his ministers were intently employed in preparing regulations, by which they hoped not only to re-establish tranquillity there, but to introduce a more perfect system of internal policy into all their settlements in the New World. It is manifest from all the events recorded in the history of America, that rapid and extensive as the Spanish conquests there had been, they were not carried on by any regular exertion of the national force, but by the occasional efforts of private adventurers. After fitting out a few of the first armaments for discovering new regions, the court of Spain, during the busy reigns of Ferdinand and of Charles V. the former the most intriguing prince of the age, and the latter the most ambitious, was encumbered with such a multiplicity of schemes, and involved in war with so many nations of Europe, that it had not leisure to attend to distant and less interesting objects. The care of prosecuting discovery, or of attempting conquest, was abandoned to individuals; and with such ardour did men push forward in this new career, on which novelty, the spirit of adventure, avarice, ambition, and the hope of meriting heaven, prompted them with combined influence to enter, that in less than half a century almost the whole of that extensive empire which Spain now possesses in the New World, was subjected to its dominion. As the Spanish court contributed no-

* Zarate, lib. iv. c. 21. Comara, c. 150. Herrera, dec. 7. lib. iii. cap. 12. lib. vi. c. 1.

thing towards the various expeditions undertaken in America, it was not entitled to claim
much from their success. The sovereignty of
the conquered provinces, with the fifth of the
gold and silver, was reserved for the crown;
every thing else was seized by the associates in
each expedition as their own right. The plunder of the countries which they invaded served
to indemnify them for what they had expended in
equipping themselves for the service, and the
conquered territory was divided among them,
according to rules which custom had introduced,
as permanent establishments which their successful
valour merited. In the infancy of those settlements, when their extent as well as their value
were unknown, many irregularities escaped observation, and it was found necessary to connive
at many excesses. The conquered people were
frequently pillaged with destructive rapacity, and
their country parcelled out among its new masters in exorbitant shares, far exceeding the highest
recompence due to their services. The rude conquerors of America, incapable of forming their
establishments upon any general or extensive plan
of policy, attentive only to private interest, unwilling to forego present gain from the prospect
of remote or public benefit, seem to have had no
object but to amass sudden wealth, without re-
garding what might be the consequences of the
means by which they acquired it. But when
time at length discovered to the Spanish court
the importance of its American possessions, the
necessity of new-modelling their whole frame became obvious, and in place of the maxims and
practices prevalent among military adventurers,

it was found requisite to substitute the institutions of regular government.

One evil in particular called for an immediate remedy. The conquerors of Mexico and Peru imitated the fatal example of their countrymen settled in the islands, and employed themselves in searching for gold and silver with the same inconsiderate eagerness. Similar effects followed. The natives, employed in this labour by masters who, in imposing tasks, had no regard either to what they felt or to what they were able to perform, pined away and perished so fast that there was reason to apprehend that Spain, instead of possessing countries peopled to such a degree as to be susceptible of progressive improvement, would soon remain proprietor only of a vast uninhabited desert.

The emperor and his ministers were so sensible of this, and so solicitous to prevent the extinction of the Indian race, which threatened to render their acquisitions of no value, that from time to time various laws, which I have mentioned, had been made for securing to that unhappy people more gentle and equitable treatment. But the distance of America from the seat of empire, the feebleness of government in the new colonies, the avarice and audacity of soldiers unaccustomed to restraint, prevented these salutary regulations from operating with any considerable influence. The evil continued to grow, and at this time the emperor found an interval of leisure from the affairs of Europe to take it into attentive consideration. He consulted not only with his ministers and the members of the council of the Indies, but called

upon several persons who had resided long in the
New World, to aid them with the result of
their experience and observation. Fortunately
for the people of America, among these was
Bartholomew de las Casas, who happened to be
then at Madrid on a mission from a chapter of
his order at Chiapa *. Though, since the mis-
carriage of his former schemes for the relief of
the Indians, he had continued shut up in his
cloister, or occupied in religious functions, his
zeal in behalf of the former objects of his pity
was so far from abating, that, from an increased
knowledge of their sufferings, its ardour had
augmented. He seized eagerly this opportunity
of reviving his favourite maxims concerning the
treatment of the Indians. With the moving
eloquence natural to a man on whose mind the
scenes which he had beheld had made a deep
impression, he described the irreparable waste of
the human species in the New World, the Indian
race almost totally swept away in the Islands in
less than fifty years, and hastening to extinction
on the continent with the same rapid decay.
With the decisive tone of one strongly prepos-
sessed with the truth of his own system, he imputed all this to a single cause, to the exactions
and cruelty of his countrymen, and contended
that nothing could prevent the depopulation of
America, but the declaring of its natives to be
freemen, and treating them as subjects, not as
slaves. Nor did he confide for the success of
this proposal in the powers of his oratory alone.
In order to enforce them, he composed his
famous treatise concerning the destruction of

* Remesal, Hist. de Chiapa, p. 146.

America *, in which he relates, with many horrid circumstances, but with apparent marks of exaggerated description, the devastation of every province which had been visited by the Spaniards.

The emperor was deeply afflicted with the recital of so many actions shocking to humanity. But as his views extended far beyond those of Las Casas, he perceived that relieving the Indians from oppression was but one step towards rendering his possessions in the New World a valuable acquisition, and would be of little avail, unless he could circumscribe the power and usurpations of his own subjects there. The conquerors of America, however great their merit had been towards their country, were mostly persons of such mean birth, and of such an abject rank in society, as gave no distinction in the eye of a monarch. The exorbitant wealth with which some of them returned, gave umbrage to an age not accustomed to see men in inferior condition elevated above their level, and rising to emulate or to surpass the ancient nobility in splendour. The territories which their leaders had appropriated to themselves were of such enormous extent †, that if the country should ever be improved in proportion to the fertility of the soil, they must grow too wealthy and too powerful for subjects. It appeared to Charles that this abuse required a remedy no less than the other, and that the regulations concerning both must be enforced by a mode of government more vigorous than had yet been introduced into America.

* Remesal, 192. 199.   † See Note CXXXIX.

With this view he framed a body of laws, containing many salutary appointments with respect to the constitution and powers of the supreme council of the Indies; concerning the station and jurisdiction of the royal audiences in different parts of America ; the administration of justice ; the order of government, both ecclesiastical and civil. These were approved of by all ranks of men. But together with them were issued the following regulations, which excited universal alarm, and occasioned the most violent convulsions : " That as the *repartimientos* or shares of land seized by several persons appeared to be excessive, the royal audiences are empowered to reduce them to a moderate extent : That upon the death of any conqueror or planter, the lands and Indians granted to him shall not descend to his widow or children, but return to the crown : That the Indians shall henceforth be exempt from personal service, and shall not be compelled to carry the baggage of travellers, to labour in the mines, or to dive in the pearl fisheries : That the stated tribute due by them to their superior shall be ascertained, and they shall be paid as servants for any work they voluntarily perform : That all persons who are or have been in public offices, all ecclesiastics of every denomination, all hospitals and monasteries, shall be deprived of the lands and Indians allotted to them, and these be annexed to the crown : That every person in Peru, who had any criminal concern in the contests between Pizarro and Almagro, should forfeit his lands and Indians *."

* Herrera, dec. 7. lib. vi. c. 5.   Fernandez, Hist. lib. i. c. i, 2.

All the Spanish ministers who had hitherto
been entrusted with the direction of American
affairs, and who were best acquainted with the
state of the country, remonstrated against those
regulations as ruinous to their infant colonies.
They represented, that the number of Spaniards
who had hitherto emigrated to the New World
was so extremely small, that nothing could be
expected from any effort of theirs towards improving the vast regions over which they were
scattered ; that the success of every scheme for
this purpose must depend upon the ministry and
service of the Indians, whose native indolence
and aversion to labour, no prospect of benefit or
promise of reward could surmount ; that the
moment the right of imposing a task, and exacting the performance of it, was taken from
their masters, every work of industry must cease,
and all the sources from which wealth begun to
pour in upon Spain must be stopt for ever.   But
Charles, tenacious at all times of his own opinions,
and so much impressed at present with the view
of the disorders which reigned in America, that
he was willing to hazard the application even of
a dangerous remedy, persisted in his resolution
of publishing the laws.   That they might be
carried into execution with greater vigour and
authority, he authorised Francisco Tello de Sandoval to repair to Mexico as *Visitador*, or super-
intendant of that country, and to co-operate
with Antonio de Mendoza, the viceroy, in enforcing them.   He appointed Blasco Nugnez
Vela to be governor of Peru, with the title of
Viceroy ; and in order to strengthen his administration, he established a court of royal audi-

ence in Lima [1543], in which four lawyers of eminence were to preside as judges *.

The viceroy and superintendent sailed at the same time ; and an account of the laws which they were to enforce reached America before them. The entry of Sandoval into Mexico was viewed as the prelude of general ruin. The unlimited grant of liberty to the Indians affected every Spaniard in America without distinction, and there was hardly one who might not on some pretext be included under the other regulations, and suffer by them. But the colony in New Spain had now been so long accustomed to the restraints of law and authority under the steady and prudent administration of Mendoza, that how much soever the spirit of the new statutes was detested and dreaded, no attempt was made to obstruct the publication of them by any act of violence unbecoming subjects. The magistrates and principal inhabitants, however, presented dutiful addresses to the viceroy and superintendent, representing the fatal consequences of enforcing them. Happily for them, Mendoza, by long residence in the country, was so thoroughly acquainted with its state, that he knew what was for its interest as well as what it could bear ; and Sandoval, though new in office, displayed a degree of moderation seldom possessed by persons just entering upon the exercise of power. They engaged to suspend, for some time, the execution of what was offensive in the new laws, and not only consented that a deputation of citizens should be sent to Europe to

* Zarate. lib. iii. c. 24. Gomara, c. 151. Vega, p. 2. lib. iii. c. 20.

lay before the emperor the apprehensions of his subjects in New Spain with respect to their tendency and effects, but they concurred with them in supporting their sentiments. Charles, moved by the opinion of men whose abilities and integrity entitled them to decide concerning what fell immediately under their own view, granted such a relaxation of the rigour of the laws as re-established the colony in its former tranquillity *.

In Peru the storm gathered with an aspect still more fierce and threatening, and was not so soon dispelled. The conquerors of Peru, of a rank much inferior to those who had subjected Mexico to the Spanish crown, farther removed from the inspection of, the parent state, and intoxicated with the sudden acquisition of wealth, carried on all their operations with greater licence and irregularity than any body of adventurers in the New World. Amidst the general subversion of law and order, occasioned by two successive civil wars, when each individual was at liberty to decide for himself, without any guide but his own interest or passions, this turbulent spirit rose above all sense of subordination. To men thus corrupted by anarchy, the introduction of regular government, the power of a viceroy, and the authority of a respectable court of judicature, would of themselves have appeared formidable restraints, to which they would have submitted with reluctance. But they

* Fernandez, Hist. lib. i. c. 3, 4, 5. Vega, p. 11. lib. iii. c. 21, 22. Herrera, dec. 7. lib. v. c. 7. lib. vii. c. 14, 15. Torquem. Mond. Ind. lib. v. c. 13.

H 2

revolted with indignation against the idea of
complying with laws by which they were to be
stripped at once of all they had earned so hardly
during many years of service and suffering.   As
the account of the new laws spread successively
through the different settlements, the inhabitants
ran together, the women in tears, and the men
exclaiming against the injustice and ingratitude
of their sovereign in depriving them, unheard and
unconvicted, of their possessions.   " Is this,"
cried they, " the recompence due to persons,
who, without public aid, at their own expence,
and by their own valour, have subjected to the
crown of Castile territories of such immense extent and opulence ? Are these the rewards bestowed for having endured unparalleled distress,
for having encountered every species of danger
in the service of their country ? Whose merit is
so great, whose conduct has been so irreproachable, that he may not be condemned by some
penal clause in regulations, conceived in terms as
loose and comprehensive, as if it had been intended that all should be entangled in their
snare ? Every Spaniard of note in Peru has held
some public office, and all, without distinction,
have been constrained to take an active part in
the contest between the two rival chiefs.   Were
the former to be robbed of their property because
they had done their duty ? Were the latter to
be punished on account of what they could not
avoid ? Shall the conquerors of this great empire, instead of receiving marks of distinction, be
deprived of the natural consolation of providing
for their widows and children, and leave them to

depend for subsistence on the scanty supply they can extort from unfeeling courtiers * ? We are not able now, continued they, to explore unknown regions in quest of more secure settlements; our constitutions, debilitated with age, and our bodies covered with wounds, are no longer fit for active service; but still we possess vigour sufficient to assert our just rights, and we will not tamely suffer them to be wrested from us †."

By discourses of this sort, uttered with vehemence, and listened to with universal approbation, their passions were inflamed to such a pitch, that they were prepared for the most violent measures; and began to hold consultations in different places, how they might oppose the entrance of the viceroy and judges, and prevent not only the execution but the promulgation of the new laws. From this, however, they were diverted by the address of Vaca de Castro, who flattered them with hopes, that, as soon as the viceroy and judges should arrive, and had leisure to examine their petitions and remonstrances, they would concur with them in endeavouring to procure some mitigation in the rigour of laws which had been framed without due attention either to the state of the country, or to the sentiments of the people. A greater degree of accommodation to these, and even some concessions on the part of government, were now become requisite to compose the present ferment, and to sooth the colonists into submission, by inspiring them with confidence in their superiors

* Herrera, dec. 7. lib. vii. c. 14, 15.

† Gomara, c. 152. Herrera, dec. 7. lib. vi. c. 10, 11. Vega, p. 14. lib. iii. c. 20. 22. lib. iv. c. 3, 4.

H 3

But without profound discernment, conciliating
manners, and flexibility of temper, such a plan
could not be carried on.   The viceroy possessed
none of these.   Of all the qualities that fit men
for high command, he was endowed only with
integrity and courage; the former, harsh and un-
complying, the latter bordering so frequently on
rashness or obstinacy, that in his situation they
were defects rather than virtues.   From the moment that he landed at Tumbez [March 4],
Nugnez Vela seems to have considered himself
merely as an executive officer, without any discretionary power; and, regardless of whatever
he observed or heard concerning the state of the
country, he adhered to the letter of the regulations with unrelenting rigour.   In all the towns
through which he passed, the natives were declared to be free, every person in public office was
deprived of his lands and servants; and as an
example of obedience to others, he would not
suffer a single Indian to be employed in carrying
his own baggage in his march towards Lima.
Amazement and consternation went before him
as he approached; and so little solicitous was he
to prevent these from augmenting, that, on entering the capital, he openly avowed that he came
to obey the orders of his sovereign, not to dispense with his laws.   This harsh declaration was
accompanied with what rendered it still more intolerable, haughtiness in deportment, a tone of
arrogance and decision in discourse, and an insolence of office, grievous to men little accustomed
to hold civil authority in high respect.   Every
attempt to procure a suspension or mitigation of
the new laws, the viceroy considered as flowing

from a spirit of disaffection that tended to rebellion. Several persons of rank were confined, and some put to death, without any form of trial. Vaca de Castro was arrested, and, notwithstanding the dignity of his former rank, and his merit in having prevented a general insurrection in the colony, he was loaded with chains, and shut up in the common jail *.

But however general the indignation was against such proceedings, it is probable the hand of authority would have been strong enough to suppress it, or to prevent it bursting out with open violence, if the malecontents had not been provided with a leader of credit and eminence to unite and to direct their efforts. From the time that the purport of the new regulations was known in Peru, every Spaniard there turned his eyes towards Gonzalo Pizarro, as the only person able to avert the ruin with which they threatened the colony. From all quarters, letters and addresses were sent to him, conjuring him to stand forth as their common protector, and offering to support him in the attempt with their lives and fortunes. Gonzalo, though inferior in talents to his other brothers, was equally ambitious, and of courage no less daring. The behaviour of an ungrateful court towards his brothers and himself, dwelt continually on his mind. Ferdinand a state prisoner in Europe, the children of the governor in custody of the viceroy, and sent aboard his fleet, himself reduced to the condition

* Zarate, lib. iv. c. 23, 24, 25. Gomara, c. 153—155. Vega, p. 11. lb. iv. c. 4, 5. Fernandez, lib. i. c. 6—10.

of a private citizen in a country, for the discovery and conquest of which Spain was indebted to his family: These thoughts prompted him to seek for vengeance, and to assert the rights of his family, of which he now considered himself as the guardian and the heir. But as no Spaniard can easily surmount that veneration for his sovereign which seems to be interwoven in his frame, the idea of marching in arms against the royal standard filled him with horror. He hesitated long, and was still unresolved, when the violence of the viceroy, the universal call of his countrymen, and the certainty of becoming soon a victim himself to the severity of the new laws, moved him to quit his residence at Chuquisaca de la Plata, and repair to Cuzco. All the inhabitants went out to meet him, and received him with transports of joy as the deliverer of the colony. In the fervour of their zeal, they elected him procurator-general of the Spanish nation in Peru, to solicit the repeal of the late regulations. They empowered him to lay their remonstrances before the royal audience in Lima, and upon pretext of danger from the Indians, authorised him to march thither in arms. [1544.] Under sanction of this nomination, Pizarro took possession of the royal treasure, appointed officers, levied soldiers, seized a large train of artillery which Vaca de Castro had deposited in Gumanga, and set out for Lima, as if he had been advancing against a public enemy. Disaffection having now assumed a regular form, and being united under a chief of such distinguished name, many persons of note resorted to his standard;

and a considerable part of the troops, raised by the viceroy to oppose his progress, deserted to him in a body *.

Before Pizarro reached Lima, a revolution had happened there, which encouraged him to proceed with almost certainty of success. The violence of the viceroy's administration was not more formidable to the Spaniards of Peru, than his overbearing haughtiness was odious to his associates, the judges of the royal audience. During their voyage from Spain, some symptoms of coldness between the viceroy and them began to appear †. But as soon as they entered upon the exercise of their respective offices, both parties were so much exasperated by frequent contests, arising from interference of jurisdiction, and contrariety of opinion, that their mutual disgust soon grew into open enmity. The judges thwarted the viceroy in every measure, set at liberty prisoners whom he had confined, justified the malecontents, and applauded their remonstrances.

At a time when both departments of government should have united against the approaching enemy, they were contending with each other for superiority. The judges at length prevailed. The viceroy, universally odious, and abandoned even by his own guards, was seized in his palace [Sept. 18], and carried to a desert island on the coast, to be kept there until he could be sent home to Spain.

* Zarate, lib. 5. c. 1. Gomara, c. 156, 157. Vega, p. 11. lib. iv. c. 4—12. Fernandez, lib. i. c. 12—17. Herrera, dec. 7. lib. vii. c. 18, &c. lib. viii. c. 1—5.
† Gomara, c. 171.

The judges, in consequence of this, having assumed the supreme direction of affairs into their own hands, issued a proclamation suspending the execution of the obnoxious laws, and sent a message to Pizarro, requiring him, as they had already granted whatever he could request, to dismiss his troops, and to repair to Lima with fifteen or twenty attendants. They could hardly expect that a man so daring and ambitious would tamely comply with this requisition. It was made, probably, with no such intention, but only to throw a decent veil over their own conduct; for Cepeda, the president of the court of audience, a pragmatical and aspiring lawyer, seems to have held a secret correspondence with Pizarro, and had already formed the plan, which he afterwards executed, of devoting himself to his service. The imprisonment of the viceroy, the usurpation of the judges, together with the universal confusion and anarchy consequent upon events so singular and unexpected, opened new and vast prospects to Pizarro. He now beheld the supreme power within his reach. Nor did he want courage to push on towards the object which fortune presented to his view. Carvajal, the prompter of his resolutions, and guide of all his actions, had long fixed his eye upon it as the only end at which Pizarro ought to aim. Instead of the inferior function of procurator for the Spanish settlements in Peru, he openly demanded to be governor and captain-general of the whole province, and required the court of audience to grant him a commission to that effect. At the head of twelve hundred men, within a mile of

Lima, where there was neither leader nor army to oppose him, such a request carried with it the authority of a command.   But the judges, either from unwillingness to relinquish power, or from a desire of preserving some attention to appearances, hesitated, or seemed to hesitate, about complying with what he demanded.   Carvajal, impatient of delay, and impetuous in all his operations, marched into the city by night, seized several officers of distinction obnoxious to Pizarro, and hanged them without the formality of a trial. Next morning the court of audience issued a commission in the emperor's name, appointing Pizarro governor of Peru, with full powers, civil as well as military, and he entered the town that day with extraordinary pomp, to take possession of his new dignity *.

Oct. 28.] But amidst the disorder and turbulence which accompanied this total dissolution of the frame of government, the minds of men, set loose from the ordinary restraints of law and authority, acted with such capricious irregularity, that events no less extraordinary than unexpected followed in a rapid succession. Pizarro had scarcely begun to exercise the new powers with which he was invested, when he beheld formidable enemies rise up to oppose him.   The viceroy having been put on board a vessel by the judges of the audience, in order that he might be carried to Spain under custody of Juan Alvarez, one of their own number ; as soon as they were out at sea, Alvarez, either touched with remorse, or moved

* Zarate, lib. v. c. 8—10. Vega. p. 11. lib. iv. c. 13 —19. Gomara, c. 159—163. Fernandez, lib. i. c. 18— 25. Herrera, dec, 7. lib. viii. c. 10—20.

by fear, kneeled down to his prisoner, declaring him from that moment to be free, and that he himself, and every person in the ship, would obey him as the legal representative of their sovereign. Nugnez Vela ordered the pilot of the vessel to shape his course towards Tumbez, and as soon as he landed there, erected the royal standard, and resumed his functions of viceroy. Several persons of note, to whom the contagion of the seditious spirit which reigned at Cuzco and Lima had not reached, instantly avowed their resolution to support his authority *. The violence of Pizarro's government, who observed every individual with the jealousy natural to usurpers, and who punished every appearance of disaffection with unforgiving severity, soon augmented the number of the viceroy's adherents, as it forced some leading men in the colony to fly to him for refuge. While he was gathering such strength at Tumbez, that his forces began to assume the appearance of what was considered as an army in America, Diego Centeno, a bold and active officer, exasperated by the cruelty and oppression of Pizarro's lieutenant-governor in the province of Charcas, formed a conspiracy against his life, cut him off, and declared for the viceroy †.

1545.] Pizarro, though alarmed with those appearances of hostility in the opposite extremes of the empire, was not disconcerted. He prepared to assert the authority to which he had attained, with the spirit and conduct of an officer

* Zarate, lib. v. c. 9. Gomara, c. 165. Fernandez, lib. 1. c. 23. Herrera. dec. 7. lib. viii. c. 15.

† Zarate, lib. v. c. 18. Gomara, c. 169. Herrera, dec. 7. lib. ix. c. 27.

accustomed to command, and marched directly against the viceroy as the enemy who was nearest as well as most formidable. As he was master of the public revenues in Peru, and most of the military men were attached to his family, his troops were so numerous, that the viceroy, unable to face them, retreated towards Quito. Pizarro followed him; and in that long march, through a wild mountainous country, suffered hardships and encountered difficulties, which no troops but those accustomed to serve in America could have endured or surmounted *. The viceroy had scarcely reached Quito, when the vanguard of Pizarro's forces appeared, led by Carvajal, who, though near fourscore, was as hardy and active as any young soldier under his command. Nugnez Vela instantly abandoned a town incapable of defence, and with a rapidity more resembling a flight than a retreat, marched into the province of Popayan. Pizarro continued to pursue; but finding it impossible to overtake him, returned to Quito. From thence he dispatched Carvajal to oppose Centeno, who was growing formidable in the southern provinces of the empire, and he himself remained there to make head against the viceroy †.

By his own activity, and the assistance of Benalcazar, Nugnez Vela soon assembled four hundred men in Popayan. As he retained, amidst all his disasters, the same elevation of mind, and the same high sense of his own dignity, he re-

* See Note CXL.
† Zarate, lib. v. c. 15, 16—24. Gomara. c. 167. Vega. p. 11. lib. iv. c. 25—28. Fernandez. lib. i. c. 34 40. Herrera. dec. 7. lib. viii. c. 16. 20—27.

jected with disdain the advice of some of his followers, who urged him to make overtures of
accommodation to Pizarro, declaring that it was
only by the sword that a contest with rebels
could be decided. With this intention he marched back to Quito [1546]. Pizarro, relying on
the superior number, and still more on the discipline and valour of his troops, advanced reso-
lutely to meet him [January 18]. The battle
was fierce and bloody, both parties fighting
like men who knew that the possession of a great
empire, the fate of their leaders, and their own
future fortune, depended upon the issue of that
day. But Pizarro's veterans pushed forward
with such regular and well-directed force, that
they soon began to make impression on their
enemies. The viceroy, by extraordinary exertions, in which the abilities of a commander and
the courage of a soldier were equally displayed,
held victory for some time in suspense. At length
he fell, pierced with many wounds; and the rout
of his followers became general. They were
hotly pursued. His head was cut off, and placed
on the public gibbet in Quito, which Pizarro
entered in triumph. The troops assembled by
Centeno were dispersed soon after by Carvajal,
and he himself compelled to fly to the mountains, where he remained for several months concealed in a cave. Every person in Peru, from
the frontiers of Popayan to those of Chili, submitted to Pizarro; and by his fleet, under Pedro
de Hinojosa, he had not only the unrivalled command of the South-Sea, but had taken possession
of Panama, and placed a garrison in Nombre de
Dios, on the opposite side of the isthmus, which

rendered him master of the only avenue of communication between Spain and Peru that was used at that period *.

After this decisive victory, Pizarro and his followers remained for some time at Quito, and during the first transports of their exultation, they ran into every excess of licentious indulgence, with the riotous spirit usual among low adventurers upon extraordinary success. But amidst this dissipation, their chief and his confidents were obliged to turn their thoughts sometimes to what was serious, and deliberated with much solicitude concerning the part that he ought now to take. Carvajal, no less bold and decisive in counsel than in the field, had from the beginning warned Pizarro, that in the career on which he was entering, it was vain to think of holding a middle course; that he must either boldly aim at all, or attempt nothing. From the time that Pizarro obtained possession of the government of Peru, he inculcated the same maxim with greater earnestness. Upon receiving an account of the victory at Quito, he remonstrated with him in a tone still more peremptory. " You have usurped (said he, in a letter written to Pizarro on that occasion) the supreme power in this country, in contempt of the emperor's commission to the viceroy. You have marched, in hostile array, against the royal standard; you have attacked the representative of your sovereign in the field, have defeated him, and cut

* Zarate, lib. v. c. 31, 32. Gomara, c. 170. Vega, p. 11. lib. iv. c. 32, 34. Fernandez, lib. i. c. 51—54. Herrera, dec. 7. lib. x. c. 12. 19—22. dec. 8. lib. i. c. 1—3. Benzo, lib. iii. c. 12.

off his head. Think not that ever a monarch will forgive such insults on his dignity, or that any reconciliation with him can be cordial or sincere. Depend no longer on the precarious favour of another. Assume yourself the sovereignty over a country, to the dominion of which your family has a title founded on the rights both of discovery and conquest. It is in your power to attach every Spaniard in Peru of any consequence inviolably to your interest by liberal grants of lands and of Indians, or by instituting ranks of nobility, and creating titles of honour similar to those which are courted with so much eagerness in Europe. By establishing orders of knighthood, with privileges and distinctions resembling those in Spain, you may bestow a gratification upon the officers in your service, suited to the ideas of military men. Nor is it to your countrymen only that you ought to attend; endeavour to gain the natives. By marrying the Coya, or daughter of the Sun next in succession to the crown, you will induce the Indians, out of veneration for the blood of their ancient princes, to unite with the Spaniards in support of your authority. Thus, at the head of the ancient inhabitants of Peru, as well as of the new settlers there, you may set at defiance the power of Spain, and repel with ease any feeble force which it can send at such a distance." Cepeda, the lawyer, who was now Pizarro's confidential counsellor, warmly seconded Carvajal's exhortations, and employed whatever learning he possessed in demonstrating, that all the founders of great monarchies had been raised to pre eminence, not by the antiquity of their lineage, or the validity of their rights, but by their own aspiring valour and personal merit *.

Pizarro listened attentively to both, and could not conceal the satisfaction with which he contemplated the object that they presented to his view. But happily for the tranquillity of the world, few men possess that superior strength of mind, and extent of abilities, which are capable of forming and executing such daring schemes, as cannot be accomplished without overturning the established order of society, and violating those maxims of duty which men are accustomed to hold sacred. The mediocrity of Pizarro's talents circumscribed his ambition within more narrow limits. Instead of aspiring at independent power, he confined his views to the obtaining from the court of Spain a confirmation of the authority which he now possessed ; and for that purpose he sent an officer of distinction thither, to give such a representation of his conduct, and of the state of the country, as might induce the emperor and his ministers, either from inclination or from necessity, to continue him in his present station.

While Pizarro was deliberating with respect to the part which he should take, consultations were held in Spain, with no less solicitude, concerning the measures which ought to be pursued in order to re-establish the emperor's authority in Peru. Though unacquainted with the last excesses of outrage to which the malecontents had proceeded in that country, the court had received an account of the insurrection against the vice-

* Vega, p. 11. lib. iv. c. 40. Fernandez, lib. i. c. 34. lib. ii. c. 1. 49. Herrera, dec. 8. lib. ii. c. 10.

roy, of his imprisonment, and the usurpation of
the government by Pizarro. A revolution so
alarming called for an immediate interposition of
the emperor's abilities and authority. But as he
was fully occupied at that time in Germany, in
conducting the war against the famous league
of Smalkalde, one of the most interesting and
arduous enterprises in his reign, the care of providing a remedy for the disorders in Peru devolved
upon his son Philip, and the counsellors whom
Charles had appointed to assist him in the government of Spain during his absence. At first
view, the actions of Pizarro and his adherents
appeared so repugnant to the duty of subjects
towards their sovereign, that the greater part of
the ministers insisted on declaring them instantly
to be guilty of rebellion, and on proceeding to
punish them with exemplary rigour. But when
the fervour of their zeal and indignation began
to abate, innumerable obstacles to the execution
of this measure presented themselves. The veteran bands of infantry, the strength and glory of
the Spanish armies, were then employed in Germany. Spain, exhausted of men and money by
a long series of wars, in which she had been involved by the restless ambition of two successive
monarchs, could not easily equip an armament of
sufficient force to reduce Pizarro. To transport
any respectable body of troops to a country so
remote as Peru, appeared almost impossible. While
Pizarro continued master of the South-Sea, the
direct route by Nombre de Dios and Panama was
impracticable. An attempt to march to Quito
by land through the new kingdom of Granada,
and the province of Popayan, across regions of

prodigious extent, desolate, unhealthy, or inhabited by fierce and hostile tribes, would be attended with insurmountable danger and hardships. The passage to the South Sea by the Straits of Magellan was so tedious, so uncertain, and so little known in that age, that no confidence could be placed in any effort carried on in a course of navigation so remote and precarious. Nothing then remained but to relinquish the system which the ardour of their loyalty had first suggested, and to attempt by lenient measures what could not be effected by force. It was manifest, from Pizarro's solicitude to represent his conduct in a favourable light to the emperor, that, notwithstanding the excesses of which he had been guilty, he still retained sentiments of veneration for his sovereign. By a proper application to these, together with some such concessions as should discover a spirit of moderation and forbearance in government, there was still room to hope that he might be yet reclaimed, or the ideas of loyalty natural to Spaniards might so far revive among his followers, that they would no longer lend their aid to uphold his usurped authority.

The success, however, of this negotiation, no less delicate than it was important, depended entirely on the abilities and address of the person to whom it should be committed. After weighing with much attention the comparative merit of various persons, the Spanish ministers fixed with unanimity of choice upon Pedro de la Gasca, a priest in no higher station than that of counsellor to the Inquisition. Though in no public office, he had been occasionally employed by government in affairs of trust and consequence, and had conducted them with no less skill than success; displaying a gentle and insinuating temper, accompanied with much firmness; probity, superior to any feeling of private interest; and a cautious circumspection in concerting measures, followed by such vigour in executing them, as is rarely found in alliance with the other. These qualities marked him out for the function to which he was destined. The emperor, to whom Gasca was not unknown, warmly approved of the choice, and communicated it to him in a letter containing expressions of goodwill and confidence, no less honourable to the prince who wrote, than to the subject who received it. Gasca, notwithstanding his advanced age and feeble constitution, and though, from the apprehensions natural to a man, who, during the course of his life, had never been out of his own country, he dreaded the effects of a long voyage, and of an unhealthy climate *, did not hesitate a moment about complying with the will of his sovereign. But as a proof that it was from this principle alone he acted, he refused a bishopric which was offered to him, in order that he might appear in Peru with a more dignified character; he would accept of no higher title than that of President of the Court of Audience in Lima; and declared that he would receive no salary on account of his discharging the duties of that office. All he required was, that the expence of supporting his family should be defrayed by the public, and as he was to go like a minister of peace, with his gown and breviary,

* Fernandez, lib. ii. c. 17.

and without any retinue but a few domestics, this would not load the revenue with any enormous burden *.

But while he discovered such disinterested moderation with respect to whatever related personally to himself, he demanded his official powers in a very different tone. He insisted, as he was to be employed in a country so remote from the seat of government, where he could not have recourse to his sovereign for new instructions on every emergence; and as the whole success of his negotiations must depend upon the confidence which the people with whom he had to treat could place in the extent of his powers, that he ought to be invested with unlimited authority; that his jurisdiction must reach to all persons and to all causes; that he must be empowered to pardon, to punish, or to reward, as circumstances and the behaviour of different men might require; that in case of resistance from the malecontents, he might be authorised to reduce them to obedience by force of arms, to levy troops for that purpose, and to call for assistance from the governors of all the Spanish settlements in America. These powers, though manifestly conducive to the great objects of his mission, appeared to the Spanish ministers to be inalienable prerogatives of royalty, which ought not to be delegated to a subject, and they refused to grant them. But the emperor's views were more enlarged. As, from the nature of his employment, Gasca must be entrusted with discretionary power in several

* Zarate, lib. vi. c 6. Gomara, c. 174. Ferrandez. lib ii. c. 14—16. Vega, p. 11. lib. v. c. 1. Herrera, dec. 8. lib. 1. c. 4, &c.

points, and all his efforts might prove ineffectual
if he was circumscribed in any one particular,
Charles scrupled not to invest him with authority
to the full extent that he demanded.   Highly
satisfied with this fresh proof of his master's confidence, Gasca hastened his departure, and, without either money or troops, set out to quell a
formidable rebellion *.

On his arrival at Nombre de Dios [July 27],
he found Herman Mexia, an officer of note,
posted there, by order of Pizarro, with a considerable body of men to oppose the landing of
any hostile forces.   But Gasca appeared in such
pacific guise, with a train so-little formidable,
and with a title of no such dignity as to excite
terror, that he was received with much respect.
From Nombre de Dios he advanced to Panama,
and met with a similar reception from Hinojosa,
whom Pizarro had entrusted with the government of that town, and the command of his fleet
stationed there.   In both places he held the same
language, declaring that he was sent by their
sovereign as a messenger of peace, not as a minister of vengeance ; that he came to redress all
their grievances, to revoke the laws which had
excited alarm, to pardon past offences, and to
re-establish order and justice in the government
of Peru.   His mild deportment, the simplicity of
his manners, the sanctity of his profession, and a
winning appearance of candour, gained credit to
his declarations.   The veneration due to a person
clothed with legal authority, and acting in virtue
of a royal commission, began to revive among
men accustomed for some time to nothing more

* Fernandez, lib. ii. c. 16—18.

respectable than an usurped jurisdiction. Hinojosa, Mexia, and several other officers of distinction, to each of whom Gasca applied separately,
were gained over to his interest, and waited only
for some decent occasion of declaring openly in
his favour *.

This the violence of Pizarro soon afforded
them. As soon as he heard of Gasca's arrival
at Panama, though he received, at the same
time, an account of the nature of his commission,
and was informed of his offers not only to render
every Spaniard in Peru easy concerning what was
past, by an act of general oblivion ; but secure
with respect to the future, by repealing the obnoxious laws ; instead of accepting with gratitude his sovereign's gracious concessions, he was
so much exasperated on finding that he was not
to be continued in his station as governor of the
country, that he instantly resolved to oppose
the president's entry into Peru, and to prevent his exercising any jurisdiction there. To
this desperate resolution he added another highly
preposterous. He sent a new deputation to
Spain to justify this conduct, and to insist, in
name of all the communities in Peru, for a confirmation of the government to himself during
life, as the only means of preserving tranquillity
there. The persons entrusted with this strange
commission, intimated the intention of Pizarro
to the president, and required him, in his name,
to depart from Panama and return to Spain.
They carried likewise secret instructions to Hinojosa, directing him to offer Gasca a present of

* Fernandez, lib. ii. c. 21, &c. Zarate, lib. vi. c. 6, 7.
Gomara, c. 175. Vega, p. 11. lib. v. c. 3.

fifty thousand pesos, if he would comply voluntarily with what was demanded of him ; and if
he should continue obstinate, to cut him off either
by assassination or poison *.

Many circumstances concurred in pushing on
Pizarro to those wild measures. Having been
once accustomed to supreme command, he could
not bear the thoughts of descending to a private
station. Conscious of his own demerit, he suspected that the emperor studied only to deceive
him, and would never pardon the outrages which
he had committed. His chief confidents, no
less guilty, entertained the same apprehensions.
The approach of Gasca without any military
force excited no terror. There were now above
six thousand Spaniards settled in Peru † ; and at
the head of these he doubted not to maintain
his own independence, if the court of Spain
should refuse to grant what he required. But
he knew not that a spirit of defection had already begun to spread among those whom he
trusted most. Hinojosa, amazed at Pizarro's
precipitate resolution of setting himself in opposition to the emperor's commission, and disdaining to be his instrument in perpetrating the
odious crimes pointed out in his secret instructions, publicly recognised the title of the president to the supreme authority in Peru. The
officers under his command did the same. Such
was the contagious influence of the example,
that it reached even the deputies who had been
sent from Peru ; and at the time when Pizarro

* Zarate, lib. vi. c. 8. Fernandez, lib. ii. c. 33, 34.
Herrera, dec. 8. lib. ii. c. 9, 10.
† Herrera, dec. 8. lib. iii. c. 1.

expected to hear either of Gasca's return to Spain, or of his death, he received an account of his being master of the fleet, of Panama, and of the troops stationed there.

1547.] Irritated almost to madness by events so unexpected, he openly prepared for war; and in order to give some colour of justice to his arms, appointed the court of audience in Lima to proceed to the trial of Gasca, for the crimes of having seized his ships, seduced his officers, and prevented his deputies from proceeding in their voyage to Spain. Cepeda, though acting as a judge in virtue of the royal commission, did not scruple to prostitute the dignity of his function by finding Gasca guilty of treason, and condemning him to death on that account.*. Wild, and even ridiculous as this proceeding was, it imposed on the low illiterate adventurers, with whom Peru was filled, by the semblance of a legal sanction warranting Pizarro to carry on hostilities against a convicted traitor. Soldiers accordingly resorted from every quarter to his standard, and he was soon at the head of a thousand men, the best equipped that had ever taken the field in Peru.

Gasca, on his part, perceiving that force must be employed in order to accomplish the purpose of his mission, was no less assiduous in collecting troops from Nicaragua, Carthagena, and other settlements on the continent; and with such success, that he was soon in a condition to detach a squadron of his fleet, with a considerable body of soldiers, to the coast of Peru, [April]. Their ap-

* Fernandez. lib. ii. c. 55. Vega, p. 11. lib. v. c. 7. Herrera, dec. 8. lib. iii. c. 6.

pearance excited a dreadful alarm; and though
they did not attempt for some time to make any
descent, they did more effectual service, by setting ashore, in different places, persons who dispersed copies of the act of general indemnity, and
the revocation of the late edicts; and who made
known everywhere the pacific intentions, as well
as mild temper, of the president. The effect of
spreading this information was wonderful. All
who were dissatisfied with Pizarro's violent administration, all who retained any sentiments of
fidelity to their sovereign, began to meditate revolt. Some openly deserted a cause which they
now deemed to be unjust. Centeno, leaving the
cave in which he lay concealed, assembled about
fifty of his former adherents, and with this feeble
half-armed band advanced boldly to Cuzco. By
a sudden attack in the night-time, in which he
displayed no less military skill than valour, he
rendered himself master of that capital, though
defended by a garrison of five hundred men.
Most of these having ranged themselves under
his banners, he had soon the command of a respectable body of troops *.

Pizarro, though astonished at beholding one
enemy approaching by sea, and another by land,
at a time when he trusted to the union of all
Peru in his favour, was of a spirit more undaunted, and more accustomed to the vicissitudes of
fortune, than to be disconcerted or appalled. As
the danger from Centeno's operations was the
most urgent, he instantly set out to oppose him.
Having provided horses for all his soldiers, he

* Zarate, lib. vi. c. 13—16.   Gomara, c. 180, 181.
Fernandez, lib. ii. c. 28. 64, &c.

marched with amazing rapidity. But every morning he found his force diminished, by numbers who had left him during the night; and though he became suspicious to excess, and punished without mercy all whom he suspected, the rage of desertion was too violent to be checked. Before he got within sight of the enemy at Huarina, near the lake Titiaca, he could not muster more than four hundred soldiers. But these he justly considered as men of tried attachment, on whom he might depend. They were indeed the boldest and most desperate of his followers, conscious, like himself, of crimes for which they could hardly expect forgiveness, and without any hope but in the success of their arms. With these he did not hesitate to attack Centeno's troops [October 20], though double to his own in number. The royalists did not decline the combat. It was the most obstinate and bloody that had hitherto been fought in Peru. At length the intrepid valour of Pizarro, and the superiority of Carvajal's military talents, triumphed over numbers, and obtained a complete victory. The booty was immense *, and the treatment of the vanquished cruel. By this signal success the reputation of Pizarro was reestablished, and being now deemed invincible in the field, his army increased daily in number †.

But events happened in other parts of Peru, which more than counterbalanced the splendid victory at Huarina. Pizarro had scarcely left

* See Note CXLI.　　　† Zarate, lib. vii. c. 2, 3. Gomara, c. 181. Vega, p. 11. lib. v. c. 18. &c. Fernandez, lib. ii. c. 79. Herrera, dec. 8. lib. iv. c. 1, 2.

Lima, when the citizens, weary of his oppressive dominion, erected the royal standard, and Aldana, with a detachment of soldiers from the fleet, took possession of the town. About the same time *, Gasca landed at Tumbez with five hundred men. Encouraged by his presence, every settlement in the low country declared for the king. The situation of the two parties was now perfectly reversed; Cuzco and the adjacent provinces were possessed by Pizarro; all the rest of the empire from Quito southward, acknowledged the jurisdiction of the president. As his numbers augmented fast, Gasca advanced into the interior part of the country. His behaviour still continued to be gentle and unassuming; he expressed, on every occasion, his ardent wish of terminating the contest without bloodshed. More solicitous to reclaim than to punish, he upbraided no man for past offences, but received them as a father receives penitent children returning to a sense of their duty. Though desirous of peace, he did not slacken his preparations for war. He appointed the general rendezvous of his troops in the fertile valley of Xauxa, on the road to Cuzco †. There he remained for some months, not only that he might have time to make another attempt towards an accommodation with Pizarro, but that he might train his new soldiers to the use of arms, and accustom them to the discipline of a camp, before he led them against a body of victorious veterans. Pizarro, intoxicated with the success which had hitherto accompanied his arms, and elated with

* Zarate, lib. vi. c. 17.
† Zarate, lib. vii. c. 9. Fernandez, lib. ii. c. 77. 82.

having again near a thousand men under his command, refused to listen to any terms, although Cepeda, together with several of his officers, and even Carvajal himself *, gave it as their advice to close with the president's offer of a general indemnity, and the revocation of the obnoxious laws †. Gasca having tried in vain every expedient to avoid embruing his hands in the blood of his countrymen, began to move towards Cuzco [Dec. 29], at the head of sixteen hundred men.

Pizarro, confident of victory, suffered the royalists to pass all the rivers which lie between Guamanga and Cuzco without opposition [1548], and to advance within four leagues of that capital, flattering himself that a defeat in such a situation as rendered escape impracticable would at once terminate the war. He then marched out to meet the enemy [April 9], and Carvajal chose his ground, and made the disposition of the troops with the discerning eye and profound knowledge in the art of war conspicuous in all his operations. As the two armies moved forwards slowly to the charge, the appearance of each was singular. In that of Pizarro, composed of men enriched with the spoils of the most opulent country in America, every officer, and almost all the private men, were clothed in stuffs of silk, or brocade, embroidered with gold and silver; and their horses, their arms, their standards, were adorned with all the pride of military pomp ‡. That of Gasca, though not so splendid, exhibited what was no less striking. He himself,

* See Note CXLII.
Vega, p. 1'. lib. v. c. 27.

† Zarate, lib. vii. c. 6.
‡ Zarate, lib. vi. c. 11.

accompanied by the archbishop of Lima, the bishops of Quito and Cuzco, and a great number of ecclesiastics, marching along the lines, blessing the men, and encouraging them to a resolute discharge of their duty.

When both armies were just ready to engage, Cepeda set spurs to his horse, galloped off, and surrendered himself to the president. Garcilasso de la Vega, and other officers of note, followed his example. The revolt of persons in such high rank struck all with amazement. The mutual confidence on which the union and strength of armies depend, ceased at once. Distrust and consternation spread from rank to rank. Some silently slipped away, others threw down their arms, the greatest number went over to the royalists. Pizarro, Carvajal, and some leaders, employed authority, threats, and entreaties, to stop them, but in vain. In less than half an hour, a body of men, which might have decided the fate of the Peruvian empire, was totally dispersed. Pizarro, seeing all irretrievably lost, cried out in amazement to a few officers who still faithfully adhered to him, " What remains for us to do ?"—" Let us rush," replied one of them, " upon the enemy's firmest battalion, and die like Romans." Dejected with such a reverse of fortune, he had not spirit to follow this soldierly counsel, and with a tameness disgraceful to his former fame, he surrendered to one of Gasca's officers. Carvajal, endeavouring to escape, was overtaken and seized.

Gasca, happy in this bloodless victory, did not stain it with cruelty. Pizarro, Carvajal, and a small number of the most distinguished or notorious offenders, were punished capitally. Pizarro was beheaded on the day after he surrendered. He submitted to his fate with a composed dignity, and seemed desirous to atone by repentance for the crimes which he had committed. The end of Carvajal was suitable to his life. On his trial he offered no defence. When the sentence adjudging him to be hanged was pronounced, he carelessly replied, " One can die but once." During the interval between the sentence and execution, he discovered no sign either of remorse for the past, or of solicitude about the future ; scoffing at all who visited him, in his usual sarcastic vein of mirth, with the same quickness of repartee and gross pleasantry as at any other period of his life. Cepeda, more criminal than either, ought to have shared the same fate ; but the merit of having deserted his associates at such a critical moment, and with such decisive effect, saved him from immediate punishment. He was sent, however, as a prisoner to Spain, and died in confinement *.

In the minute detail which the contemporary historians have given of the civil dissensions that raged in Peru, with little interruption, during ten years, many circumstances occur so striking, and which indicate such an uncommon state of manners, as to merit particular attention.

Though the Spaniards who first invaded Peru were of the lowest order in society, and the greater part of those who afterwards joined them were persons of desperate fortune, yet in all the

* Zarate, lib. vii. c. 6, 7, 8. Gomara. c. 186 c. 186. Vega, p. 11. lib. v. c. 30, &c. Fernandez, lib. ii. c. 86, &c. Herrera, dec. 8. lib. iv. c. 14, &c.

bodies of troops brought into the field by the different leaders who contended for superiority, not one man acted as a hired soldier, that follows his standard for pay. Every adventurer in Peru considered himself as a conqueror, entitled, by his services, to an establishment in that country which had been acquired by his valour. In the contests between the rival chiefs, each chose his side as he was directed by his own judgment or affections. He joined his commander as a companion of his fortune, and disdained to degrade himself by receiving the wages of a mercenary. It was to their sword, not to pre-eminence in office, or nobility of birth, that most of the leaders whom they followed were indebted for their elevation; and each of their adherents hoped, by the same means, to open a way for himself to the possession of power and wealth *.

But though the troops in Peru served without any regular pay, they were raised at immense expence. Among men accustomed to divide the spoils of an opulent country, the desire of obtaining wealth acquired incredible force. The ardour of pursuit augmented in proportion to the hope of success. Where all were intent on the same object, and under the dominion of the same passion, there was but one mode of gaining men, or of securing their attachment. Officers of name and influence, besides the promise of future establishments, received in hand large gratuities from the chief with whom they engaged. Gonzalo Pizarro, in order to raise a thousand men, advanced five hundred thousand pesos †. Gasca

* Vega, p. 11. lib iv. c. 38. 41.
† Fernandez, lib. ii. c. 54.

expended, in levying the troops which he led against Pizarro, nine hundred thousand pesos *. The distribution of property, bestowed as the reward of services, was still more exorbitant. Cepeda, as the recompence of his perfidy and address, in persuading the court of royal audience to give the sanction of its authority to the usurped jurisdiction of Pizarro, received a grant of lands which yielded an annual income of a hundred and fifty thousand pesos †. Hinojosa, who, by his early defection from Pizarro, and surrender of the fleet to Gasca, decided the fate of Peru, obtained a district of country affording two hundred thousand pesos of yearly value ‡. While such rewards were dealt out to the principal officers, with more than royal munificence, proportional shares were conferred upon those of inferior rank.

Such a rapid change of fortune produced its natural effects. It gave birth to new wants, and new desires. Veterans, long accustomed to hardship and toil, acquired of a sudden a taste for profuse and inconsiderate dissipation, and indulged in all the excesses of military licentiousness. The riot of low debauchery occupied some ; a relish for expensive luxuries spread among others §. The meanest soldier in Peru would have thought himself degraded by marching on foot ; and at a time when the prices of horses in that country were exorbitant, each insisted on being furnished with one before he would take the field. But though less patient under the fatigue and hardships of service, they were ready to face danger

---

* Zarate, lib. vii. c. 10.   Herrera, dec. 8. lib. v. c. 7.
† Gomara, c. 164.   ‡ Vega, p. 11. lib. vi. c. 3.
§ Herrera, dec. 5. lib. ii. c. 3. dec. 8. lib. viii. c. 10.

and death with as much intrepidity as ever ; and ahimated by the hope of new rewards, they never failed, on the day of battle, to display all their ancient valour.

Together with their courage, they retained all the ferocity by which they were originally distinguished. Civil discord never raged with a more fell spirit than among the Spaniards in Peru. To all the passions which usually envenom contests among countrymen, avarice was added, and rendered their enmity more rancorous. Eagerness to seize the valuable forfeitures expected upon the death of every opponent, shut the door against mercy. To be wealthy, was of itself sufficient to expose a man to accusation, or to subject him to punishment. On the slightest suspicions, Pizarro condemned many of the most opulent inhabitants in Peru to death. Carvajal, without searching for any pretext to justify his cruelty, cut off many more. The number of those who suffered by the hand of the executioner, was not much inferior to what fell in the field *; and the greater part was condemned without the formality of any legal trial.

The violence with which the contending parties treated their opponents was not accompanied with its usual attendants, attachment and fidelity to those with whom they acted. The ties of honour, which ought to be held sacred among soldiers, and the principle of integrity, interwoven as thoroughly in the Spanish character as in that of any nation, seem to have been equally forgotten. Even regard for decency, and the sense of shame, were totally lost. During their dissen-

* See Note CXLIII.

sions, there was hardly a Spaniard in Peru who did not abandon the party which he had originally espoused, betray the associates with whom he had united, and violate the engagements under which he had come. The viceroy Nugnez Vela was ruined by the treachery of Cepeda and the other judges of the royal audience, who were bound by the duties of their function to have supported his authority. The chief advisers and companions of Gonzalo Pizarro's revolt were the first to forsake him, and submit to his enemies. His fleet was given up to Gasca by the man whom he had singled out among his officers to entrust with that important command. On the day that was to decide his fate, an army of veterans, in sight of the enemy, threw down their arms without striking a blow, and deserted a leader who had often conducted them to victory. Instances of such general and avowed contempt of the principles and obligations which attach man to man, and bind them together in social union, rarely occur in history. It is only where men are far removed from the seat of government, where the restraints of law and order are little felt, where the prospect of gain is unbounded, and where immense wealth may cover the crimes by which it is acquired, that we can find any parallel to the levity, the rapaciousness, the perfidy and corruption prevalent among the Spaniards in Peru.

On the death of Pizarro, the malecontents in every corner of Peru laid down their arms, and tranquillity seemed to be perfectly re-established. But two very interesting objects still remained to occupy the president's attention. The one

was to find immediately such employment for a
multitude of turbulent and daring adventurers
with which the country was filled, as might prevent them from exciting new commotions; the
other, to bestow proper gratifications upon those
to whose loyalty and valour he had been indebted for his success. The former of these was
in some measure accomplished, by appointing
Pedro de Valdivia to prosecute the conquest of
Chili; and by empowering Diego Centeno to
undertake the discovery of the vast regions bordering on the river De la Plata. The reputation
of those leaders, together with the hopes of acquiring wealth, and of rising to consequence in
some unexplored country, alluring many of the
most indigent and desperate soldiers to follow
their standards, drained off no inconsiderable portion of that mutinous spirit which Gasca dreaded.

The latter was an affair of greater difficulty,
and to be adjusted with a more attentive and delicate hand. The *repartimientos*, or allotments
of lands and Indians which fell to be distributed,
in consequence of the death or forfeiture of the
former possessors, exceeded two millions of pesos
of yearly rent *. Gasca, when now absolute master of this immense property, retained the same
disinterested sentiments which he had originally
professed, and refused to reserve the smallest
portion of it for himself. But the number of
claimants was great; and whilst the vanity or
avarice of every individual fixed the value of his
own services, and estimated the recompence which
he thought due to him, the pretensions of each
were so extravagant, that it was impossible to

* Vega, p. 11. lib. vi. c. 4.

satisfy all. Gasca listened to them one by one, with the most patient attention; and that he might have leisure to weigh the comparative merit of their several claims with accuracy, he retired, with the archbishop of Lima and a single secretary, to a village twelve leagues from Cuzco. There he spent several days in allotting to each a district of lands and number of Indians, in proportion to his idea of their past services and future importance. But that he might get beyond the reach of the fierce storm of clamour and rage which he foresaw would burst out on the publication of his decree, notwithstanding the impartial equity with which he had framed it, he set out for Lima, leaving the instrument of partition sealed up, with orders not to open it for some days after his departure.

The indignation excited by publishing the decree of partition [Aug. 24] was not less than Gasca had expected. Vanity, avarice, emulation, envy, shame, rage, and all the other passions which most vehemently agitate the minds of men when both their honour and their interest are deeply affected, conspired in adding to it violence. It broke out with all the fury of military insolence. Calumny, threats, and curses, were poured out openly upon the president. He was accused of ingratitude, of partiality, and of injustice. Among soldiers prompt to action, such seditious discourse would have been soon followed by deeds no less violent, and they already began to turn their eyes towards some discontented leaders, expecting them to stand forth in redress of their wrongs. By some vigorous interpositions of government, a timely check was given to this mutinous spirit, and the danger of another civil war was averted for the present *.

1549.] Gasca, however, perceiving that the flame was suppressed rather than extinguished, laboured with the utmost assiduity to sooth the malecontents, by bestowing large gratuities on some, by promising *repartimientos*, when they fell vacant, to others, and by caressing and flattering all. But that the public security might rest on a foundation more stable than their good affection, he endeavoured to strengthen the hands of his successors in office, by re-establishing the regular administration of justice in every part of the empire. He introduced order and simplicity into the mode of collecting the royal revenue. He issued regulations concerning the treatment of the Indians, well calculated to protect them from oppression, and to provide for their instruction in the principles of religion, without depriving the Spaniards of the benefit accruing from their labour. Having now accomplished every object of his mission [1550], Gasca, longing to return again to a private station, committed the government of Peru to the court of audience, and set out for Spain [Feb. 1]. As, during the anarchy and turbulence of the four last years, there had been no remittance made of the royal revenue, he carried with him thirteen hundred thousand pesos of public money, which the economy and order of his administration enabled him to save, after paying all the expences of the war.

* Zarate, lib. vii. c. 9. Gomara, c. 187. Vega, p. 11. lib. vii. c. 1, &c. Fernandez, p. 11. lib. i. c. 1, &c. Herrera, dec. 8. lib. iv. c. 17, &c.

He was received in his native country with universal admiration of his abilities, and of his virtue. Both were, indeed, highly conspicuous. Without army, or fleet, or public funds; with a train so simple, that only three thousand ducats were expended in equipping him *, he set out to oppose a formidable rebellion. By his address and talents he supplied all those defects, and seemed to create instruments for executing his designs. He acquired such a naval force, as gave him the command of the sea. He raised a body of men able to cope with the veteran bands which gave law to Peru. He vanquished their leader, on whose arms victory had hitherto attended, and in place of anarchy and usurpation, he established the government of laws, and the authority of the rightful sovereign. But the praise bestowed on his abilities was exceeded by that which his virtue merited. After residing in a country where wealth presented allurements which had seduced every person who had hitherto possessed power there, he returned from that trying station with integrity not only untainted but unsuspected. After distributing among his countrymen possessions of greater extent and value than had ever been in the disposal of a subject in any age or nation, he himself remained in his original state of poverty; and at the very time when he brought such a large recruit to the royal treasury he was obliged to apply by petition for a small sum to discharge some petty debts which he had contracted during the course of his service † Charles was not insensible to such disinterest

* Fernandez, lib. ii. c. 18.   † M

L 2

merit. Gasca was received by him with the most distinguishing marks of esteem, and being promoted to the bishopric of Palencia, he passed the remainder of his days in the tranquillity of retirement, respected by his country, honoured by his sovereign, and beloved by all.

Notwithstanding all Gasca's wise regulations, the tranquillity of Peru was not of long continuance. In a country where the authority of government had been almost forgotten during the long prevalence of anarchy and misrule, where there were disappointed leaders ripe for revolt, and seditious soldiers ready to follow them, it was not difficult to raise combustion. Several successive insurrections desolated the country for some years. But as those, though fierce, were only transient storms, excited rather by the ambition and turbulence of particular men, than by general or public motives, the detail of them is not the object of this history. These commotions in Peru, like every thing of extreme violence either in the natural or political body, were not of long duration, and by carrying off the corrupted humours which had given rise to the disorders, they contributed in the end to strengthen the society which at first they threatened to destroy. During their fierce contests, several of the first invaders of Peru, and many of those licentious adventurers whom the fame of their success had allured thither, fell by each other's hands. Each of the parties, as they alternately prevailed in the struggle, gradually cleared the country of a number of turbulent spirits, by executing, proscribing, or banishing their opponents. Men less enterprising,

less desperate, and more accustomed to move in
the path of sober and peaceable industry, settled
in Peru ; and the royal authority was gradually
established as firmly there as in the other Spanish colonies.

BOOK VII.

As the conquest of the two great empires of
Mexico and Peru forms the most splendid and interesting period in the history of America, a view
of their political institutions, and a description
of their national manners, will exhibit the human
species to the contemplation of intelligent observers in a very singular stage of its progress *.

When compared with other parts of the New
World, Mexico and Peru may be considered as
polished states. Instead of small, independent,
hostile tribes, struggling for subsistence amidst
woods and marshes, strangers to industry and
arts, unacquainted with subordination, and almost
without the appearance of regular government,
we find countries of great extent subjected to
the dominion of one sovereign, the inhabitants
collected together in cities, the wisdom and foresight of rulers employed in providing for the
maintenance and security of the people, the
empire of laws in some measure established, the
authority of religion recognised, many of the

* See Note CXLIV.

L 3

arts essential to life brought to some degree of maturity, and the dawn of such as are ornamental beginning to appear.

But if the comparison be made with the people of the ancient continent, the inferiority of America in improvement will be conspicuous, and neither the Mexicans nor Peruvians will be entitled to rank with those nations which merit the name of civilized. The people of both the great empires in America, like the rude tribes around them, were totally unacquainted with the useful metals, and the progress which they had made in extending their dominion over the animal creation was inconsiderable. The Mexicans had gone no farther than to tame and rear turkeys, ducks, a species of small dogs, and rabbits *. By this feeble essay of ingenuity, the means of subsistence were rendered somewhat more plentiful and secure, than when men depend solely on hunting ; but: hey had no idea of attempting to subdue the more robust animals, or of deriving any aid from their ministry in carrying on works of labour. The Peruvians seem to have neglected the inferior animals, and had not rendered any of them domestic except the duck ; but they were more fortunate in taming the Llama, an animal peculiar to their country, of a form which bears some resemblance to a deer, and some to a camel, and is of a size somewhat larger than a sheep. Under the protection of man, this species multiplied greatly. Its wool furnished the Peruvians with clothing, its flesh with food. It was even employed as a beast of burden, and carried a moderate load with much

* Herrera, dec. 11. lib. vii. c. 12.

patience and docility *.   It was never used for
draught ; and the breed being confined to the
mountainous country, its service, if we may judge
by incidents which occur in the early Spanish
writers, was not very extensive among the Peruvians in their original state.

In tracing the line by which nations proceed
towards civilization. the discovery of the useful
metals, and the acquisition of dominion over the
animal creation, have been marked as steps of
capital importance in their progress.   In our
continent, long after men had attained both,
society continued in that state which is denominated barbarous.   Even with all that command over nature which these confer, many ages
elapse, before industry becomes so regular as to
render subsistence secure, before the arts which
supply the wants and furnish the accommodations
of life are brought to any considerable degree of
perfection, and before any idea is conceived of
various institutions requisite in a well-ordered
society.   The Mexicans and Peruvians, without
knowledge of the useful metals, or the aid of domestic animals, laboured under disadvantages
which must have greatly retarded their progress,
and in their highest state of improvement their
power was so limited, and their operations so
feeble, that they can hardly be considered as
having advanced beyond the infancy of civil
life.

After this general observation concerning the
most singular and distinguishing circumstances in
the state of both the great empires in America,
I shall endeavour to give such a view of the con-

* Vega, p. i. lib. viii. c. 16.   Zarate, lib. i. e. 14.

stitution and interior police of each, as may enable us to ascertain their place in the political scale, to allot them their proper station between the rude tribes in the New World, and the polished states of the ancient, and to determine how far they had risen above the former, as well as how much they fell below the latter.

Mexico was first subjected to the Spanish crown. But our acquaintance with its laws and manners is not, from that circumstance, more complete. What I have remarked concerning the defective and inaccurate information on which we must rely with respect to the condition and customs of the savage tribes in America, may be applied likewise to our knowledge of the Mexican empire. Cortes, and the rapacious adventurers who accompanied him, had not leisure or capacity to enrich either civil or natural history with new observations. They undertook their expedition in quest of one object, and seemed hardly to have turned their eyes towards any other. Or if, during some short interval of tranquillity, when the occupations of war ceased, and the ardour of plunder was suspended, the institutions and manners of the people whom they had invaded drew their attention, the inquiries of illiterate soldiers were conducted with so little sagacity and precision, that the accounts given by them of the policy and order established in the Mexican monarchy are superficial, confused, and inexplicable. It is rather from incidents which they relate occasionally, than from their own deductions and remarks, that we are enabled to form some idea of the genius and manners of that people. The obscurity in which

the ignorance of its conquerors involved the annals of Mexico, was augmented by the superstition of those who succeeded them.   As the
memory of past events was preserved among the
Mexicans by figures painted on skins, on cotton
cloth, on a kind of pasteboard, or on the bark
of trees, the early missionaries, unable to comprehend their meaning, and struck with their
uncouth forms, conceived them to be monuments of idolatry which ought to be destroyed,
in order to facilitate the conversion of the Indians.   In obedience to an edict issued by Juan
de Zummaraga, a Franciscan monk, the first
bishop of Mexico, as many records of the ancient Mexican story as could be collected were
committed to the flames.   In consequence of
this fanatical zeal of the monks who first visited
New Spain (which their successors soon began to
lament), whatever knowledge of remote events
such rude monuments contained was almost entirely lost, and no information remained concerning the ancient revolutions and policy of the
empire, but what was derived from tradition, or
from some fragments of their historical paintings
that escaped the barbarous researches of Zummaraga *.   From the experience of all nations it
is manifest, that the memory of past transactions
can neither be long preserved, nor be transmitted
with any fidelity, by tradition.   The Mexican
paintings, which are supposed to have served as
annals of their empire, are few in number, and
of ambiguous meaning.   Thus, amidst the uncertainty of the former, and the obscurity of the

* Acosta, lib. vi. c. 7. Torquem. Proem. lib. ii. lib. iii.
c. 6. lib. xiv. c. 6.

latter, we must glean what intelligence can be collected from the scanty materials scattered in the Spanish writers *.

* In the first edition, I observed that in consequence of the destruction of the ancient Mexican paintings, occasioned by the zeal of Zummaraga, whatever knowledge they might have conveyed was *entirely* lost. Every candid reader must have perceived that the expression was inaccurate; as in a few lines afterwards I mention some ancient paintings to be still extant. M. Clavigero, not satisfied with laying hold of this inaccuracy, which I corrected in the subsequent editions, labours to render it more glaring, by the manner in which he quotes the remaining part of the sentence. He reprehends with great asperity the account which I gave of the scanty materials for writing the ancient history of Mexico. Vol. I. Account of Writers, p. xxvj. Vol. II. 380. My words, however, are almost the same with those of Torquemada, who seems to have been better acquainted with the ancient monuments of the Mexicans than any Spanish author whose works I have seen. Lib. xiv. c. 6. M. Clavigero himself gives a description of the destruction of ancient paintings in almost the same terms I have used; and mentions, as an additional reason of there being so small a number of ancient paintings known to the Spaniards, that the natives have become so solicitous to preserve and conceal them, that it is " difficult, if not impossible, to " make them part with one of them." Vol. I. 407. II. 194. No point can be more ascertained than that few of the Mexican historical paintings have been preserved. Though several Spaniards have carried on inquiries into the antiquities of the Mexican empire, no engravings from Mexican paintings have been communicated to the public, except those by Purchas, Gemelli Carreri, and Lorenzana. It affords me some satisfaction, that in the course of my researches, I have discovered two collections of Mexican paintings which were unknown to former inquirers. The cut which I published is an exact copy of the original, and gives no high idea of the progress which the Mexicans had made in the art of painting. I cannot conjecture what could induce M. Clavigero to express some dissatisfaction with me for having published it without the same colour

According to the account of the Mexicans themselves, their empire was not of long duration. Their country, as they relate, was originally possessed, rather than peopled, by small independent tribes, whose mode of life and manners resemble those of the rudest savages which we have described. But about a period corresponding to the beginning of the tenth century in the Christian era, several tribes moved in successive migrations from unknown regions towards the north and north-west, and settled in different provinces of *Anahuac*, the ancient name of New Spain. These, more civilized than the original inhabitants, began to form them to the arts of social life. At length, towards the commencement of the thirteenth century, the Mexicans, a people more polished than any of the former, advanced from the border of the Californian

it has in the original painting, p. xxix. He might have recollected, that neither Purchas, nor Gemelli Carreri, nor Lorenzana, thought it necessary to colour the prints which they have published, and they have never been censured on that account. He may rest assured, that though the colours in the paintings in the Imperial Library are remarkably bright, they are laid on without art, and without " any of that regard to light and shade, or the rules of " perspective," which M. Clavigero requires. Vol. II. 378. If the public express any desire to have the seven paintings still in my possession engraved, I am ready to communicate them. The print published by Gemelli Carreri, of the route of the ancient Mexicans when they travelled towards the lake on which they built the capital of their empire, Churchill, Vol. IV. p. 481, is the most finished monument of art brought from the New World, and yet a very slight inspection of it will satisfy every one, that the annals of a nation conveyed in this manner must be very meagre and imperfect.

gulf, and took possession of the plains adjacent
to the great lake near the centre of the country.
After residing there about fifty years, they
founded a town, since distinguished by the name
of *Mexico*, which from humble beginnings soon
grew to be the most considerable city in the New
World. The Mexicans, long after they were
established in their new possessions, continued,
like other martial tribes in America, unacquainted
with regal dominion, and were governed in peace,
and conducted in war, by such as were entitled
to pre-eminence by their wisdom or their valour.
But among them, as in other states whose power
and territories become extensive, the supreme
authority centered at last in a single person ;
and when the Spaniards under Cortes invaded
the country, Montezuma was the ninth monarch
in order who had swayed the Mexican sceptre,
not by hereditary right, but by election.

Such is the traditional tale of the Mexicans
concerning the progress of their own empire.
According to this, its duration was very short.
From the first migration of their parent tribe,
they can reckon little more than three hundred
years. From the establishment of monarchical
government, not above a hundred and thirty
years, according to one account *, or a hundred
and ninety-seven, according to another computation †, had elapsed. If, on one hand, we
s ppose the Mexican state to have been of higher
antiquity, and to have subsisted during such a
length of time as the Spanish accounts of its

---

* Acost. Hist. lib. vii. c. 8, &c.
† Purchas, Pilgr. iii. p. 1068, &c.

civilization would naturally lead us to conclude, it is difficult to conceive how, among a people who possessed the art of recording events by pictures, and who considered it as an essential part of their national education, to teach their children to repeat the historical songs which celebrated the exploits of their ancestors *, the knowledge of past transactions should be so slender and limited. If, on the other hand, we adopt their own system with respect to the antiquities of their nation, it is no less difficult to account either for that improved state of society, or for the extensive dominion to which their empire had attained, when first visited by the Spaniards. The infancy of nations is so long, and, even when every circumstance is favourable to their progress, they advance so slowly towards any maturity of strength or policy, that the recent origin of the Mexicans seems to be a strong presumption of some exaggeration, in the splendid descriptions which have been given of their government and manners.

But it is not by theory or conjectures that history decides with regard to the state or character of nations. It produces facts as the foundation of every judgment which it ventures to pronounce. In collecting those which must regulate our opinion in the present inquiry, some occur that suggest an idea of considerable progress in civilization in the Mexican empire, and others which seem to indicate that it had advanced but little beyond the savage tribes around it. Both shall be exhibited to the view of the reader, that, from comparing them, he may

* Herrera, dec. 3. lib. ii. c. 18.

determine on which side the evidence prepon-
derates.

In the Mexican empire, the right of private
property was perfectly understood, and established
in its full extent. Among several savage tribes,
we have seen, that the idea of a title to the separate and exclusive possession of any object was
hardly known; and that among all, it was extremely limited and ill defined. But in Mexico,
where agriculture and industry had made some
progress, the distinction between property in land
and property in goods had taken place. Both
might be transferred from one person to another
by sale or barter; both might descend by inheritance. Every person who could be denominated
a freeman had property in land. This, however, they held by various tenures. Some possessed it in full right, and it descended to their
heirs. The title of others to their lands was
derived from the office or dignity which they
enjoyed; and when deprived of the latter, they
lost possession of the former. Both these modes
of occupying land were deemed noble, and peculiar to citizens of the highest class. The
tenure by which the great body of the people
held their property, was very different. In every
district a certain quantity of land was measured
out in proportion to the number of families.
This was cultivated by the joint labour of the
whole; its produce was deposited in a common
storehouse, and divided among them according
to their respective exigencies. The members
of the *Calpullee*, or associations, could not alienate
their share of the common estate; it was an indi-
visible, permanent property, destined for the sup-

port of their families *. In consequence of this distribution of the territory of the state, every man had an interest in its welfare, and the happiness of the individual was connected with the public security.

Another striking circumstance, which distinguishes the Mexican empire from those nations in America we have already described, is the number and greatness of its cities. While society continues in a rude state, the wants of men are so few, and they stand so little in need of mutual assistance, that their inducements to crowd together are extremely feeble. Their industry at the same time is so imperfect, that it cannot secure subsistence for any considerable number of families settled in one spot. They live dispersed, at this period, from choice as well as from necessity, or at the utmost assemble in small hamlets on the banks of the river which supplies them with food, or on the border of some plain left open by nature, or cleared by their own labour. The Spaniards, accustomed to this mode of habitation among all the savage tribes with which they were hitherto acquainted, were astonished, on entering New Spain, to find the natives residing in towns of such extent as resembled those of Europe. In the first fervour of their admiration, they compared Zempoalla, though a town only of the second or third size, to the cities of greatest note in their own country. When, afterwards, they visited in succession Tlascala, Cholula, Tacuba, Tezeuco, and Mexico itself, their amazement increased so

* Herrera, dec. 3. lib. iv. c. 15. Torquem. Mon Ind. lib. xiv. c. 7. Corita, MS.

M 2

much, that it led them to convey ideas of their magnitude and populousness bordering on what is incredible. Even when there is leisure for observation, and no interest that leads to deceive, conjectural estimates of the number of people in cities are extremely loose, and usually much exaggerated. It is not surprising, then, that Cortes and his companions, little accustomed to such computations, and powerfully tempted to magnify, in order to exalt the merit of their own discoveries and conquests, should have been betrayed into this common error, and have raised their descriptions considerably above truth. For this reason, some considerable abatement ought to be made from their calculations of the number of inhabitants in the Mexican cities, and we may fix the standard of their population much lower than they have done; but still they will appear to be cities of such consequence, as are not to be found but among people who have made some considerable progress in the arts of social life *. From their accounts, we can hardly suppose Mexico, the capital of the empire, to have contained fewer than sixty thousand inhabitants.

The separation of professions among the Mexicans is a symptom of improvement no less remarkable. Arts, in the early ages of society, are so few and so simple, that each man is sufficiently master of them all, to gratify every demand of his own limited desires. The savage can form his bow, point his arrows, rear his hut, and hollow his canoe, without calling in the aid of any hand more skilful than his own.

* See Note CXLV.

Time must have augmented the wants of men, and ripened their ingenuity, before the productions of art became so complicated in their structure, or so curious in their fabric, that a particular course of education was requisite towards forming the artificer to expertness in contrivance and workmanship. In proportion as refinement spreads, the distinction of professions increases, and they branch out into more numerous and minute subdivisions. Among the Mexicans, this separation of the arts necessary in life had taken place to a considerable extent. The functions of the mason, the weaver, the goldsmith, the painter, and of several other crafts, were carried on by different persons. Each was regularly instructed in his calling. To it alone his industry was confined; and, by assiduous application to one object, together with the persevering patience peculiar to Americans, their artizans attained to a degree of neatness and perfection in work, far beyond what could have been expected from the rude tools which they employed. Their various productions were brought into commerce; and by the exchange of them in the stated markets held in the cities, not only were their mutual wants supplied *, in such orderly intercourse as characterises an improved state of society, but their industry was daily rendered persevering and inventive.

The distinction of ranks established in the Mexican empire, is the next circumstance that merits attention. In surveying the savage tribes

* Cortes, Relat. ap. Ramus. iii. 239, &c. Gom. Cron. c. 79. Torquem lib. xiii. c. 34. Herrera, dec. 2. lib. vii. c. 15, &c.

M 3

of America, we observed that consciousnes of
equality, and impatience of subordination, are
sentiments natural to man in the infancy of civil
life.   During peace, the authority of a superior
is hardly felt among them, and even in war it
is but little acknowledged.   Strangers to the
idea of property, the difference in condition resulting from the inequality of it is unknown.
Birth or titles confer no pre-eminence; it is only by personal merit and accomplishments that
distinction can be acquired.   The form of society
was very different among the Mexicans.   The
great body of the people was in a most humiliating state.   A considerable number, known by
the name of *Mayeques*, nearly resembling in condition those peasants who, under various denominations, were considered, during the prevalence of the feudal system, as instruments of
labour attached to the soil. The *Mayeques* could
not change their place of residence without
permission of the superior on whom they depended.   They were conveyed, together with
the lands on which they were settled, from one
proprietor to another; and were bound to cultivate the ground, and to perform several kinds
of servile work *.   Others were reduced to the
lowest form of subjection, that of domestic servitude, and felt the utmost rigour of that wretched state.   Their condition was held to be so
vile, and their lives deemed to be of so little value, that a person who killed one of these slaves
was not subjected to any punishment †.   Even
those considered as freemen were treated by

* Herrera, dec. 3. lib. iv. c. 17.   Corita, MS.
† Herrera, dec. 3. lib. iv. c. 7.

their haughty lords as beings of an inferior
species.   The nobles, possessed of ample territories, were divided into various classes, to
each of which peculiar titles of honour belonged.
Some of these titles, like their lands, descended
from father to son in perpetual succession.
Others were annexed to particular offices, or
conferred during life as marks of personal distinction *.   The monarch, exalted above all, enjoyed extensive power, and supreme dignity.
Thus the distinction of ranks was completely
established, in a line of regular subordination,
reaching from the highest to the lowest member
of the community.   Each of these knew what
he could claim, and what he owed.   The people, who were not allowed to wear a dress of
the same fashion, or to dwell in houses of a
form similar to those of the nobles, accosted
them with the most submissive reverence.   In
the presence of their sovereign, they durst not
lift their eyes from the ground, or look him in
the face †.   The nobles themselves, when admitted to an audience of their sovereign, entered
bare-footed, in mean garments, and, as his
slaves, paid him homage approaching to ador-
ation.   This respect, due from inferiors to those
above them in rank, was prescribed with such
ceremonious accuracy, that it incorporated with
the language, and influenced its genius and idiom.
The Mexican tongue abounded in expressions of
reverence and courtesy.   The style and appellations used in the intercourse between equals,
would have been so unbecoming in the mouth of

* Herrera, dec. 3. lib. iv. c. 15.   Corita, MS.
† Herrera, dec. 3. lib. ii. c. 14.

one in a lower sphere, when he accosted a person in higher rank, as to be deemed an insult [*]. It is only in societies, which time and the institution of regular government have moulded into form, that we find such an orderly arrangement of men into different ranks, and such nice attention paid to their various rights.

The spirit of the Mexicans, thus familiarized and bended to subordination, was prepared for submitting to monarchical government. But the descriptions of their policy and laws by the Spaniards who overturned them, are so inaccurate and contradictory, that it is difficult to delineate the form of their constitution with any precision. Sometimes they represent the monarchs of Mexico as absolute, deciding according to their pleasure, with respect to every operation of the state. On other occasions, we discover the traces of established customs and laws, framed in order to circumscribe the power of the crown, and we meet with rights and privileges of the nobles which seem to be opposed as barriers against its encroachments. This appearance of inconsistency has arisen from inattention to the innovations of Montezuma upon the Mexican policy. His aspiring ambition subverted the original system of government, and introduced a pure despotism. He disregarded the ancient laws, violated the privileges held most sacred, and reduced his subjects of every order to the level of slaves [†]. The chiefs, or nobles of the first rank, submitted to the yoke with such reluctance, that, from impatience to shake it off,

<hr>

[*] See Note CXLVI.   [†] Herrera, dec. 3. lib. ii. c. 14. Torquem. lib. ii. c. 69.

and hope of recovering their rights, many of them courted the protection of Cortes, and joined a foreign power against their domestic oppressor *. It is not then under the dominion of Montezuma, but under the government of his predecessors, that we can discover what was the original form and genius of Mexican policy. From the foundation of the monarchy to the election of Montezuma, it seems to have subsisted with little variation. That body of citizens, which may be distinguished by the name of nobility, formed the chief and most respectable order in the state. They were of various ranks, as has been already observed, and their honours were acquired and transmitted in different manners. Their number seems to have been great. According to an author accustomed to examine with attention what he relates, there were in the Mexican empire thirty of this order, each of whom had in his territories about an hundred thousand people, and subordinate to these, there were about three thousand nobles of a lower class †. The territories belonging to the chiefs of Tezeuco and Tacuba were hardly inferior in extent to those of the Mexican monarch ‡. Each of these possessed complete territorial jurisdiction, and levied taxes from their own vassals. But all followed the standard of Mexico in war, serving with a number of men in proportion to their domain, and most of them paid tribute to its monarch as their superior lord.

* Herrera, dec. 2. lib. v. c. 10, 11.   Torquem. lib. iv. c. 49.   † Herrera, dec. 2. lib. viii. c. 12.   ‡Torquem. lib. ii. c. 57.   Corita, MS.

In tracing those great lines of the Mexican constitution, an image of feudal policy, in its most rigid form, rises to view, and we discern its three distinguishing characteristics, a nobility possessing almost independent authority, a people depressed into the lowest state of subjection, and a king entrusted with the executive power of the state. Its spirit and principles seem to have operated in the New World in the same manner as in the ancient. The jurisdiction of the crown was extremely limited. All real and effective authority was retained by the Mexican nobles in their own hands, and the shadow of it only left to the king. Jealous to excess of their own rights, they guarded with the most vigilant anxiety against the encroachments of their sovereigns. By a fundamental law of the empire, it was provided that the king should not determine concerning any point of general importance, without the approbation of a council composed of the prime nobility *. Unless he obtained their consent, he could not engage the nation in war, nor could he dispose of the most considerable branch of the public revenue at pleasure ; it was appropriated to certain purposes from which it could not be diverted by the regal authority alone †. In order to secure full effect to those constitutional restraints, the Mexican nobles did not permit their crown to descend by inheritance, but disposed of it by election. The right of election seems to have been originally vested in the whole body of no-

* Herrera, dec. 3. lib. ii. c. 19. Id. dec. 3. lib. iv. c. 16. Corita, MS. † Herrera, dec. 3. lib. iv. c. 17.

bility, but was afterwards committed to six electors, of whom the chiefs of Tezeuco and Tacuba were always two. From respect for the family of their monarchs, the choice fell generally upon some person sprung from it. But as the activity and valour of their prince were of greater moment to a people perpetually engaged in war, than a strict adherence to the order of birth, collaterals of mature age or of distinguished merit were often preferred to those who were nearer the throne in direct descent *. To this maxim in their policy, the Mexicans appear to be indebted for such a succession of able and warlike princes, as raised their empire in a short period to that extraordinary height of power which it had attained when Cortes landed in New Spain.

While the jurisdiction of the Mexican monarchs continued to be limited, it is probable that it was exercised with little ostentation. But as their authority became more extensive, the splendour of their government augmented. It was in this last state that the Spaniards beheld it ; and struck with the appearance of Montezuma's court, they describe its pomp at great length, and with much admiration. The number of his attendants, the order, the silence, and the reverence with which they served him ; the extent of his royal mansion, the variety of its apartments allotted to different officers, and the ostentation with which his grandeur was displayed, whenever he permitted his subjects to behold him, seem to resemble the magnifi-

* Acosta, lib. vi. c. 24. Herrera, dec. 3. lib. ii. c. 13. Corita, MS.

cence of the ancient monarchies in Asia, rather than the simplicity of the infant states in the New World.

But it was not in the mere parade of royalty that the Mexican potentates exhibited their power; they manifested it more beneficially in the order and regularity with which they conducted the internal administration and police of their dominions. Complete jurisdiction, civil as well as criminal, over its own immediate vassals, was vested in the crown. Judges were appointed for each department, and if we may rely on the account which the Spanish writers give of the maxims and laws upon which they founded their decisions with respect to the distribution of property, and the punishment of crimes, justice was administered in the Mexican empire with a degree of order and equity resembling what takes place in societies highly civilized.

Their attention in providing for the support of government was not less sagacious. Taxes were laid upon land, upon the acquisitions of industry, and upon commodities of every kind exposed to sale in the public markets. These duties were considerable, but not arbitrary or unequal. They were imposed according to established rules, and each knew what share of the common burden he had to bear. As the use of money was unknown, all the taxes were paid in kind, and thus not only the natural productions of all the different provinces in the empire, but every species of manufacture, and every work of ingenuity and art, were collected in the public storehouses. From those

the emperor supplied his numerous train of attendants in peace, and his armies during war,
with food, with clothes, and ornaments.   People
of inferior condition, neither possessing land nor
engaged in commerce, were bound to the performance of various services.   By their stated
labour the crown-lands were cultivated, public
works were carried on, and the various houses
belonging to the emperor were built and kept
in repair *.

The improved state of government among the
Mexicans is conspicuous, not only in points essential to the being of a well-ordered society, but
in several regulations of inferior consequence
with respect to police.   The institution which
I have already mentioned, of public couriers,
stationed at proper intervals, to convey intelligence from one part of the empire to the other,
was a refinement in police not introduced into
any kingdom of Europe at that period.   The
structure of the capital city in a lake, with artificial dikes, and causeways of great length,
which served as avenues to it from different
quarters, erected in the water, with no less ingenuity than labour, seems to be an idea that
could not have occurred to any but a civilized
people.   The same observation may be applied
to the structure of the aqueducts, or conduits,
by which they conveyed a stream of fresh water,
from a considerable distance, into the city, along
one of the causeways †.   The appointment of a
number of persons to clean the streets, to light
them by fires kindled in different places, and to

* Herrera, dec. 2. lib. vii. c. 13. dec. 3. lib. iv. c. 16. 17
See Note CXLVII.   † See Note CXLVIII.

patrole as watchmen during the night *, discovers a degree of attention which even polished
nations are late in acquiring.

The progress of the Mexicans in various arts,
is considered as the most decisive proof of their
superior refinement.   Cortes, and the early
Spanish authors, describe this with rapture, and
maintain, that the most celebrated European
artists could not surpass or even equal them in
ingenuity and neatness of workmanship.   They
represented men, animals, and other objects, by
such a disposition of various-coloured feathers, as
is said to have produced all the effects of light
and shade, and to have imitated nature with truth
and delicacy.   Their ornaments of gold and silver have been described to be of a fabric no less
curious.   But in forming any idea, from general
descriptions, concerning the state of arts among
nations imperfectly polished, we are extremely
ready to err.   In examining the works of people whose advances in improvement are nearly
the same with our own, we view them with a
critical, and often with a jealous eye.   Whereas,
when conscious of our own superiority, we survey the arts of nations comparatively rude, we
are astonished at works executed by them under
such manifest disadvantages, and, in the warmth
of our admiration, are apt to represent them as
productions more finished than they really are.
To the influence of this illusion, without supposing any intention to deceive, we may impute
the exaggeration of some Spanish authors, in
their accounts of the Mexican arts.

* Herrera, dec. 2. lib. viii. c. 4.   Torribio, MS.

It is not from those descriptions, but from considering such specimens of their arts as are still preserved, that we must decide concerning their degree of merit.   As the ship in which Cortes sent to Charles V. the most curious productions of the Mexican artisans, which were collected by the Spaniards when they first pillaged the empire, was taken by a French corsair *, the remains of their ingenuity are less numerous than those of the Peruvians.   Whether any of their works with feathers, in imitation of painting, be still extant in Spain, I have not learned ; but many of their ornaments in gold and silver, as well as various utensils employed in common life, are deposited in the magnificent cabinet of natural and artificial productions, lately opened by the king of Spain ; and I am informed by persons on whose judgment and taste I can rely, that these boasted efforts of their art are uncouth representations of common objects, or very coarse images of the human and some other forms, destitute of grace and propriety †.   The justness of these observations is confirmed by inspecting the wooden prints and copperplates of their paintings, which have been published by various authors.   In them every figure of men, of quadrupeds, or birds, as well as every representation of inanimated nature, is extremely rude and awkward ‡.   The

* Relac. de Cort. Ramus. iii. 294, F.
† See Note CXLIX.
‡ As a specimen of the spirit and style in which M. Clavigero makes his strictures upon my History of America, I shall publish his remarks upon this passage: " Thus far " Robertson ; to whom we answer, first, That there is " no reason to believe that those rude works were really

N 2

hardest Egyptian style, stiff and imperfect as it was, is more elegant. The scrawls of children delineate objects almost as accurately.

"Mexican; secondly, That neither do we know whether "those persons in whose judgment he confides, may be "persons fit to merit our faith, because we have observ- "ed that Robertson trusts frequently to the testimony of "Gage, Correal, Ibagnez, and other such authors, who "are entirely undeserving of credit.—Thirdly, It is more "probable that the arms of copper, believed by those in- "telligent judges to be certainly Oriental, are really "Mexican." Vol. II. 391.——When an author, not en- tirely destitute of integrity or discernment, and who has some solicitude about his own character, asserts that he received his information concerning any particular point from persons " on whose judgment and taste he can re- ly;" a very slender degree of candour, one should think, might induce the reader to believe that he does not en- deavour to impose upon the public by an appeal to testi- mony altogether unworthy of credit. My information concerning the Mexican works of art deposited in the king of Spain's cabinet, was received from the late Lord Grantham, ambassador extraordinary from the court of London to that of Madrid, and from Mr. Archdeacon Waddilove, chaplain to the embassy; and it was upon their authority that I pronounced the coat of armour, mentioned in the note, to be of Oriental fabric. As they were both at Madrid in their public character when the first edition of the History of America was published, I thought it improper at that time to mention their names. Did their decision concerning a matter of taste, or their testimony concerning a point of fact, stand in need of confirmation, I might produce the evidence of an intel- ligent traveller, who, in describing the royal cabinet of Madrid, takes notice that it contains " Specimens of " Mexican and Peruvian utensils, vases, &c. in earthen " ware, wretched both in taste and execution." Dillon's Travels through Spain, p. 77. As Gage composed his *Survey of New Spain* with all the zeal and acrimony of a new convert, I have paid little regard to his testimony with respect to points relating to religion. But as he re- sided in several provinces in New Spain which travel-

But however low the Mexican paintings may be ranked, when viewed merely as works of art, a very different station belongs to them, when considered as the records of their country, as historical monuments of its policy and transactions; and they become curious as well as interesting objects of attention. The noblest and most beneficial invention of which human ingenuity can boast, is that of writing. But the first essays of this art, which hath contributed more than all others to the improvement of the species, were very rude, and it advanced towards perfection slowly, and by a gradual progression. When the warrior, eager for fame, wished to transmit some knowledge of his exploits to succeeding ages; when the gratitude of a people to their sovereign prompted them to hand down an account of his beneficent deeds to posterity; the first method of accomplishing this which seems to have occurred to them, was to delineate, in the best manner they could, figures representing the action of which they were solicitous to preserve the memory. Of this, which has very properly been called *picture-writing* *, we find traces among

lers seldom visit, and as he seems to have observed their manners and laws with an intelligent eye, I have availed myself of his information with respect to matters where religious opinion could have little influence. Correal I have seldom quoted, and never rested upon his evidence alone. The station in which Ibagnez was employed in America, as well as the credit given to his veracity by printing his Regno Jesuitico among the large collection of documents published (as I believe by authority) at Madrid, A. D. 1767, justifies me for appealing to his authority.

* Divine Legat. of Moses, iii. 73.

some of the most savage tribes of America. When a leader returns from the field, he strips a tree of its bark, and with red paint scratches upon it some uncouth figures which represent the order of his march, the number of his followers, the enemy whom he attacked, the scalps and captives which he brought home. To those simple annals he trusts for renown, and sooths himself with hope that by their means he shall receive praise from the warriors of future times *.

Compared with those awkward essays of their savage countrymen, the paintings of the Mexicans may be considered as works of composition and design. They were not acquainted, it is true, with any other method of recording transactions, than that of delineating the objects which they wished to represent. But they could exhibit a more complex series of events in progressive order, and describe, by a proper disposition of figures, the occurrences of a king's reign from his accession to his death; the progress of an infant's education from its birth until it attain to the years of maturity; the different recompences and marks of distinction conferred upon warriors, in proportion to the exploits which they had performed. Some singular specimens of this picture-writing have been preserved, which are justly considered as the most curious monuments of art brought from the New World. The most valuable of these was published by Purchas in sixty-six plates. It is divided into three parts. The first contains

* Sir W. Johnson Philos Transact. vol. lxiii. p. 143. Mem. de la Hontan. ii. 191.   Lafitau, Mœurs de Sauv. ii. 43.

the history of the Mexican empire under its ten
monarchs.   The second is a tribute-roll, representing what each conquered town paid into the
royal treasury.   The third is a code of their institutions, domestic, political, and military.   Another specimen of Mexican painting has been
published in thirty-two plates, by the present
archbishop of Toledo.   To both are annexed a
full explanation of what the figures were intended to represent, which was obtained by the Spaniards from Indians well acquainted with their
own arts.   The style of painting in all these is
the same.   They represent *things*, not *words*.
They exhibit images to the eye, not ideas to the
understanding.   They may, therefore, be considered as the earliest and most imperfect essay
of men in their progress towards discovering the
art of writing.   The defects in this mode of recording transactions must have been early felt.
To paint every occurrence was, from its nature,
a very tedious operation ; and as affairs became
more complicated, and events multiplied in any
society, its annals must have swelled to an enormous bulk.   Besides this, no objects could be delineated but those of sense ; the conceptions of the
mind had no corporeal form, and as long as picture-writing could not convey an idea of these, it
must have been a very imperfect art.   The necessity of improving it must have roused and sharp-
ened invention ; and the human mind, holding the
same course in the New World as in the Old,
might have advanced by the same successive steps,
first, from an actual picture to the plain hieroglyphic ; next, to the allegorical symbol ; then to the

arbitrary character; until at length an alphabet of letters was discovered, capable of expressing all the various combinations of sound employed in speech. In the paintings of the Mexicans we accordingly perceive that this progress was begun among them. Upon an attentive inspection of the plates which I have mentioned, we may observe some approach to the plain or simple hieroglyphic, where some principal part or circumstance in the subject is made to stand for the whole. In the annals of their kings, published by Purchas, the towns conquered by each are uniformly represented in the same manner by a rude delineation of a house; but in order to point out the particular towns which submitted to their victorious arms, peculiar emblems, sometimes natural objects, and sometimes artificial figures, are employed. In the tribute-roll published by the archbishop of Toledo, the house, which was properly the picture of the town, is omitted, and the emblem alone is employed to represent it. The Mexicans seem even to have made some advances beyond this, towards the use of the more figurative and fanciful hieroglyphic. In order to describe a monarch who had enlarged his dominions by force of arms, they painted a target ornamented with darts, and placed it between him and those towns which he subdued. But it is only in one instance, the notation of numbers, that we discern any attempt to exhibit ideas which had no corporeal form. The Mexican painters had invented artificial marks, or *signs of convention*, for this purpose. By means of these, they computed the years of their kings' reigns, as well as the amount of tribute to be paid into the royal treasury. The figure of a circle represented unit, and in small numbers the computation was made by repeating it. Larger numbers were expressed by a peculiar mark, and they had such as denoted all integral numbers, from twenty to eight thousand. The short duration of their empire prevented the Mexicans from advancing farther in that long course which conducts men from the labour of delineating real objects, to the simplicity and ease of alphabetic writing. Their records, notwithstanding some dawn of such ideas as might have led to a more perfect style, can be considered as little more than a species of picture-writing, so far improved as to mark their superiority over the savage tribes of America; but still so defective, as to prove that they had not proceeded far beyond the first stage in that progress which must be completed before any people can be ranked among polished nations *.

Their mode of computing time may be considered as a more decisive evidence of their progress in improvement. They divided their year into eighteen months, each consisting of twenty days, amounting in all to three hundred and sixty. But as they observed that the course of the sun was not completed in that time, they added five days to the year. These, which were properly intercalary days, they termed *supernumerary* or *waste;* and as they did not belong to any month, no work was done, and no sacred rite performed on them; they were devoted wholly to festivity and pastime †. This near approach to philoso-

* See Note CL.   † Acosta, lib. vi. c. 2.

phical accuracy is a remarkable proof that the Mexicans had bestowed some attention upon inquiries and speculations, to which men in a very rude state never turn their thoughts *.

Such are the most striking particulars in the manners and policy of the Mexicans, which exhibit them to view as a people considerably refined. But from other circumstances, one is apt to suspect that their character, and many of their institutions, did not differ greatly from those of the other inhabitants of America.

Like the rude tribes around them, the Mexicans were incessantly engaged in war, and the motives which prompted them to hostility seem to have been the same. They fought, in order to gratify their vengeance, by shedding the blood of their enemies. In battle they were chiefly intent on taking prisoners, and it was by the number of these that they estimated the glory of victory. No captive was ever ransomed or spared. All were sacrificed without mercy, and their flesh devoured with the same barbarous joy as among the fiercest savages. On some occasions it rose to even wilder excesses. Their principal warriors covered themselves with the skins of the unhappy victims, and danced about the streets, boasting of their own valour, and exulting over their enemies †. Even in their civil institutions we dis-

* The Mexican mode of computing time, and every other particular relating to their chronology, have been considerably elucidated by M. Clavigero, Vol. I. 288; Vol II. 225. &c. The observations and theories of the Mexicans concerning those subjects, discover a greater progress in speculative science than we find among any people in the New World.

† Herrera, dec. 3. lib. 2. c. 15. Gom. Cron. c. 217.

cover traces of that barbarous disposition which
their system of war inspired. The four chief
counsellors of the empire were distinguished by
titles, which could have been assumed only by a
people who delighted in blood *. This ferocity
of character prevailed among all the nations of
New Spain. The Tlascalans, the people of
Mechoacan, and other states at enmity with the
Mexicans, delighted equally in war, and treated
their prisoners with the same cruelty. In proportion as mankind combine in social union, and
live under the influence of equal laws and regular
policy, their manners soften, sentiments of humanity arise, and the rights of the species come
to be understood. The fierceness of war abates,
and even while engaged in hostility, men remember what they owe one to another. The savage
fights to destroy, the citizen to conquer. The
former neither pities nor spares, the latter has
acquired sensibility which tempers his rage. To
this sensibility the Mexicans seem to have been
perfect strangers, and among them war was carried on with so much of its original barbarity,
that we cannot but suspect their degree of civilization to have been very imperfect.

Their funeral rites were not less bloody than
those of the most savage tribes. On the death of
any distinguished personage, especially of the emperor, a certain number of his attendants were
chosen to accompany him to the other world,
and those unfortunate victims were put to death
without mercy, and buried in the same tomb †.

* See Note CLI.
† Herrera, dec. 3. lib. ii. c. 18. Gom. Cron. c. 202.

Though their agriculture was more extensive than that of the roving tribes who trusted chiefly to their bow for food, it seems not to have supplied them with such subsistence as men require when engaged in efforts of active industry. The Spaniards appear not to have been struck with any superiority of the Mexicans over the other people of America in bodily vigour. Both, according to their observation, were of such a feeble frame as to be unable to endure fatigue, and the strength of one Spaniard exceeded that of several Indians. This they imputed to their scanty diet, on poor fare, sufficient to preserve life, but not to give firmness to the constitution. Such a remark could hardly have been made with respect to any people furnished plentifully with the necessaries of life. The difficulty which Cortes found in procuring subsistence for his small body of soldiers, who were often constrained to live on the spontaneous productions of the earth, seems to confirm the remark of the Spanish writers, and gives no high idea of the state of cultivation in the Mexican empire *.

A practice that was universal in New Spain appears to favour this opinion. The Mexican women gave suck to their children for several years, and during that time they did not cohabit with their husbands †. This precaution against a burdensome increase of progeny, though necessary, as I have already observed, among savages, who, from the hardships of their condition, and

* Relat. ap Ramus. iii. 306, A. Herrera, dec. iii. lib. iv. c. 17. dec. 2. lib. vi. c. 16.
† Gom. Cron. c. 208. Herrera, dec. 3. lib. iv. c. 16.

the precariousness of their subsistence, find it impossible to rear a numerous family, can hardly be supposed to have continued among a people who lived at ease and in abundance.

The vast extent of the Mexican empire, which has been considered, and with justice, as the most decisive proof of a considerable progress in regular government and police, is one of those facts in the history of the New World which seems to have been admitted without due examination or sufficient evidence. The Spanish historians, in order to magnify the valour of their countrymen, are accustomed to represent the dominion of Montezuma as stretching over all the provinces of New Spain from the Northern to the Southern Ocean. But a great part of the mountainous country was possessed by the *Otomies*, a fierce uncivilized people, who seem to have been the residue of the original inhabitants. The provinces towards the north and west of Mexico were occupied by the *Chichemeccas*, and others tribes of hunters. None of these recognised the Mexican monarch as their superior. Even in the interior and more level country, there were several cities and provinces which had never submitted to the Mexican yoke. Tlascala, though only twenty-one leagues from the capital of the empire, was an independent and hostile republic. Cholula, though still nearer, had been subjected only a short time before the arrival of the Spaniards. Tepeaca, at the distance of thirty leagues from Mexico, seems to have been a separate state governed by its own laws *. Mechoacan, the fron-

---

* Herrera, dec. 3. lib. 10. c. 15. 21.   B. Diaz, c. 130.

tier of which extended within forty leagues of Mexico, was a powerful kingdom, remarkable for its implacable enmity to the Mexican name *. By these hostile powers the Mexican empire was circumscribed in every quarter, and the high ideas which we are apt to form of it from the description of the Spanish historians, should be considerably moderated.

In consequence of this independence of several states in New Spain upon the Mexican empire, there was not any considerable intercourse between its various provinces. Even in the interior country not far distant from the capital, there seem to have been no roads to facilitate the communication of one district with another; and when the Spaniards first attempted to penetrate into its several provinces, they had to open their way through forests and marshes †. Cortes, in his adventurous march from Mexico to Honduras, in 1525, met with obstructions, and endured hardships, little inferior to those with which he must have struggled in the most uncivilized regions of America. In some places he could hardly force a passage through impervious woods, and plains overflowed with water. In others he found so little cultivation, that his troops were frequently in danger of perishing by famine. Such facts correspond ill with the pompous description which the Spanish writers give of Mexican police and industry, and convey an idea of a country nearly similar to that possessed by the Indian tribes in North America. Here and there a trading or a war path, as they are called in North

* Herrera, dec. 3. lib. ii. c. 10.
† B. Diaz, c. 166. d. 176.

America, led from one settlement to another *, but generally there appeared no sign of any established communication, few marks of industry, and fewer monuments of art.

A proof of this imperfection in their commercial intercourse no less striking, is their want of money, or some universal standard, by which to estimate the value of commodities. The discovery of this is among the steps of greatest consequence in the progress of nations. Until it has been made, all their transactions must be so awkward, so operose, and so limited, that we may boldly pronounce that they have advanced but a little way in their career. The invention of such a commercial standard is of such high antiquity in our hemisphere, and rises so far beyond the era of authentic history, as to appear almost coeval with the existence of society. The precious metals seem to have been early employed for this purpose, and from their permanent value, their divisibility, and many other qualities, they are better adapted to serve as a common standard than any other substance of which nature has given us the command. But in the New World, where these metals abound most, this use of them was not known. The exigencies of rude tribes, or of monarchies imperfectly civilized, did not call for it. All their commercial intercourse was carried on by barter, and their ignorance of any common standard by which to facilitate that exchange of commodities which contributes so much towards the comfort of life, may be justly mentioned as an evidence of the infant state of their policy. But even in the New World the inconvenience of wanting some gene-

* Herrera, dec. 3. lib. vii. c. 8.

ral instrument of commerce began to be felt, and some efforts were made towards supplying that defect. The Mexicans, among whom the number and greatness of their cities gave rise to a more extended commerce than in any other part of America, had begun to employ a common standard of value, which rendered smaller transactions much more easy. As chocolate was the favourite drink of persons in every rank of life, the nuts or almonds of cacao, of which it is composed, were of such universal consumption, that, in their stated markets, these were willingly received in return for commodities of small price. Thus they came to be considered as the instrument of commerce, and the value of what one wished to dispose of was estimated by the number of nuts of the cacao which he might expect to exchange for it. This seems to be the utmost length which the Americans had advanced towards the discovery of any expedient for supplying the use of money. And if the want of it is to be held, on one hand, as a proof of their barbarity, this expedient for supplying that want should be admitted, on the other, as an evidence no less satisfying, of some progress which the Mexicans had made in refinement and civilization beyond the savage tribes around them.

In such a rude state were many of the Mexican provinces when first visited by their conquerors. Even their cities, extensive and populous as they were, seem more fit to be the habitation of men just emerging from barbarity, than the residence of a polished people. The description of Tlascala nearly resembles that of an Indian village. A number of low straggling huts, scattered about irregularly, according to the caprice of each proprietor, built with turf and stone, and thatched with reeds, without any light but what they received by a door, so low that it could not be entered upright *.   In Mexico, though, from the peculiarity of its situation, the disposition of the houses was more orderly, the structure of the greater part was equally mean. Nor does the fabric of their temples, and other public edifices, appear to have been such as entitled them to the high praises bestowed upon them by many Spanish authors.   As far as one can gather from their obscure and inaccurate descriptions, the great temple of Mexico, the most famous in New Spain, which has been represented as a magnificent building, raised to such a height that the ascent to it was by a flight of a hundred and fourteen steps, was a solid mass of earth of a square form, faced partly with stone.   Its base on each side extended ninety feet, and decreasing gradually as it advanced in height, it terminated in a quadrangle of about thirty feet, where were placed a shrine of the deity, and two altars on which the victims were sacrificed †.   All the other celebrated temples of New Spain exactly resembled that of Mexico ‡.   Such structures convey no high idea of progress in art and ingenuity; and one can hardly conceive that a form more rude and simple could have occurred to a nation in its first efforts towards erecting any great work.

Greater skill and ingenuity were displayed, if we may believe the Spanish historians, in the houses of the emperor and in those of the princi-

* Herrera, dec. 7. lib. vi. c. 12.
† Herrera, dec. 2. lib. vii. c. 17.   ‡ See Note CLII.

pal nobility. There, some elegance of design was visible, and a commodious arrangement of the apartments was attended to. But if buildings corresponding to such descriptions had ever existed in the Mexican cities, it is probable that some remains of them would still be visible. From the manner in which Cortes conducted the siege of Mexico, we can indeed easily account for the total destruction of whatever had any appearance of splendor in that capital. But as only two centuries and a half have elapsed since the conquest of New Spain, it seems altogether incredible that in a period so short, every vestige of this boasted elegance and grandeur should have disappeared; and that in the other cities, particularly in those which did not suffer by the destructive hand of the conquerors, there are any ruins which can be considered as monuments of their ancient magnificence.

Even in a village of the rudest Indians, there are buildings of greater extent and elevation than common dwelling-houses. Such as are destined for holding the council of the tribe, and in which all assemble on occasions of public festivity, may be called stately edifices, when compared with the rest. As among the Mexicans the distinction of ranks was established, and property was unequally divided, the number of distinguished structures in their towns would of course be greater than in other parts of America. But these seem not to have been either so solid or magnificent as to merit the pompous epithets which some Spanish authors employ in describing them. It is probable that, though more ornamented, and built on a larger scale, they were erected with the same flight materials which the Indians employed in their common buildings *, and time, in a space much less than two hundred and fifty years, may have swept away all the remains of them †.

From this enumeration of facts, it seems, upon the whole, to be evident, that the state of society in Mexico was considerably advanced beyond that of the savage tribes which we have delineated. But it is no less manifest, that with respect to many particulars, the Spanish accounts of their progress appear to be highly embellished. There is not a more frequent or a more fertile source of deception, in describing the manners and arts of savage nations, or of such as are imperfectly civilized, than that of applying to them the names and phrases appropriated to the institutions and refinements of polished life. When the leader of a small tribe, or the head of a rude community, is dignified with the name of king or emperor, the place of his residence can receive no other name but that of his palace; and whatever his attendants may be, they must be called his court. Under such appellations they acquire, in our estimation, an importance and dignity which does not belong to them. The illusion spreads, and giving a false colour to every part of the narrative, the imagination is so much carried away with the resemblance, that it becomes difficult to discern objects as they really are. The Spaniards, when they first touched on the Mexican coast, were so much struck with the appearance of attainments in policy and in the arts of life, far superior to those of the rude tribes with which they were hitherto acquainted, that they fancied they

* See Note CLIII.   † See Note CLIV.

had at length discovered a civilized people in the New World. This comparison between the people of Mexico and their uncultivated neighbours, they appear to have kept constantly in view, and observing with admiration many things which marked the pre-eminence of the former, they employ, in describing their imperfect policy and infant arts, such terms as are applicable to the institutions of men far beyond them in improvement. Both these circumstances concur in detracting from the credit due to the descriptions of Mexican manners by the early Spanish writers. By drawing a parallel between them and those of people so much less civilized, they raised their own ideas too high. By their mode of describing them, they conveyed ideas to others no less exalted above truth. Later writers have adopted the style of the original historians, and improved upon it. The colours with which De Solis delineates the character, and describes the actions of Montezuma, the splendour of his court, the laws and policy of his empire, are the same that he must have employed in exhibiting to view the monarch and institutions of an highly polished people.

But though we may admit, that the warm imagination of the Spanish writers has added some embellishment to their descriptions, this will not justify the decisive and peremptory tone with which several authors pronounce all their accounts of the Mexican power, policy, and laws, to be the fictions of men who wished to deceive, or who delighted in the marvellous. There are few historical facts that can be ascertained by evidence more unexceptionable, than may be produced in support of the material articles, in the description of the Mexican constitution and manners. Eye witnesses relate what they beheld. Men who had resided among the Mexicans, both before and after the conquest, describe institutions and customs which were familiar to them. Persons of professions so different that objects must have presented themselves to their view under every various aspect; soldiers, priests, and lawyers, all concur in their testimony. Had Cortes ventured to impose upon his sovereign, by exhibiting to him a picture of imaginary manners, there wanted not enemies and rivals who were qualified to detect his deceit, and who would have rejoiced in exposing it. But according to the just remark of an author, whose ingenuity has illustrated, and whose eloquence has adorned the history of America *, this supposition is in itself as improbable as the attempt would have been audacious. Who among the destroyers of this great empire was so enlightened by science, or so attentive to the progress and operations of men in social life, as to frame a fictitious system of policy so well combined, and so consistent, as that which they delineate, in their accounts of the Mexican government? Where could they have borrowed the idea of many institutions in legislation and police, to which, at that period, there was nothing parallel in the nations with which they were acquainted? There was not, at the beginning of the sixteenth century, a regular establishment of posts for conveying intelligence to the sovereign of any kingdom in Europe. The same observation will apply to

* M. l'Abbe Raynal Hist. Philos. & Polit. &c. iii. 127.

what the Spaniards relate, with respect to the structure of the city of Mexico, the regulations concerning its police, and various laws established for the administration of justice, or securing the happiness of the community. Whoever is accustomed to contemplate the progress of nations, will often, at very early stages of it, discover a premature and unexpected dawn of those ideas, which give rise to institutions that are the pride and ornament of its most advanced period. Even in a state as imperfectly polished as the Mexican empire, the happy genius of some sagacious observer, excited or aided by circumstances unknown to us, may have introduced institutions which are seldom found but in societies highly refined. But it is almost impossible that the illiterate conquerors of the New World should have formed, in any one instance, a conception of customs and laws beyond the standard of improvement in their own age and country. Or if Cortes had been capable of this, what inducement had those by whom he was superseded to continue the deception? Why should Corita, or Motolinea, or Acosta, have amused their sovereign or their fellow-citizens with a tale purely fabulous?

In one particular, however, the guides whom we must follow have represented the Mexicans to be more barbarous, perhaps, than they really were. Their religious tenets, and the rites of their worship, are described by them as wild and cruel in an extreme degree. Religion, which occupies no considerable place in the thoughts of a savage, whose conceptions of any superior power are obscure, and his sacred rites few as well as simple, was formed, among the Mexicans, into a regular system, with its complete train of priests, temples, victims, and festivals. This, of itself, is a clear proof that the state of the Mexicans was very different from that of the ruder American tribes. But from the extravagance of their religious notions, or the barbarity of their rites, no conclusion can be drawn with certainty concerning the degree of their civilization. For nations, long after their ideas begin to enlarge, and their manners to refine, adhere to systems of superstition founded on the crude conceptions of early ages. From the genius of the Mexican religion, we may, however, form a most just conclusion with respect to its influence upon the character of the people. The aspect of superstition in Mexico was gloomy and atrocious. Its divinities were clothed with terror, and delighted in vengeance. They were exhibited to the people under detestable forms, which created horror. The figures of serpents, of tygers, and of other destructive animals, decorated their temples. Fear was the only principle that inspired their votaries. Fasts, mortifications, and penances, all rigid, and many of them excruciating to an extreme degree, were the means employed to appease the wrath of their gods, and the Mexicans never approached their altars without sprinkling them with blood drawn from their own bodies. But, of all offerings, human sacrifices were deemed the most acceptable. This religious belief, mingling with the implacable spirit of vengeance, and adding new force to it, every captive taken in war was brought to the temple, was devoted as a victim to the deity, and sacrificed with rites no less solemn than cruel *. The heart and head were the portion consecrated to the gods; the warrior, by whose prowess the prisoner had been seized, carried off the body to feast upon it with his friends. Under the impression of ideas so dreary and terrible, and accustomed daily to scenes of bloodshed rendered awful by religion, the heart of man must harden, and be steeled to every sentiment of humanity. The spirit of the Mexicans was accordingly unfeeling, and the genius of their religion so far counterbalanced the influence of policy and arts, that notwithstanding their progress in both, their manners, instead of softening, became more fierce. To what circumstances it was owing that superstition assumed such a dreadful form among the Mexicans, we have not sufficient knowledge of their history to determine. But its influence is visible, and produced an effect that is singular in the history of the human species. The manners of the people in the New World who had made the greatest progress in the arts of policy, were, in several respects, the most ferocious, and the barbarity of some of their customs exceeded even those of the savage state.

The empire of Peru boasts of an higher antiquity than that of Mexico. According to the traditionary accounts collected by the Spaniards, it had subsisted four hundred years, under twelve successive monarchs. But the knowledge of their ancient story which the Peruvians could communicate to their conquerors,

---

* Cort. Relat. ap. Ramus. iii. 240, &c. B. Diaz, c. 83. Acosta, lib. v. c. 13, &c. Herrera, dec. 3. lib, ii. c, 15, &c. Gomara Cron. c. 80, &c. See Note CLV.

must have been both imperfect and uncertain *. Like the other American nations, they were totally unacquainted with the art of writing, and destitute of the only means by which the memory of past transactions can be preserved with any degree of accuracy. Even among people to whom the use of letters is known, the era where the authenticity of history commences, is much posterior to the introduction of writing. That noble invention continued every where to be long subservient to the common business and wants of life, before it was employed in recording events, with a view of conveying information from one age to another. But in no country did ever tradition alone carry down historical knowledge, in any full continued stream, during a period of half the length that the monarchy of Peru is said to have subsisted.

The *Quipos*, or knots on cords of different colours, which are celebrated by authors fond of the marvellous, as if they had been regular annals of the empire, imperfectly supplied the place of writing. According to the obscure description of them by Acosta †, which Garcilasso de la Vega has adopted with little variation and no improvement, the quipos seem to have been a device for rendering calculation more expeditious and accurate. By the various colours different objects were denoted, and by each knot a distinct number. Thus an account was taken, and a kind of register kept, of the inhabitants in each province, or of the several productions collected there for public use. But as by these

* See Note CLVI.   † Hist. lib. vi. c. 8.

knots, however varied or combined, no moral
or abstract idea, no operation or quality of the
mind, could be represented, they contributed little
towards preserving the memory of ancient events
and institutions. By the Mexican paintings and
symbols, rude as they were, more knowledge of
remote transactions seems to have been conveyed
than the Peruvians could derive from their boasted quipos. Had the latter been even of more extensive use, and better adapted to supply the
place of written records, they perished so generally, together with other monuments of Peruvian ingenuity, in the wreck occasioned by the
Spanish conquest, and the civil wars subsequent
to it, that no accession of light or knowledge
comes from them. All the zeal of Garcilasso de
la Vega for the honour of that race of monarchs from whom he descended, all the industry
of his researches, and the superior advantages
with which he carried them on, opened no source
of information unknown to the Spanish authors
who wrote before him. In his *Royal Com-
mentaries*, he confines himself to illustrate what
they had related concerning the antiquities
and institutions of Peru * ; and his illustra-
tions, like their accounts, are derived entirely
from the traditionary tales current among his
countrymen.

Very little credit then is due to the minute details which have been given of the exploits, the
battles, the conquests, and private character of
the early Peruvian monarchs. We can rest upon
nothing in their story as authentic, but a few
facts, so interwoven in the system of their religion

* Lib. i. c. 10.

and policy, as preserved the memory of them from being lost; and upon the description of such customs and institutions as continued in force at the time of the conquest, and fell under the immediate observation of the Spaniards. By attending carefully to these, and endeavouring to separate them from what appears to be fabulous, or of doubtful authority, I have laboured to form an idea of the Peruvian government and manners.

The people of Peru, as I have already observed *, had not advanced beyond the rudest form of savage life, when Manco Capac, and his consort Mama Ocollo, appeared to instruct and civilize them. Who these extraordinary personages were, whether they imported their system of legislation and knowledge of arts from some country more improved, or, if natives of Peru, how they acquired ideas so far superior to those of the people whom they addressed, are circumstances with respect to which the Peruvian tradition conveys no information. Manco Capac and his consort, taking advantage of the propensity in the Peruvians to superstition, and particularly of their veneration for the Sun, pretended to be children of that glorious luminary, and to deliver their instructions in his name, and by authority from him. The multitude listened and believed. What reformation in policy and manners the Peruvians ascribe to those founders of their empire, and how, from the precepts of the Inca and his consort, their ancestors gradually acquired some knowledge of those arts, and some relish for that industry, which render subsistence

* Book vi. vol. ii. p. 332, &c.

P 2

secure, and life comfortable, hath been formerly
related. Those blessings were originally confined
within narrow precincts ; but in process of time
the successors of Manco Capac extended their
dominion over all the regions that stretch to the
west of the Andes from Chili to Quito, establishing in every province their peculiar policy
and religious institutions.

The most singular and striking circumstance
in the Peruvian government, is the influence of
religion upon its genius and laws. Religious ideas
make such a feeble impression on the mind of a
savage, that their effect upon his sentiments and
manners is hardly perceptible. Among the Mexicans, religion, reduced into a regular system,
and holding a considerable place in their public
institutions, operated with conspicuous efficacy
in forming the peculiar character of that people.
But in Peru, the whole system of civil policy was
founded on religion. The Inca appeared not
only as a legislator, but as a messenger of Heaven. His precepts were received not merely as
the injunctions of a superior, but as the mandates
of the Deity. His race was to be held sacred ;
and in order to preserve it distinct, without being
polluted by any mixture of less noble blood, the
sons of Manco Capac married their own sisters,
and no person was ever admitted to the throne
who could not claim it by such a pure descent.
To those *Children of the Sun*, for that was the
appellation bestowed upon all the offspring of the
first Inca, the people looked up with the reverence due to beings of a superior order. They were
deemed to be under the immediate protection of
the deity from whom they issued, and by him

every order of the reigning Inca was supposed
to be dictated.

From those ideas two consequences resulted.
The authority of the Inca was unlimited and absolute, in the most extensive meaning of the
words. Whenever the decrees of a prince are
considered as the commands of the Divinity, it
is not only an act of rebellion, but of impiety,
to dispute or oppose his will. Obedience becomes a duty of religion; and as it would be
prophane to control a monarch who is believed
to be under the guidance of Heaven, and pre-
sumptuous to advise him, nothing remains but to
submit with implicit respect. This must necessarily be the effect of every government established on pretensions of intercourse with superior powers. Such accordingly was the blind
submission which the Peruvians yielded to their
sovereigns. The persons of highest rank and
greatest power in their dominions acknowledged
them to be of a more exalted nature; and in
testimony of this, when admitted into their presence, they entered with a burden upon their
shoulders, as an emblem of their servitude, and
willingness to bear whatever the Inca was pleased to impose. Among their subjects, force was
not requisite to second their commands. Every
officer entrusted with the execution of them was
revered, and, according to the account of an intelligent observer of Peruvian manners *, he might
proceed alone, from one extremity of the empire
to another, without meeting opposition; for, on
producing a fringe from the royal *Borla*, an ornament of the head peculiar to the reigning Inca,

* Zarate, lib. i. c. 13.

the lives and fortunes of the people were at his disposal.

Another consequence of establishing government in Peru on the foundation of religion was, that all crimes were punished capitally. They were not considered as transgressions of human laws, but as insults offered to the Deity. Each, without any distinction between such as were slight and such as were atrocious, called for vengeance, and could be expiated only by the blood of the offender. Consonantly to the same ideas, punishment followed the trespass with inevitable certainty, because an offence against Heaven was deemed such an high enormity as could not be pardoned *. Among a people of corrupted morals, maxims of jurisprudence so severe and unrelenting, by rendering men ferocious and desperate, would be more apt to multiply crimes than to restrain them. But the Peruvians, of simple manners and unsuspicious faith, were held in such awe by this rigid discipline, that the number of offenders was extremely small. Veneration for monarchs enlightened and directed, as they believed, by the divinity whom they adored, prompted them to their duty; the dread of punishment, which they were taught to consider as unavoidable vengeance inflicted by offended Heaven, withheld them from evil.

The system of superstition on which the Incas ingrafted their pretensions to such high authority, was of a genius very different from that established among the Mexicans. Manco Capac turned the veneration of his followers entirely towards natural objects. The Sun, as the great

* Vega, lib. ii. c. 6.

source of light, of joy, and fertility in the creation, attracted their principal homage. The Moon and Stars, as co-operating with him, were entitled to secondary honours. Wherever the propensity in the human mind, to acknowledge and to adore some superior power, takes this direction, and is employed in contemplating the order and beneficence that really exist in nature, the spirit of superstition is mild. Wherever imaginary beings, created by the fancy and the fears of men, are supposed to preside in nature, and become the objects of worship, superstition always assumes a more severe and atrocious form. Of the latter we have an example among the Mexicans, of the former among the people of Peru. The Peruvians had not, indeed, made such progress in observation or inquiry, as to have attained just conceptions of the Deity ; nor was there in their language any proper name or appellation of the Supreme Power, which intimated that they had formed any idea of him as the Creator and Governor of the World *. But by directing their veneration to that glorious luminary, which, by its universal and vivifying energy, is the best emblem of divine beneficence, the rites and observances which they deemed acceptable to him were innocent and humane. They offered to the sun a part of those productions which his genial warmth had called forth from the bosom of the earth, and reared to maturity. They sacrificed, as an oblation of gratitude, some of the animals which were indebted to his influence for nourishment. They presented to him choice specimens of those works of ingenuity which his

* Acosta, lib. v. c. 3.

light had guided the hand of man in forming. But the Incas never stained his altars with human blood, nor could they conceive that their beneficent father the Sun would be delighted with such horrid victims *. Thus the Peruvians, unacquainted with those barbarous rites which extinguish sensibility, and suppress the feelings of nature at the sight of human sufferings, were formed, by the spirit of the superstition which they had adopted, to a national character, more gentle than that of any people in America.

The influence of this superstition operated in the same manner upon their civil institutions, and tended to correct in them whatever was adverse to gentleness of character. The dominion of the Incas, though the most absolute of all despotisms, was mitigated by its alliance with religion. The mind was not humbled and depressed by the idea of a forced subjection to the will of a superior: Obedience, paid to one who was believed to be clothed with divine authority, was willingly yielded, and implied no degradation. The sovereign, conscious that the submissive reverence of his people flowed from their belief of his heavenly descent, was continually reminded of a distinction which prompted him to imitate that beneficent power which he was supposed to represent. In consequence of those impressions, there hardly occurs in the traditional history of Peru, any instance of rebellion against the reigning prince; and among twelve successive monarchs, there was not one tyrant.

Even the wars in which the Incas engaged, were carried on with a spirit very different from

* See Note CLVII.

that of other American nations.   They fought
not like savages, to destroy and exterminate;
or, like the Mexicans, to glut blood-thirsty divinities with human sacrifices.   They conquered, in
order to reclaim and civilize the vanquished, and
to diffuse the knowledge of their own institutions
and arts.   Prisoners seem not to have been exposed to the insults and tortures, which were
their lot in every other part of the New
World.   The Incas took the people whom they
subdued under their protection, and admitted
them to a participation of all the advantages enjoyed by their original subjects.   This practice,
so repugnant to American ferocity, and resembling the humanity of the most polished nations,
must be ascribed, like other peculiarities which
we have observed in the Peruvian manners, to the
genius of their religion.   The Incas, considering
the homage paid to any other object than to the
heavenly powers which they adored as impious,
were fond of gaining proselytes to their favourite
system.   The idols of every conquered province
were carried in triumph to the great temple at
Cuzco *, and placed there as trophies of the superior power of the divinity who was the protector of the empire.   The people were treated
with lenity, and instructed in the religious tenets
of their new masters †, that the conqueror might
have the glory of having added to the number
of the votaries of his father the Sun.

The state of property in Peru was no less singular than that of religion, and contributed, likewise, towards giving a mild turn of character to

* Herrera, dec. 5. lib. iv. c. 4.   Vega, lib. v. c. 12.
† Herrera, dec. 5. lib. iv. c. 8.

the people. All the lands capable of cultivation were divided into three shares. One was consecrated to the Sun, and the product of it was applied to the erection of temples, and furnishing what was requisite towards celebrating the public rites of religion. The second belonged to the Inca, and was set apart as the provision made by the community for the support of government. The third and largest share was reserved for the maintenance of the people, among whom it was parcelled out. Neither individuals, however, nor communities, had a right of exclusive property in the portion set apart for their use. They possessed it only for a year, at the expiration of which a new division was made in proportion to the rank, the number, and exigencies of each family. All those lands were cultivated by the joint industry of the community. The people, summoned by a proper officer, repaired in a body to the fields, and performed their common task, while songs and musical instruments cheered them to their labour *. By this singular distribution of territory, as well as by the mode of cultivating it, the idea of a common interest, and of mutual subserviency, was continually inculcated. Each individual felt his connection with those around him, and knew that he depended on their friendly aid for what increase he was to reap. A state thus constituted may be considered as one great family, in which the union of the members was so complete, and the exchange of good offices so perceptible, as to create stronger attachment, and to bind man to man in closer intercourse, than subsisted under any form of so-

* Herrera, dec. 5. lib. iv. c. 2. Vega, lib. v. c. 5.

ciety established in America.   From this resulted gentle manners, and mild virtues unknown in
the savage state, and with which the Mexicans
were little acquainted.

But, though the institutions of the Incas were
so framed as to strengthen the bonds of affection
among their subjects, there was great inequality
in their condition.   The distinction of ranks was
fully established in Peru.   A great body of the
inhabitants, under the denomination of *Yana-
conas*, were held in a state of servitude.   Their
garb and houses were of a form different from
those of freemen.   Like the *Tamemes* of Mexico,
they were employed in carrying burdens, and
in performing every other work of drudgery *.
Next to them in rank, were such of the people
as were free, but distinguished by no official or
hereditary honours.   Above them were raised
those whom the Spaniards call *Orejones*, from
the ornaments worn in their ears.   They formed
what may be denominated the order of nobles,
and in peace as well as war held every office of
power or trust †.   At the head of all were the
children of the Sun, who, by their high descent
and peculiar privileges, were as much exalted
above the Orejones, as these were elevated above
the people.

Such a form of society, from the union of its
members, as well as from the distinction in their
ranks, was favourable to progress in the arts.
But the Spaniards having been acquainted with
the improved state of various arts in Mexico,
several years before they discovered Peru, were

---

* Herrera, dec. 5. lib. iii. c. 4. lib. x. c. 8.
† Herrera, dec. 5. lib. iv. c. 1.

not so much struck with what they observed in the latter country, and describe the appearances of ingenuity there with less warmth of admiration. The Peruvians, nevertheless, had advanced far beyond the Mexicans, both in the necessary arts of life, and in such as have some title to the name of elegant.

In Peru, agriculture, the art of primary necessity in social life, was more extensive, and carried on with greater skill, than in any part of America. The Spaniards, in their progress through the country, were so fully supplied with provisions of every kind, that in the relation of their adventures we meet with few of those dismal scenes of distress occasioned by famine, in which the conquerors of Mexico were so often involved. The quantity of soil under cultivation was not left to the discretion of individuals, but regulated by public authority in proportion to the exigencies of the community. Even the calamity of an unfruitful season was but little felt, for the product of the lands consecrated to the Sun, as well as those set apart for the Incas, being deposited in the *Tambos*, or public storehouses, it remained there as a stated provision for times of scarcity *. As the extent of cultivation was determined with such provident attention to the demands of the state, the invention and industry of the Peruvians were called forth to extraordinary exertions, by certain defects peculiar to their climate and soil. All the vast rivers that flow from the Andes take their course eastward to the Atlantic Ocean. Peru is watered only by some streams which rush down from the moun-

* Zarate, lib. i. c. 14.   Vega, lib. i. c. 8.

tains like torrents. A great part of the low country is sandy and barren, and never refreshed with rain. In order to render such an unpromising region fertile, the ingenuity of the Peruvians had recourse to various expedients. By means of artificial canals, conducted with much patience and considerable art from the torrents that poured across their country, they conveyed a regular supply of moisture to their fields *. They enriched the soil by manuring it with the dung of sea-fowls, of which they found an inexhaustible store on all the islands scattered along their coasts †. In describing the customs of any nation thoroughly civilized, such practices would hardly draw attention, or be mentioned as in any degree remarkable; but in the history of the improvident race of men in the New World, they are entitled to notice as singular proofs of industry and of art. The use of the plough, indeed, was unknown to the Peruvians. They turned up the earth with a kind of mattock of hard wood ‡. Nor was this labour deemed so degrading as to be devolved wholly upon the women. Both sexes joined in performing this necessary work. Even the children of the Sun set an example of industry, by cultivating a field near Cuzco with their own hands, and they dignified this function by denominating it their triumph over the earth §.

The superior ingenuity of the Peruvians is obvious, likewise, in the construction of their

---

* Zarate, lib. i. c. 4.   Vega, lib. v. c. 1. & 24.
† Acosta, lib. iv. c. 37.   Vega, lib. v. c. 3.   See Note CLVIII.
‡ Zarate, lib. i. c. 6.   § Vega, lib. v. c. 2.

houses and public buildings. In the extensive plains which stretch along the Pacific Ocean, where the sky is perpetually serene, and the climate mild, their houses were very properly of a fabric extremely slight. But in the higher regions, where rain falls, where the vicissitude of seasons is known, and their rigour felt, houses were constructed with greater solidity. They were generally of a square form, the walls about eight feet high, built with bricks hardened in the sun, without any windows, and the door low and strait. Simple as these structures were, and rude as the materials may seem to be of which they were formed, they were so durable, that many of them still subsist in different parts of Peru, long after every monument that might have conveyed to us any idea of the domestic state of the other American nations has vanished from the face of the earth. But it was in the temples consecrated to the Sun, and in the buildings destined for the residence of their monarchs, that the Peruvians displayed the utmost extent of their art and contrivance. The descriptions of them by such of the Spanish writers as had an opportunity of contemplating them, while in some measure entire, might have appeared highly exaggerated, if the ruins which still remain did not vouch the truth of their relations. These ruins of sacred or royal buildings are found in every province of the empire, and by their frequency demonstrate that they are monuments of a powerful people, who must have subsisted, during a period of some extent, in a state of no inconsiderable improvement. They appear to have been edifices various in their dimensions. Some of a moderate size, many of immense extent, all remarkable for solidity, and resembling each other in the style of architecture. The temple of Pachacamac, together with a palace of the Inca, and a fortress, were so connected together as to form one great structure, above half a league in circuit. In this prodigious pile, the same singular taste in building is conspicuous as in other works of the Peruvians. As they were unacquainted with the use of the pulley, and other mechanical powers, and could not elevate the large stones and bricks which they employed in building to any considerable height, the walls of this edifice, in which they seem to have made their greatest effort towards magnificence, did not rise above twelve feet from the ground. Though they had not discovered the use of mortar, or of any other cement in building, the bricks or stones were joined with so much nicety, that the seams can hardly be discerned *. The apartments, as far as the distribution of them can be traced in the ruins, were ill disposed, and afforded little accommodation. There was not a single window in any part of the building; and as no light could enter but by the door, all the apartments of largest dimension must either have been perfectly dark, or illuminated by some other means. But with all these, and many other imperfections that might be mentioned in their art of building, the works of the Peruvians which still remain, must be considered as stupendous efforts of a people unacquainted with the use of iron, and convey to us an high idea of the power possessed by their ancient monarchs.

* See Note CLIX.

Q 2

These, however, were not the noblest or most useful works of the Incas. The two great roads from Cuzco to Quito, extending, in an uninterrupted stretch, above fifteen hundred miles, are entitled to still higher praise. The one was conducted through the interior and mountainous country, the other through the plains on the seacoast. From the language of admiration in which some of the early writers express their astonishment when they first viewed those roads, and from the more pompous descriptions of later writers, who labour to support some favourite theory concerning America, one might be led to compare this work of the Incas to the famous military ways which remain as monuments of the Roman power. But in a country where there was no tame animal except the Llama, which was never used for draught, and but little as a beast of burden, where the high roads were seldom trod by any but a human foot, no great degree of labour or art was requisite in forming them. The Peruvian roads were only fifteen feet in breadth *, and in many places so slightly formed, that time has effaced every vestige of the course in which they ran. In the low country, little more seems to have been done, than to plant trees or to fix posts at certain intervals, in order to mark the proper route to travellers. To open a path through the mountainous country was a more arduous task. Eminences were levelled, and hollows filled up, and for the preservation of the road it was fenced with a bank of turf. At proper distances, Tambos, or storehouses, were

* Cieca, c. 6a.

erected for the accommodation of the Inca and
his attendants, in their progress through his dominions.   From the manner in which the road
was originally formed in this higher and more
impervious region, it has proved more durable;
and though, from the inattention of the Spaniards to every object but that of working their
mines, nothing has been done towards keeping
it in repair, its course may still be traced *.
Such was the celebrated road of the Incas; and
even from this description, divested of every
circumstance of manifest exaggeration, or of suspicious aspect, it must be considered as a striking
proof of an extraordinary progress in improvement and policy.   To the savage tribes of America, the idea of facilitating communication with
places at a distance had never occurred.   To the
Mexicans it was hardly known.   Even in the most
civilized countries of Europe, men had advanced far in refinement, before it became a regular
object of national police to form such roads as
render intercourse commodious.   It was a capital
object of Roman policy to open a communication
with all the provinces of their extensive empire,
by means of those roads which are justly considered as one of the noblest monuments both of
their wisdom and their power.   But during the
long reign of barbarism, the Roman roads were
neglected or destroyed; and at the time when
the Spaniards entered Peru, no kingdom in Europe could boast of any work of public utility

---

* Xerez, p. 189—191.   Zarate, lib. i. c. 12. 14.   Vega, lib. ix. c. 13.   Boguer Voyage, p. 105.   Ulloa Entre-
tenemientos, p 365.

Q 3

that could be compared with the great roads
formed by the Incas.

The formation of those roads introduced another improvement in Peru equally unknown over
all the rest of America. In its course from south
to north, the road of the Incas was intersected
by all the torrents which roll from the Andes towards the Western Ocean. From the rapidity
of their course, as well as from the frequency
and violence of their inundation, these were not
fordable. Some expedient, however, was to be
found for passing them. The Peruvians, from
their unacquaintance with the use of arches, and
their inability to work in wood, could not con-
struct bridges either of stone or timber. But
necessity, the parent of invention, suggested a
device which supplied that defect. They formed
cables of great strength, by twisting together
some of the pliable withs or osiers with which
their country abounds ; six of these cables they
stretched across the stream parallel to one another, and made them fast on each side. These
they bound firmly together by interweaving smaller ropes so close, as to form a compact piece of
net-work, which being covered with branches of
trees and earth, they passed along it with tolerable security *. Proper persons were appointed
to attend at each bridge, to keep it in repair,
and to assist passengers †. In the level country,
where the rivers became deep and broad and still,
they are passed in *Balzas*, or floats ; in the con-

---

* See Note CLX.
† Sancho ap. Ram. iii. 376, B. Zarate, lib. i. c. 14.
Vega, lib. iii. c. 7, 8. Herrera, dec. 5. lib. iv, c. 3, 4.

struction, as well as navigation of which, the ingenuity of the Peruvians appears to be far superior to that of any people in America. These had advanced no farther in naval skill than the use of the paddle, or oar; the Peruvians ventured to raise a mast, and spread a sail, by means of which their balzas not only went nimbly before the wind, but could veer and tack with great celerity *.

Nor were the ingenuity and art of the Peruvians confined solely to objects of essential utility. They had made some progress in arts, which may be called elegant. They possessed the precious metals in greater abundance than any people of America. They obtained gold in the same manner with the Mexicans, by searching in the channels of rivers, or washing the earth in which particles of it were contained. But in order to procure silver, they exerted no inconsiderable degree of skill and invention. They had not indeed, attained the art of sinking a shaft into the bowels of the earth, and penetrating to the riches concealed there; but they hollowed deep caverns on the banks of rivers and the sides of mountains, and emptied such veins as did not dip suddenly beyond their reach. In other places, where the vein lay near the surface, they dug pits to such a depth, that the person who worked below could throw out the ore, or hand it up in baskets †. They had discovered the art of smelting and refining this, either by the simple application of fire, or, where the ore was more stubborn, and impregnated with foreign substances, by placing it in small ovens or fur-

* Ulloa Voy. i. 167, &c.   † Ramusio, iii. 414, A.

naces, on high grounds, so artificially constructed, that the draught of air performed the function of a bellows, an engine with which they
were totally unacquainted. By this simple device,
the purer ores were smelted with facility, and the
quantity of silver in Peru was so considerable,
that many of the utensils employed in the functions of common life were made of it *. Several
of those vessels and trinkets are said to have
merited no small degree of estimation, on account of the neatness of the workmanship, as
well as the intrinsic value of the materials. But
as the conquerors of America were well acquainted with the latter, but had scarcely any conception of the former, most of the silver vessels and
trinkets were melted down, and rated according
to the weight and fineness of the metal in the division of the spoil.

In other works of mere curiosity or ornament,
their ingenuity has been highly celebrated. Many
specimens of those have been dug out of the
Guacas, or mounds of earth, with which the
Peruvians covered the bodies of the dead.
Among these are mirrors of various dimensions,
of hard shining stones highly polished ; vessels of
earthen ware of different forms ; hatchets and
other instruments, some destined for war, and
others for labour. Some were of flint, some of
copper, hardened to such a degree by an unknown process, as to supply the place of iron on
several occasions. Had the use of those tools
formed of copper been general, the progress of
the Peruvians in the arts might have been such,

* Acosta, lib. iv. c 4, 5. Vega, p. 1. lib. viii. c. 25.
Ulloa Entreten. 258.

as to emulate that of more cultivated nations.
But either the metal was so rare, or the operation
by which it was hardened so tedious, that their
instruments of copper were few, and so extremely small, that they seem to have been employed
only in slighter works.   But even to such a circumscribed use of this imperfect metal, the Peruvians were indebted for their superiority to the
other people of America in various arts *.   The
same observation, however, may be applied to
them, which I formerly made with respect to the
arts of the Mexicans.   From several specimens
of Peruvian utensils and ornaments, which are deposited in the royal cabinet of Madrid, and from
some preserved in different collections in other
parts of Europe, I have reason to believe that
the workmanship is more to be admired on account of the rude tools with which it was executed, than on account of its intrinsic neatness
and elegance; and that the Peruvians, though
the most improved of all the Americans, were
not advanced beyond the infancy of arts.

But notwithstanding so many particulars,
which seem to indicate an high degree of improvement in Peru, other circumstances occur
that suggest the idea of a society still in the
first stages of its transition from barbarism to civilization.   In all the dominions of the Incas,
Cuzco was the only place that had the appearance, or was entitled to the name of a city.
Every where else, the people lived mostly in detached habitations, dispersed over the country,
or, at the utmost, settled together in small vil-

* Ulloa Voy. tom. i. 381, &c.   Id. Entreten. p. 369, &c.

lages *.   But until men are brought to assemble
in numerous bodies, and incorporated in such
close union as to enjoy frequent intercourse,
and to feel mutual dependence, they never imbibe
perfectly the spirit, or assume the manners of
social life.   In a country of immense extent,
with only one city, the progress of manners, and
the improvement either of the necessary or more
refined arts, must have been so slow, and carried on under such disadvantages, that it is more
surprising the Peruvians should have advanced so
far in refinement, than that they did not proceed
farther.

In consequence of this state of imperfect union,
the separation of professions in Peru was not so
complete as among the Mexicans.   The less
closely men associate, the more simple are their
manners, and the fewer their wants.   The crafts
of common and most necessary use in life do not,
in such a state, become so complex or difficult,
as to render it requisite that men should be trained to them by any particular course of education.
All the arts, accordingly, which were of daily
and indispensable utility, were exercised by every
Peruvian indiscriminately.   None but the artists,
employed in works of mere curiosity or ornament,
constituted a separate order of men, or were distinguished from other citizens †.

From the want of cities in Peru, another consequence followed.   There was little commercial
intercourse among the inhabitants of that great
empire.   The activity of commerce is coeval with

* Zarate, lib. i. c. 9.   Herrera, dec. 5. lib. vi. c. 4.
† Acosta, lib. vi. c. 15.   Vega, lib. v. c. 9.   Herrera,
dec. 5. lib. iv. c. 4.

the foundation of cities; and from the moment that the members of any community settle in considerable numbers in one place, its operations become vigorous. The citizen must depend for subsistence on the labour of those who cultivate the ground. They, in return, must receive some equivalent. Thus mutual intercourse is established, and the productions of art are regularly exchanged for the fruits of agriculture. In the towns of the Mexican empire, stated markets were held, and whatever could supply any want or desire of man was an object of commerce. But in Peru, from the singular mode of dividing property, and the manner in which the people were settled, there was hardly any species of commerce carried on between different provinces [*], and the community was less acquainted with that active intercourse, which is at once a bond of union, and an incentive to improvement.

But the unwarlike spirit of the Peruvians was the most remarkable, as well as most fatal defect in their character [†]. The greater part of the rude nations of America opposed their invaders with undaunted ferocity, though with little conduct or success. The Mexicans maintained the struggle in defence of their liberties with such persevering fortitude, that it was with difficulty the Spaniards triumphed over them. Peru was subdued at once, and almost without resistance; and the most favourable opportunities of regaining their freedom, and of crushing their oppressors, were lost through the timidity of the peo-

[*] Vega, lib. vi. c. 8.
[†] Xerez, 190. Sancho ap. Ram. iii. 372. Herrera dec. 5. lib. i. c. 3.

ple.   Though the traditional history of the Peruvians represents all the Incas as warlike princes,
frequently at the head of armies, which they led
to victory and conquest ; few symptoms of such,
a martial spirit appear in any of their operations
subsequent to the invasion of the Spaniards.   The
influence, perhaps, of those institutions which
rendered their manners gentle, gave their minds
this unmanly softness ; perhaps, the constant se-
renity and mildness of the climate may have ener-
vated the vigour of their frame ; perhaps, some
principle in their government, unknown to us,
was the occasion of this political debility.   Whatever may have been the cause, the fact is certain,
and there is not an instance in history of any people so little advanced in refinement, so totally
destitute of military enterprise.   This character
hath descended to their posterity.   The Indians
of Peru are now more tame and depressed than
any people of America.   Their feeble spirits,
relaxed in lifeless inaction, seem hardly capable
of any bold or manly exertion.

But, besides those capital defects in the political state of Peru, some detached circumstances
and facts occur in the Spanish writers, which
discover a considerable remainder of barbarity in
their manners.   A cruel custom, that prevailed
in some of the most savage tribes, subsisted among
the Peruvians.   On the death of the Incas, and
of other eminent persons, a considerable number
of their attendants was put to death, and in-
terred around their Guacas, that they might appear in the next world with their former dignity,
and be served with the same respect.   On the
death of Huana Capac, the most powerful of

their monarchs, above a thousand victims were doomed to accompany him to the tomb *. In one particular, their manners appear to have been more barbarous than those of most rude tribes. Though acquainted with the use of fire in preparing maize, and other vegetables for food, they devoured both flesh and fish perfectly raw, and astonished the Spaniards with a practice repugnant to the ideas of all civilized people †.

But though Mexico and Peru are the possessions of Spain in the New World, which, on account both of their ancient and present state, have attracted their greatest attention, her other dominions there are far from being inconsiderable either in extent or value. The greater part of them was reduced to subjection, during the first part of the sixteenth century, by private adventurers, who fitted out their small armaments either in Hispaniola or in Old Spain; and were we to follow each leader in his progress, we should discover the same daring courage, the same persevering ardour, the same rapacious desire of wealth, and the same capacity of enduring and surmounting every thing in order to attain it, which distinguished the operations of the Spaniards in their greater American conquests. But, instead of entering into a detail, which, from the similarity of the transactions, would appear almost a repetition of what has been already related, I shall satisfy myself with such a

* Acosta, lib. 5. c. 7.
† Xerez, p. 190. Sancho, Ram. iii. 372, C. Herrera, dec. 5. lib. i. c. 3.

view of those provinces of the Spanish empire
in America, which have not hitherto been mentioned, as may convey to my readers an adequate idea of its greatness, fertility, and opulence.

I begin with the countries contiguous to the
two great monarchies, of whose history and institutions I have given some account, and shall
then briefly describe the other districts of Spanish
America. The jurisdiction of the viceroy of
New Spain extends over several provinces which
were not subject to the dominion of the Mexicans.
The countries of Cinaloa and Sonora, that stretch
along the east side of the Vermilion Sea, or gulph
of California, as well as the immense kingdoms
of New Navarre and New Mexico, which bend
towards the west and north, did not acknowledge
the sovereignty of Montezuma, or his predecessors. These regions, not inferior in magnitude
to all the Mexican empire, are reduced some to
a greater, others to a less degree of subjection to
the Spanish yoke. They extend through the
most delightful part of the temperate zone; their
soil is, in general, remarkably fertile, and all
their productions, whether animal or vegetable,
are most perfect in their kind. They have all
a communication either with the Pacific Ocean,
or with the Gulph of Mexico, and are watered
by rivers which not only enrich them, but may
become subservient to commerce. The number
of Spaniards settled in those vast countries, is
indeed extremely small. They may be said to
have subdued rather than to have occupied them.
But if the population in their ancient establishments in America shall continue to increase, they

may gradually spread over those provinces, of which, however inviting, they have not hither-to been able to take full possession.

One circumstance may contribute to the speedy population of some districts.   Very rich mines both of gold and silver have been discovered in many of the regions which I have mentioned. Wherever these are opened, and worked with success, a multitude of people resort.   In order to supply them with the necessaries of life, cultivation must be increased, artisans of various kinds must assemble, and industry as well as wealth will be gradually diffused.   Many examples of this have occurred in different parts of America since they fell under the dominion of the Spaniards.   Populous villages and large towns have suddenly arisen amidst uninhabited wilds and mountains ; and the working of mines, though far from being the most proper object towards which the attention of an infant society should be turned, may become the means both of promoting useful activity, and of augmenting the number of people.   A recent and singular instance of this has happened, which, as it is but little known in Europe, and may be productive of great effects, merits attention.   The Spaniards settled in the provinces of Cinaloa and Sonora, had been long disturbed by the depredations of some fierce tribes of Indians.   In the year 1765, the incursions of those savages became so frequent, and so destructive, that the Spanish inhabitants, in despair, applied to the Marquis de Croix, viceroy of Mexico, for such a body of troops as might enable them to drive those formidable invaders from their places of re-

R 2

treat in the mountains. But the treasury of
Mexico was so much exhausted by the large
sums drawn from it, in order to support the late
war against Great Britain, that the viceroy could
afford them no aid. The respect due to his
virtues, accomplished what his official power
could not effect. He prevailed with the merchants of New Spain to advance about two hundred thousand pesos for defraying the expence
of the expedition. The war was conducted by
an officer of abilities; and after being protracted
for three years, chiefly by the difficulty of pur-
suing the fugitives over mountains and through
defiles which were almost impassable, it terminated in the year 1771, in the final submission of
the tribes, which had been so long the object of
terror to the two provinces. In the course of
this service, the Spaniards marched through
countries into which they seem not to have penetrated before that time, and discovered mines
of such value, as was astonishing even to men acquainted with the riches contained in the mountains of the New World. At Cineguilla, in the
province of Sonora, they entered a plain of fourteen leagues in extent, in which, at the depth of
only sixteen inches, they found gold in grains of
such a size, that some of them weighed nine
marks, and in such quantities, that in a short
time, with a few labourers, they collected a thousand marks of gold in grains, even without taking
time to wash the earth that had been dug, which
appeared to be so rich, that persons of skill computed that it might yield what would be equal
in value to a million of pesos. Before the end of
the year 1771, above two thousand persons were

settled in Cineguilla, under the government of proper magistrates, and the inspection of several ecclesiastics. . As several other mines, not inferior in richness to that of Cineguilla, have been discovered, both in Sonora and Cinaloa *, it is probable, that these neglected and thinly inhabited provinces, may soon become as populous and valuable as any part of the Spanish empire in America.

The peninsula of California, on the other side of the Vermilion Sea, seems to have been less known to the ancient Mexicans than the provinces which I have mentioned. It was discovered by Cortes in the year 1536 †. During a long period it continued to be so little frequented, that even its form was unknown, and in most charts it was represented as an island, not as a peninsula ‡. Though the climate of this country, if we may judge from its situation, must be very desirable, the Spaniards have made small progress in peopling it. Towards the close of the last century, the Jesuits, who had great merit in exploring this neglected province, and in civilizing its rude inhabitants, imperceptibly acquired a dominion over it as complete as that which they possessed in their missions in Paraguay, and they laboured to introduce into it the same policy, and to govern the natives by the same maxims. In order to prevent the court of Spain from conceiving any jealousy of their designs and operations, they seem studiously to have depreciated the country, by representing the climate

* See Note CLXI.
† Book v. vol. ii p. 312.   ‡ See Note CLXII

as so disagreeable and unwholesome, and the soil as so barren, that nothing but a zealous desire of converting the natives could have induced them to settle there *. Several public-spirited citizens endeavoured to undeceive their sovereigns, and to give them a better view of California; but in vain. At length, on the expulsion of the Jesuits from the Spanish dominions, the court of Madrid, as prone at that juncture to suspect the purity of the Order's intentions, as formerly to confide in them with implicit trust, appointed Don Joseph Galvez, whose abilities have since raised him to the high rank of minister for the Indies, to visit that peninsula. His account of the country was favourable; he found the pearl fishery on its coasts to be valuable, and he discovered mines of gold of a very promising appearance †. From its vicinity to Cinaloa and Sonora, it is probable, that if the population of these provinces shall increase in the manner which I have supposed, California may by degrees receive from them such a recruit of inhabitants, as to be no longer reckoned among the desolate and useless districts of the Spanish empire.

On the east of Mexico, Yucatan and Honduras are comprehended in the government of New Spain, though anciently they can hardly be said to have formed a part of the Mexican empire. These large provinces, stretching, from the Bay of Campeachy beyond Cape Gracias a Dios, do not, like the other territories of Spain

---

* Venegas, Hist. of California, i. 26.
† Lorenzano, 349, 350.

in the New World, derive their value either from the fertility of their soil or the richness of their mines ; but they produce, in greater abundance than any part of America, the logwood tree, which in dying some colours, is so far preferable to any other material, that the consumption of it in Europe is considerable, and it has become an article in commerce of great value. During a long period, no European nation intruded upon the Spaniards in those provinces, or attempted to obtain any share in this branch of trade. But after the conquest of Jamaica by the English, it soon appeared what a formidable rival was now seated in the neighbourhood of the Spanish territories. One of the first objects which tempted the English settled in that island, was the great profit arising from the logwood trade, and the facility of wresting some portion of it from the Spaniards. Some adventurers from Jamaica made the first attempt at Cape Catoche, the south-east promontory of Yucatan, and by cutting logwood there, carried on a gainful traffic. When most of the trees near the coast in that place were felled, they removed to the island of Trist, in the Bay of Campeachy ; and in later times, their principal station has been in the Bay of Honduras. The Spaniards, alarmed at this encroachment, endeavoured by negotiation, remonstrances, and open force, to prevent the English from obtaining any footing on that part of the American continent. But after struggling against it for more than a century, the disasters of last war extorted from the court of Madrid a reluctant consent to tolerate this settle-

ment of foreigners in the heart of its territories *.
The pain which this humbling concession occasioned, seems to have prompted the Spaniards to
devise a method of rendering it of little consequence, more effectual than all the efforts of
negotiation or violence. The logwood produced
on the west coast of Yucatan, where the soil is
drier, is in quality far superior to that which
grows on the marshy grounds where the English
are settled. By encouraging the cutting of this,
and permitting the importation of it into Spain
without paying any duty †, such vigour has been
given to this branch of commerce, and the logwood which the English bring to market has
sunk so much in value, that their trade to the
Bay of Honduras has gradually declined ‡ since
it obtained a legal sanction; and, it is probable,
will soon be finally abandoned. In that event,
Yucatan and Honduras will become possessions
of considerable importance to Spain.

Still farther east than Honduras lie the two
provinces of Costa Rica and Veragua, which
likewise belong to the viceroyalty of New Spain;
but both have been so much neglected by the
Spaniards, and are apparently of such small
value, that they merit no particular attention.

The most important province depending on the
viceroyalty of Peru, is Chili. The Incas had
established their dominion in some of its northern
districts; but in the greater part of the country,
its gallant and high-spirited inhabitants main-

---

* Treaty of Paris, Art. xviii.
† Real Cedula, Campomanes, iii. 145.
‡ See Note CLXIII.

tained their independence. The Spaniards, allured by the fame of its opulence, early attempted the conquest of it under Diego Almagro; and after his death, Pedro de Valdivia resumed the design. Both met with fierce opposition. The former relinquished the enterprise in the manner which I have mentioned *. The latter, after having given many displays both of courage and military skill, was cut off, together with a considerable body of troops under his command. Francisco de Villagra, Valdivia's lieutenant, by his spirited conduct, checked the natives in their career, and saved the remainder of the Spaniards from destruction. By degrees, all the champaign country along the coast was subjected to the Spanish dominion. The mountainous country is still possessed by the Puelches, Araucos, and other tribes of its original inhabitants, formidable neighbours to the Spaniards; with whom, during the course of two centuries, they have been obliged to maintain almost perpetual hostility, suspended only by a few intervals of insecure peace.

That part of Chili then which may properly be deemed a Spanish province, is a narrow district, extended along the coast from the desert of Atacamas to the island of Chiloe, above nine hundred miles. Its climate is the most delicious in the New World, and is hardly equalled by that of any region on the face of the earth. Though bordering on the torrid zone, it never feels the extremity of heat, being screened on the east by the Andes, and refreshed from the west by cooling sea-breezes. The temperature

* Book vi. vol. iii. p. 34, &c.

of the air is so mild and equable, that the Spaniards give it the preference to that of the southern provinces in their native country. The fertility of the soil corresponds with the benignity of the climate, and is wonderfully accommodated to European productions. The most valuable of these, corn, wine, and oil, abound in Chili, as if they had been native to the country. All the fruits imported from Europe attain to full maturity there. The animals of our hemisphere not only multiply, but improve in this delightful region. The horned cattle are of larger size than those of Spain. Its breed of horses surpasses, both in beauty and in spirit, the famous Andalusian race, from which they sprung. Nor has nature exhausted her bounty on the surface of the earth; she has stored its bowels with riches. Valuable mines of gold, of silver, of copper, and of lead, have been discovered in various parts of it.

A country distinguished by so many blessings, we may be apt to conclude, would early become a favourite station of the Spaniards, and must have been cultivated with peculiar predilection and care. Instead of this, a great part of it remains unoccupied. In all this extent of country, there are not above eighty thousand white inhabitants, and about three times that number of negroes and people of a mixed race. The most fertile soil in America lies uncultivated, and some of its most promising mines remain unwrought. Strange as this neglect of the Spaniards to avail themselves of advantages which seemed to court their acceptance, may appear, the causes of it can be traced. The only inter-

course of Spain with its colonies in the South
Sea, was carried on during two centuries by the
annual fleet to Porto-Bello. All the produce of
these colonies was shipped in the ports of Callao,
or Arica in Peru, for Panama, and carried from
thence across the isthmus. All the commodities which they received from the mother-country,
were conveyed from Panama to the same harbours. Thus both the exports and imports of
Chili passed through the hands of merchants
settled in Peru. These had of course a profit on
each ; and in both transactions the Chilese felt
their own subordination ; and having no direct
intercourse with the parent state, they depended
upon another province for the disposal of their
productions, as well as for the supply of their
wants. Under such discouragements, population could not increase, and industry was destitute of one chief incitement. But now that
Spain, from motives which I shall mention here-
after, has adopted a new system, and carries on
her commerce with the colonies in the South
Sea by ships which go round Cape Horn, a direct intercourse is opened between Chili and the
mother country. The gold, the silver, and the
other commodities of the province, will be exchanged in its own harbours for the manufactures
of Europe. Chili may speedily rise into that
importance among the Spanish settlements to
which it is entitled by its natural advantages.
It may become the granary of Peru, and the
other provinces along the Pacific Ocean. It
may supply them with wine, with cattle, with
horses, with hemp, and many other articles for
which they now depend upon Europe. Though

the new system has been established only a few
years, those effects of it begin already to be
observed *.   If it shall be adhered to with any
steadiness for half a century, one may venture
to foretel, that population, industry, and opulence, will advance in this province with rapid
progress.

To the east of the Andes, the provinces of
Tucaman and Rio de la Plata border on Chili,
and like it were dependent on the viceroyalty
of Peru.   These regions of immense extent
stretch in length from north to south above
thirteen hundred miles, and in breadth more
than a thousand.   This country, which is larger
than most European kingdoms, naturally forms
itself into two great divisions, one on the north,
and the other on the south of Rio de la Plata.
The former comprehends Paraguay, the famous
missions of the Jesuits, and several other districts.   But as disputes have long subsisted between the courts of Spain and Portugal, concerning its boundaries, which, it is probable, will
be soon finally ascertained, either amicably, or
by the decision of the sword, I choose to reserve
my account of this northern division until I enter upon the history of Portuguese America,
with which it is intimately connected ; and, in
relating it, I shall be able, from authentic materials, supplied both by Spain and Portugal, to
give a full and accurate description of the operations and views of the Jesuits, in rearing that
singular fabric of policy in America, which has
drawn so much attention, and has been so imperfectly understood.   The latter division of the

* Campomanes, ii. 157.

province contains the governments of Tucuman and Buenos-Ayres, and to these I shall at present confine my observations.

The Spaniards entered this part of America by the river De la Plata; and though a succession of cruel disasters befel them in their early attempts to establish their dominion in it, they were encouraged to persist in the design, at first by the hopes of discovering mines in the interior country, and afterwards by the necessity of occupying it, in order to prevent any other nation from settling there, and penetrating by this route into their rich possessions in Peru. But except at Buenos-Ayres, they have made no settlement of any consequence in all the vast space which I have mentioned. There are, indeed, scattered over it a few places on which they have bestowed the name of towns, and to which they have endeavoured to add some dignity, by erecting them into bishoprics; but they are no better than paltry villages, each with two or three hundred inhabitants. One circumstance, however, which was not originally foreseen, has contributed to render this district, though thinly peopled, of considerable importance. The province of Tucuman, together with the country to the south of the Plata, instead of being covered with wood like other parts of America, forms one extensive open plain, almost without a tree. The soil is a deep fertile mould, watered by many streams descending from the Andes, and clothed in perpetual verdure. In this rich pasturage, the horses and cattle imported by the Spaniards from Europe have multiplied to a degree which almost exceeds belief. This has

Vol. III.   S

enabled the inhabitants not only to open a lucrative trade with Peru, by supplying it with
cattle, horses, and mules, but to carry on a commerce no less beneficial, by the exportation of
hides to Europe. From both, the colony has
derived great advantages.   But its commodious
situation for carrying on contraband trade, has
been the chief source of its prosperity.   While
the court of Madrid adhered to its ancient
system, with respect to its communication with
America, the river De la Plata lay so much out
of the course of Spanish navigation, that interlopers, almost without any risk of being either
observed or obstructed, could pour in European
manufactures in such quantities, that they not
only supplied the wants of the colony, but were
conveyed into all the eastern districts of Peru.
When the Portuguese in Brasil extended their
settlements to the banks of Rio de la Plata, a
new channel was opened, by which prohibited
commodities flowed into the Spanish territories,
with still more facility, and in greater abundance.   This illegal traffic, however detrimental
to the parent state, contributed to the increase
of the settlement, which had the immediate benefit of it, and Buenos-Ayres became gradually
a populous and opulent town.   What may be
the effect of the alteration lately made in the
government of this colony, the nature of which
s all be described in the subsequent Book, cannot hitherto be known.

All the other territories of Spain in the New
World, the islands excepted, of whose discovery
and reduction I have formerly given an account,
are comprehended under two great divisions; the

former denominated the kingdom of Tierra Firmé, the provinces of which stretch along the Atlantic, from the eastern frontier of New Spain to the mouth of the Orinoco ; the latter, the New kingdom of Granada, situated in the interior country. With a short view of these I shall close this part of my work.

To the east of Veragua, the last province subject to the viceroy of Mexico, lies the isthmus of Darien. Though it was in this part of the continent that the Spaniards first began to plant colonies, they have made no considerable progress in peopling it. As the country is extremely mountainous, deluged with rain during a good part of the year, remarkably unhealthful, and contains no mines of great value, the Spaniards would probably have abandoned it altogether, if they had not been allured to continue by the excellence of the harbour of Porto-Bello on the one sea, and that of Panama on the other. These have been called the keys to the communication between the North and South Sea, between Spain and her most valuable colonies. In consequence of this advantage, Panama has become a considerable and thriving town. The peculiar noxiousness of its climate has prevented Porto-Bello from increasing in the same proportion. As the intercourse with the settlements in the Pacific Ocean is now carried on by another channel, it is probable that both Porto-Bello and Panama will decline, when no longer nourished and enriched by that commerce to which they were indebted for their prosperity, and even their existence.

S 2

The provinces of Carthagena and Santa Martha stretch to the eastward of the isthmus of Darien. The country still continues mountainous, but its valleys begin to expand, are well watered, and extremely fertile. Pedro de Heredia subjected this part of America to the crown of Spain, about the year 1532. It is thinly peopled, aud of course ill cultivated. It produces, however, a variety of valuable drugs, and some precious stones, particularly emeralds. But its chief importance is derived from the harbour of Carthagena, the safest and best fortified of any in the American dominions of Spain. In a situation so favourable, commerce soon began to flourish. As early as the year 1544, it seems to have been a town of some note. But when Carthagena was chosen as the port in which the galeons should first begin to trade on their arrival from Europe, and to which they were directed to return, in order to prepare for their voyage homeward, the commerce of its inhabitants was so much favoured by this arrangement, that it soon became one of the most populous, opulent, and beautiful cities in America. There is, however, reason to apprehend, that it has reached its highest point of exaltation, and that it will be so far affected by the change in the Spanish system of trade with America, which has withdrawn from it the desirable visits of the galeons, as to feel at least a temporary decline. But the wealth now collected there will soon find or create employment for itself, and may be turned with advantage into some new channel. Its harbour is so safe, and so

conveniently situated for receiving commodities
from Europe, its merchants have been so long
accustomed to convey these into all the adjacent
provinces, that it is probable they will still retain this branch of trade, and Carthagena continue to be a city of great importance.

The province contiguous to Santa Martha on
the east, was first visited by Alonso de Ojeda,
in the year 1499 *; and the Spaniards, on their
landing there, having observed some huts in an
Indian village built upon piles, in order to raise
them above the stagnated water which covered
the plain, were led to bestow upon it the name of
Venezuela, or Little Venice, by their usual propensity to find a resemblance between what they
discovered in America, and the objects which
were familiar to them in Europe. They made
some attempts to settle there, but with little success. The final reduction of the province was accomplished by means very different from those to
which Spain was indebted for its other acquisitions in the New World. The ambition of
Charles V. often engaged him in operations of
such variety and extent, that his revenues were
not sufficient to defray the expence of carrying
them into execution. Among other expedients
for supplying the deficiency of his funds, he had
borrowed large sums from the Velsers of Augs-
burgh, the most opulent merchants at that time
in Europe. By way of retribution for these, or
in hopes, perhaps, of obtaining a new loan, he
bestowed upon them the province of Venezuela,
to be held as an hereditary fief from the crown of

* Book ii. vol. i. p. 164.

Castile, on condition that within a limited time they should render themselves masters of the country, and establish a colony there. Under the direction of such persons, it might have been expected that a settlement would have been established on maxims very different from those of the Spaniards, and better calculated to encourage such useful industry as mercantile proprietors might have known to be the most certain source of prosperity and opulence. But unfortunately, they committed the execution of their plan to some of those soldiers of fortune with which Germany abounded in the sixteenth century. These adventurers, impatient to amass riches, that they might speedily abandon a station which they soon discovered to be very uncomfortable, instead of planting a colony in order to cultivate and improve the country, wandered from district to district in search of mines, plundering the natives with unfeeling rapacity, or oppressing them by the imposition of intolerable tasks. In the course of a few years, their avarice and exactions, in comparison with which those of the Spaniards were moderate, desolated the province so completely, that it could hardly afford them subsistence, and the Velsers relinquished a property from which the inconsiderate conduct of their agents left them no hope of ever deriving any advantage[*]. When the wretched remainder of the Germans deserted Venezuela, the Spaniards again took possession of it; but notwithstanding many natural advantages, it is one of their most languishing and unproductive settlements.

[*] Ovedo y Bagnos Hist. de Venezuela, p. 11, &c.

The provinces of Caraccas and Cumana are the last of the Spanish territories on this coast; but in relating the origin and operations of the mercantile company, in which an exclusive right of trade with them has been vested, I shall here-after have occasion to consider their state and productions.

The New Kingdom of Granada is entirely an inland country of great extent. This important addition was made to the dominions of Spain a-bout the year 1536, by Sebastian de Benalcazar and Gonzalo Ximenes de Quesada, two of the bravest and most accomplished officers employed in the conquest of America. The former, who commanded at that time in Quito, attacked it from the south; the latter made his invasion from Santa Martha on the north. As the ori-ginal inhabitants of this region were farther ad-vanced in improvement than any people in A-merica but the Mexicans and Peruvians, they defended themselves with great resolution and good conduct. The abilities and perseverance of Benalcazar and Quesada surmounted all op-position, though not without encountering many dangers, and reduced the country into the form of a Spanish province.

The New Kingdom of Granada is so far ele-vated above the level of the sea, that though it approaches almost to the equator, the climate is remarkably temperate. The fertility of its val-leys is not inferior to that of the richest districts in America, and its higher grounds yield gold and precious stones of various kinds. It is not by digging into the bowels of the earth that this gold is found; it is mingled with the soil near the surface, and separated from it by repeated washing with water. This operation is carried on wholly by negro slaves; for though the chill subterranean air has been discovered, by experience, to be so fatal to them that they cannot be employed with advantage in the deep silver mines, they are more capable of performing the other species of labour than Indians. As the natives in the New Kingdom of Granada are exempt from that service, which has wasted their race so rapidly in other parts of America, the country is still remarkably populous. Some districts yield gold with a profusion no less wonderful than that in the vale of Cineguilla, which I have formerly mentioned, and it is often found in large *pepitas*, or grains, which manifest the abundance in which it is produced. On a rising ground near Pamplona, single labourers have collected in a day what was equal in value to a thousand pesos *. A late governor of Santa Fé brought with him to Spain a lump of pure gold, estimated to be worth seven hundred and forty pounds sterling. This, which is perhaps the largest and finest specimen ever found in the New World, is now deposited in the royal cabinet of Madrid. But without founding any calculation on what is rare and extraordinary, the value of the gold usually collected in this country, particularly in the provinces of Popayan and Choco, is of considerable amount. Its towns are populous and flourishing. The number of inhabitants in almost every part of the country daily increases. Cultivation

* Piedrahita Hist. del N. Reyno, p. 481. MS. *penes me*

and industry of various kinds begin to be encouraged and to prosper. A considerable trade is carried on with Carthagena, the produce of the mines and other commodities being conveyed down the great river of St. Magdalen to that city. On another quarter, the New Kingdom of Granada has a communication with the Atlantic by the river Orinoco; but the country which stretches along its banks towards the east is little known, and imperfectly occupied by the Spaniards.

BOOK VIII.

AFTER tracing the progress of the Spaniards in their discoveries and conquests during more than half a century, I have conducted them to that period when their authority was established over almost all the vast regions in the New World still subject to their dominion. The effect of their settlements upon the countries of which they took possession, the maxims which they adopted in forming their new colonies, the interior structure and policy of these, together with the influence of their progressive improvement upon the parent state, and upon the commercial intercourse of nations, are the objects to which we now turn our attention.

The first visible consequence of the establishments made by the Spaniards in America, was the diminution of the ancient inhabitants, to a degree equally astonishing and deplorable. I

have already, on different occasions, mentioned
the disastrous influence under which the connection of the Americans with the people of our
hemisphere commenced, both in the islands, and
in several parts of the continent, and have touched upon various causes of their rapid consumption. Wherever the inhabitants of America had
resolution to take arms in defence of their liberty and rights, many perished in the unequal contest, and were cut off by their fierce invaders.
But the greatest desolation followed after the
sword was sheathed, and the conquerors were
settled in tranquillity. It was in the islands, and
in those provinces of the continent which stretch
from the Gulf of Trinidad to the confines of
Mexico, that the fatal effects of the Spanish dominion were first and most sensibly felt. All
these were occupied either by wandering tribes
of hunters, or by such as had made but small progress in cultivation and industry. When they
were compelled by their new masters to take up
a fixed residence, and to apply to regular labour;
when tasks were imposed upon them dispropor-
tioned to their strength, and were exacted with
unrelenting severity, they possessed not vigour
either of mind or of body to sustain this unusual
load of oppression. Dejection and despair drove
many to end their lives by violence. Fatigue
and famine destroyed more. In all those extensive regions, the original race of inhabitants
wasted away; in some it was totally extinguished.
In Mexico, where a powerful and martial people distinguished their opposition to the Spaniards by efforts of courage worthy of a better
fate, great numbers fell in the field; and there,

as well as in Peru, still greater numbers, perished under the hardships of attending the Spanish armies in their various expeditions and civil wars, worn out with the incessant toil of carrying their baggage, provisions, and military stores.

But neither the rage nor cruelty of the Spaniards were so destructive to the people of Mexico and Peru, as the inconsiderate policy with which they established their new settlements. The former were temporary calamities, fatal to individuals; the latter was a permanent evil, which, with gradual consumption, wasted the nation. When the provinces of Mexico and Peru were divided among the conquerors, each was eager to obtain a district, from which he might expect an instantaneous recompence for all his services. Soldiers, accustomed to the carelessness and dissipation of a military life, had neither industry to carry on any plan of regular cultivation, nor patience to wait for its slow but certain returns. Instead of settling in the valleys occupied by the natives, where the fertility of the soil would have amply rewarded the diligence of the planter, they chose to fix their stations in some of the mountainous regions, frequent both in New Spain and in Peru. To search for mines of gold and silver, was the chief object of their activity. The prospects which this opens, and the alluring hopes which it continually presents, correspond wonderfully with the spirit of enterprise and adventure that animated the first emigrants to America in every part of their conduct. In order to push forward those favourite projects, so many hands were wanted that the service of the natives became indispenably requisite. They were accordingly compelled to abandon their ancient habitations in the plains, and driven in crowds to the mountains. This sudden transition from the sultry climate of the valleys, to the chill penetrating air peculiar to high lands in the torrid zone; exorbitant labour, scanty or unwholesome nourishment, and the despondency occasioned by a species of oppression to which they were not accustomed, and of which they saw no end, affected them nearly as much as their less industrious countrymen in the islands. They sunk under the united pressure of those calamities, and melted away with almost equal rapidity *. In consequence of this, together with the introduction of the small-pox, a malady unknown in America, and extremely fatal to the natives †, the number of people both in New Spain and Peru was so much reduced, that in a few years the accounts of their ancient population appeared almost incredible ‡.

Such are the most considerable events and causes which, by their combined operation, contributed to depopulate America. Without attending to these, many authors, astonished at the suddenness of the desolation, have ascribed this unexampled event to a system of policy no less profound than atrocious. The Spaniards, as they pretend, conscious of their own inability to occupy the vast regions which they had discovered, and foreseeing the impossibility of maintaining their authority over a people infinitely superior to themselves in number, in order to

* Torquemada, i. 613. † B. Diaz, c. 124. Herrera, dec. 2. lib. x. c. 4. Ulloa Entreten. 206. ‡ Torquem. 615. 642, 643. See Note CLXIV.

preserve the possession of America, resolved to exterminate the inhabitants, and by converting a great part of the country into a desert, endeavoured to secure their own dominion over it *. But nations seldom extend their views to objects so remote, or lay their plans so deep; and for the honour of humanity we may observe, that no nation ever deliberately formed such an execrable scheme. The Spanish monarchs, far from acting upon any such system of destruction, were uniformly solicitous for the preservation of their new subjects. With Isabella, zeal for propagating the Christian faith, together with the desire of communicating the knowledge of truth, and the consolations of religion, to people destitute of spiritual light, were more than ostensible motives for encouraging Columbus to attempt his discoveries. Upon his success, she endeavoured to fulfil her pious purpose, and manifested the most tender concern to secure not only religious instruction, but mild treatment, to that inoffensive race of men subjected to her crown †. Her successors adopted the same ideas; and, on many occasions which I have mentioned, their authority was interposed in the most vigorous exertions to protect the people of America from the oppression of their Spanish subjects. Their regulations for this purpose were numerous, and often repeated. They were framed with wisdom, and dictated by humanity. After their possessions in the New World became so extensive, as might have excited some apprehensions of difficulty in retaining their dominion over them, the

* See Note CLXV.　　　† See Note CLXVI.

spirit of their regulations was as mild as when their
settlements were confined to the islands alone.
Their solicitude to protect the Indians seems rather to have augmented as their acquisitions increased; and from ardour to accomplish this,
they enacted, and endeavoured to enforce the
execution of laws, which excited a formidable
rebellion in one of their colonies, and spread
alarm and disaffection through all the rest.   But
the avarice of individuals was too violent to be
controlled by the authority of laws.   Rapacious
and daring adventurers, far removed from the
seat of government, little accustomed to the restraints of military discipline while in service, and
still less disposed to respect the feeble jurisdiction
of civil power in an infant colony, despised or
eluded every regulation that set bounds to their
exactions and tyranny.   The parent state, with
persevering attention, issued edicts to prevent
the oppression of the Indians; the colonists, regardless of these, or trusting to their distance
for impunity, continued to consider and treat
them as slaves.   The governors themselves, and
other officers employed in the colonies, several
of whom were as indigent and rapacious as the
adventurers over whom they presided, were too
apt to adopt their contemptuous ideas of the
conquered people; and instead of checking, encouraged or connived at their excesses.   The
desolation of the New World should not then be
charged on the court of Spain, or be considered
as the effect of any system of policy adopted
there.   It ought to be imputed wholly to the
indigent and often unprincipled adventurers,
whose fortune it was to be the conquerors and

first planters of America, who, by measures no less inconsiderate than unjust, counteracted the edicts of their sovereign, and have brought disgrace upon their country.

With still greater injustice, have many authors represented the intolerating spirit of the Roman Catholic religion as the cause of exterminating the Americans, and have accused the Spanish ecclesiastics of animating their countrymen to the slaughter of that innocent people, as idolators and enemies of God. But the first missionaries who visited America, though weak and illiterate, were pious men. They early espoused the defence of the natives, and vindicated their character from the aspersions of their conquerors, who, describing them as incapable of being formed to the offices of civil life, or of comprehending the doctrines of religion, contended, that they were a subordinate race of men, on whom the hand of nature had set the mark of servitude. From the accounts which I have given of the humane and persevering zeal of the Spanish missionaries, in protecting the helpless flock committed to their charge, they appear in a light which reflects lustre upon their function. They were ministers of peace, who endeavoured to wrest the rod from the hands of oppressors. To their powerful interposition the Americans were indebted for every regulation tending to mitigate the rigour of their fate. The clergy in the Spanish settlements, regular as well as secular, are still considered by the Indians as their natural guardians, to whom they have recourse under the hardships and exactions to which they are too often exposed *.

* See Note CLXVII.

But, notwithstanding the rapid depopulation of America, a very considerable number of the native race still remains both in Mexico and Peru, especially in those parts which were not exposed to the first fury of the Spanish arms, or desolated by the first efforts of their industry, still more ruinous. In Guatimala, Chiapa, Nicaragua, and the other delightful provinces of the Mexican empire which stretch along the South-Sea, the race of Indians is still numerous. Their settlements in some places are so populous, as to merit the name of cities *. In the three audiences into which New Spain is divided, there are at least two millions of Indians ; a pitiful remnant, indeed, of its ancient population, but such as still forms a body of people superior in number to that of all the other inhabitants of this extensive country †. In Peru, several districts, particularly in the kingdom of Quito, are occupied almost entirely by Indians. In other provinces they are mingled with the Spaniards, and in many of their settlements are almost the only persons who practice the mechanic arts, and fill most of the inferior stations in society. As the inhabitants both of Mexico and Peru were accustomed to a fixed residence, and to a certain degree of regular industry, less violence was requisite in bringing them to some conformity with the European modes of civil life. But wherever the Spaniards settled among the savage tribes of America, their attempts to incorporate with them have been always fruitless, and often fatal to the natives. Impatient of restraint, and disdaining labour as a mark of servility, they either abandoned their

* See Note CLXVIII.   † See Note CLXIX.

original seats, and sought for independence in mountains and forests inaccessible to their oppressors, or perished when reduced to a state repugnant to their ancient ideas and habits. In the districts adjacent to Carthagena, to Panama, and to Buenos-Ayres, the desolation is more general than even in those parts of Mexico and Peru, of which the Spaniards have taken most full possession.

But the establishments of the Spaniards in the New World, though fatal to its ancient inhabitants, were made at a period when that monarchy was capable of forming them to best advantage. By the union of all its petty kingdoms, Spain was become a powerful state, equal to so great an undertaking. Its monarchs, having extended their prerogative far beyond the limits which once circumscribed the regal power in every kingdom of Europe, were hardly subject to controul either in concerting or in executing their measures. In every wide-extended empire, the form of government must be simple, and the sovereign authority such, that its resolutions may be taken with promptitude, and may pervade the whole with sufficient force. Such was the power of the Spanish monarchs, when they were called to deliberate concerning the mode of establishing their dominion over the most remote provinces which had ever been subjected to any European state. In this deliberation, they felt themselves under no constitutional restraint, and that, as independent masters of their own resolves, they might issue the edicts requisite for modelling the government of the new colonies by a mere act of prerogative.

T 3

This early interposition of the Spanish crown, in order to regulate the policy and trade of its colonies, is a peculiarity which distinguishes their progress from that of the colonies of any other European nation. When the Portuguese, the English, and French, took possession of the regions in America which they now occupy, the advantages which these promised to yield were so remote and uncertain, that their colonies were suffered to struggle through a hard infancy, almost without guidance or protection from the parent state. But gold and silver, the first productions of the Spanish settlements in the New World, were more alluring, and immediately attracted the attention of their monarchs. Though they had contributed little to the discovery, and almost nothing to the conquest of the New World, they instantly assumed the function of its legislators ; and having acquired a species of dominion formerly unknown, they formed a plan for exercising it, to which nothing similar occurs in the history of human affairs.

The fundamental maxim of Spanish jurisprudence with respect to America, is to consider what has been acquired there as vested in the crown, rather than in the state. By the bull of Alexander VI. on which, as its great charter, Spain founded its right, all the regions that had been, or should be discovered, were bestowed as a free gift upon Ferdinand and Isabella. They and their successors were uniformly held to be the universal proprietors of the vast territories which the arms of their subjects conquered in the New World. From them all grants of land there flowed, and to them they finally returned. The leaders who conducted the various expeditions, the governors who presided over the different colonies, the officers of justice, and the ministers of religion, were all appointed by their authority, and removable at their pleasure. The people who composed infant settlements were entitled to no privileges independent of their sovereign, or that served as a barrier against the power of the crown. It is true, that when towns were built, and formed into bodies corporate, the citizens were permitted to elect their own magistrates, who governed them by laws which the community enacted. Even in the most despotic states, this feeble spark of liberty is not extinguished. But in the cities of Spanish America, this jurisdiction is merely municipal, and is confined to the regulation of their own interior commerce and police. In whatever relates to public government, and the general interest, the will of the sovereign is law. No political power originates from the people. All centres in the crown, and in the officers of its nomination.

When the conquests of the Spaniards in America were completed, their monarchs, in forming the plan of internal policy for their new dominions, divided them into two immense governments, one subject to the viceroy of New Spain, the other to the viceroy of Peru. The jurisdiction of the former extended over all the provinces belonging to Spain in the northern division of the American continent. Under that of the latter, was comprehended whatever she possessed in South America. This arrangement, which, from the beginning, was attended with many inconveniencies, became intolerable when the re-

mote provinces of each viceroyalty began to
improve in industry and population. The people complained of their subjection to a superior
whose place of residence was so distant, or so inaccessible, as almost excluded them from any intercourse with the seat of government. The authority of the viceroy over districts so far removed from his own eye and observation, was una-
voidably both feeble and ill directed. As a remedy for those evils, a third viceroyalty has been
established in the present century, at Santo Fé de
Bogota, the capital of the New Kingdom of Granada, the jurisdiction of which extends over the
whole kingdom of Tierre Firmé, and the province of Quito *. Those viceroys not only represent the person of their sovereign, but possess
his regal prerogatives within the precincts of their
own governments, in their utmost extent. Like
him, they exercise supreme authority in every
department of government, civil, military, and
criminal. They have the sole right of nominating the persons who hold many offices of the
highest importance, and the occasional privilege
of supplying those which, when they become vacant by death, are in the royal gift, until the successor appointed by the king shall arrive. The
external pomp of their government is suited to its
real dignity and power. Their courts are formed
upon the model of that at Madrid, with horse
and foot guards, a household regularly established, numerous attendants, and ensigns of
command, displaying such magnificence as hardly
retains the appearance of delegated authority †.

* Voy. de Ulloa, i. 23. 255.　　† Ulloa, Voy. i. 432.
Gage 61.

But as the viceroys cannot discharge in person the functions of a supreme magistrate in every part of their extensive jurisdiction, they are aided in their government by officers and tribunals similar to those in Spain.   The conduct of civil affairs in the various provinces and districts into which the Spanish dominions in America are divided, is committed to magistrates of various orders and denominations ; some appointed by the king ; others by the viceroy, but all subject to the command of the latter, and amenable to his jurisdiction.   The administration of justice is vested in tribunals, known by the name of *Audiences*, and formed upon the model of the court of Chancery in Spain.   These are eleven in number, and dispense justice to as many districts, into which the Spanish dominions in America are divided *.   The number of judges in the court of audience is various, according to the extent and importance of their jurisdiction.   The station is no less honourable than lucrative, and is commonly filled by persons of such abilities and merit as renders this tribunal extremely respectable. Both civil and criminal causes come under their cognizance, and, for each, peculiar judges are set apart.   Though it is only in the most despotic governments that the sovereign exercises in person the formidable prerogative of administering justice to his subjects, and, in absolving or condemning, consults no law but what is deposited in his own breast ; though, in all the monarchies of Europe, judicial authority is committed to magistrates, whose decisions are regulated by

* See Note CLXX.

known laws and established forms, the Spanish
viceroys have often attempted to intrude themselves into the seat of justice, and with an ambition which their distance from the controul of
a superior rendered bold, have aspired to a
power which their master does not venture to
assume. In order to check an usurpation which
must have annihilated justice and security in the
Spanish colonies, by subjecting the lives and property of all to the will of a single man, the viceroys have been prohibited, in the most explicit
terms, by repeated laws, from interfering in the
judicial proceedings of the courts of Audience,
or from delivering an opinion, or giving a voice
with respect to any point litigated before them*.
In some particular cases, in which any question
of civil right is involved, even the political regulations of the viceroy may be brought under the
review of the court of Audience, which, in those
instances, may be deemed an intermediate power
placed between him and the people, as a constitutional barrier to circumscribe his jurisdiction.
But as legal restraints on a person who represents
the sovereign, and is clothed with his authority,
are little suited to the genius of Spanish policy ;
the hesitation and reserve with which it confers
this power on the courts of Audience are remarkable. They may advise, they may remonstrate ; but, in the event of a direct collision between their opinion and the will of the viceroy,
what he determines must be carried into execution, and nothing remains for them, but to lay
the matter before the king and the council of

* Recop. lib. ii. tit. xv. l. 35. 38. 44. lib. iii. tit. iii.
l. 36. 37.

the Indies *.   But to be entitled to remonstrate,
and inform against a person before whom all
others must be silent, and tamely submit to his
decrees, is a privilege which adds dignity to the
courts of Audience.   This is farther augmented
by another circumstance.   Upon the death of a
viceroy, without any provision of a successor by
the king, the supreme power is vested in the court
of Audience resident in the capital of the viceroyalty, and the senior judge, assisted by his brethren, exercises all the functions of the viceroy
while the office continues vacant †.   In matters
which come under the cognizance of the Audiences, in the course of their ordinary jurisdiction,
as courts of justice, their sentences are final in
every litigation concerning property of less value
than six thousand pesos ; but when the subject in
dispute exceeds that sum, their decisions are
subject to review, and may be carried by appeal
before the royal council of the Indies ‡.

In this council, one of the most considerable in
the monarchy for dignity and power, is vested
the supreme government of all the Spanish dominions in America. It was first established by
Ferdinand, in the year 1511, and brought into
a more perfect form by Charles V. in the year
1524. Its jurisdiction extends to every department, ecclesiastical, civil, military, and commercial. All laws and ordinances relative to the
government and police of the colonies originate
there, and must be approved of by two-thirds of

---

* Solorz. de Jure Ind. lib. iv. c. 3. n. 40, 41. Recop.
lib. ii. tit. xv. l. 35. lib. iii. tit. iii. l. 34. lib. v. tit. ix. l. 1.
† Recop. lib. ii. tit. xv. l. 57. &c.
‡ Ibid. lib. v. tit. xiii. l. i, &c.

the members, before they are issued in the name
of the king. All the offices, of which the nomination is reserved to the crown, are conferred
in this council. To it each person employed in
America, from the viceroy downwards, is ac-
countable. It reviews their conduct, rewards
their services, and inflicts the punishments due to
their malversations *. Before it is laid whatever
intelligence, either public or secret, is received
from America, and every scheme of improving
the administration, the police, or the commerce
of the colonies, is submitted to its consideration. From the first institution of the council
of the Indies, it has been the constant object of
the catholic monarchs to maintain its authority,
and to make such additions from time to time,
both to its power and its splendour, as might
render it formidable to all their subjects in the
New World. Whatever degree of public order
and virtue still remains in that country, where
so many circumstances conspire to relax the
former, and to corrupt the latter, may be ascribed in a great measure to the wise regulations
and vigilant inspection of this respectable tribunal †.

As the king is supposed to be always present
in his council of the Indies, its meetings are held
in the place where he resides. Another tribunal
has been instituted, in order to regulate such
commercial affairs as required the immediate and
personal inspection of those appointed to super-
intend them. This is called *Casa de la Contratacion*, or the house of trade, and was established

* Recop. lib. i. tit. ii. l. 1, 2, &c.
† Solorz. de Jure Ind. lib. iv. l. 12.

in Seville, the port to which commerce with the
New World was confined, as early as the year
1501. It may be considered both as a board of
trade, and as a court of judicature.　In the former
capacity, it takes cognizance of whatever relates
to the intercourse of Spain with America, it re-
gulates what commodities should be exported
thither, and has the inspection of such as are
received in return.　It decides concerning the
departure of the fleets for the West Indies, the
freight and burden of the ships, their equipment
and destination.　In the latter capacity, it judges
with respect to every question, civil, commercial,
or criminal, arising in consequence of the transactions of Spain with America; and in both these
departments, its decisions are exempted from the
review of any court but that of the council of the
Indies *.

Such is the great outline of that system of
government, which Spain has established in her
American colonies.　To enumerate the various
subordinate boards and officers employed in the
administration of justice, in collecting the public
revenue, and in regulating the interior police of
the country; to describe their different functions,
and to inquire into the mode and effect of their
operations; would prove a detail no less intricate
than minute and uninteresting.

The first object of the Spanish monarchs was
to secure the productions of the colonies to the
parent state, by an absolute prohibition of any
intercourse with foreign nations.　They took
possession of America by right of conquest, and

* Recop. lib. ix. tit. 1.　Veitia Norte de la Contratacion,
lib. i. c. 1.

conscious not only of the feebleness of their infant settlments, but aware of the difficulty in
establishing their dominion over regions so extensive, or in retaining so many reluctant nations
under the yoke, they dreaded the intrusion of
strangers; they even shunned their inspection,
and endeavoured to keep them at a distance from
their coasts. This spirit of jealousy and exclusion, which at first was natural, and perhaps
necessary, augmented as their possessions in America extended, and the value of them came to be
more fully understood. In consequence of it, a
system of colonizing was introduced, to which
there had hitherto been nothing similar among
mankind. In the ancient world, it was not uncommon to send forth colonies. But they were of
two kinds only. They were either migrations,
which served to disburden a state of its superflu-
ous subjects, when they multiplied too fast for
the territory which they occupied; or they were
military detachments, stationed as garrisons in
a conquered province. The colonies of some
Greek republics, and the swarms of northern
barbarians which settled in different parts of Europe, were of the first species. The Roman
colonies were of the second. In the former, the
connection with the mother country quickly
ceased, and they became independent states. In
the latter, as the disjunction was not complete,
the dependence continued. In their American
settlements, the Spanish monarchs took what
was peculiar to each, and studied to unite them.
By sending colonies to regions so remote, by
establishing in each a form of interior policy and
administration, under distinct governors, and with

peculiar laws, they disjoined them from the mother country.   By retaining in their own hands the rights of legislation, as well as that of imposing taxes, together with the power of nominating the persons who filled every department of executive government, civil or military, they secured their dependence upon the parent state. Happily for Spain, the situation of her colonies was such as rendered it possible to reduce this new idea into practice.   Almost all the countries which she had discovered and occupied lay within the tropics.   The productions of that large portion of the globe are different from those of Europe, even in its most southern provinces. The qualities of the climate and of the soil naturally turn the industry of such as settle there into new channels.   When the Spaniards first took possession of their dominions in America, the precious metals which they yielded, were the only object that attracted their attention.   Even when their efforts began to take a better direction, they employed themselves almost wholly in rearing such peculiar productions of the climate, as, from their rarity or value, were of chief demand in the mother country.   Allured by vast prospects of immediate wealth, they disdained to waste their industry on what was less lucrative, but of superior moment.   In order to render it impossible to correct this error, and to prevent them from making any efforts in industry which might interfere with those of the mother country, the establishment of several species of manufactures, and even the culture of the vine, or olive, are prohibited in the Spanish colonies *, under severe

* See Note CLXXI.

U 2

penalties *. They must trust entirely to the mother country for the objects of primary necessity. Their clothes, their furniture, their instruments of labour, their luxuries, and even a considerable part of the provisions which they consume, were imported from Spain. During a great part of the sixteenth century, Spain, possessing an extensive commerce and flourishing manufactures, could supply with ease the growing demands of her colonies from her own stores. The produce of their mines and plantations was given in exchange for these. But all that the colonies received, as well as all that they gave, was conveyed in Spanish bottoms. No vessel belonging to the colonies was ever permitted to carry the commodities of America to Europe. Even the commercial intercourse of one colony with another, was either absolutely prohibited, or limited by many jealous restrictions. All that America yields flows into the ports of Spain ; all that it consumes must issue from them. No foreigner can enter its colonies without express permission ; no vessel of any foreign nation is received into their harbours ; and the pains of death, with confiscation of moveables, are denounced against every inhabitant who presumes to trade with them †. Thus the colonies are kept in a state of perpetual pupillage ; and by the introduction of this commercial dependence, a refinement in policy of which Spain set the first example to the European nations, the supremacy of the parent state hath been maintained over remote colonies during two centuries and a half.

* B. Ulloa Retab. des Manuf. &c. p. 206.
† Recopil. lib. ix. tit. xxvii. l. i. 4. 7, &c.

Such are the capital maxims to which the Spanish monarchs seem to have attended in forming their new settlements in America. But they could not plant with the same rapidity that they had destroyed; and from many concurring causes, their progress has been extremely slow, in filling up the immense void which their devastations had occasioned. As soon as the rage for discovery and adventure began to abate, the Spaniards opened their eyes to dangers and distresses, which at first they did not perceive, or had despised. The numerous hardships with which the members of infant colonies have to struggle, the diseases of unwholesome climates, fatal to the constitution of Europeans; the difficulty of bringing a country covered with forests into culture; the want of hands necessary for labour in some provinces, and the slow reward of industry in all, unless where the accidental discovery of mines enriched a few fortunate adventurers, were evils universally felt and magnified. Discouraged by the view of these, the spirit of migration was so much damped, that sixty years after the discovery of the New World, the number of Spaniards in all its provinces is computed not to have exceeded fifteen thousand *.

The mode in which property was distributed in the Spanish colonies, and the regulations established with respect to the transmission of it, whether by descent or by sale, were extremely unfavourable to population. In order to promote a rapid increase of people in any new settlement, property in land ought to be divided into small shares, and the alienation of it should be ren-

* See Note CLXXII.

U 3

dered extremely easy *. But the rapaciousness
of the Spanish conquerors of the New World
paid no regard to this fundamental maxim of
policy; and, as they possessed power, which enabled them to gratify the utmost extravagance
of their wishes, many seized districts of great extent, and held them as *encomiendas*. By degrees
they obtained the privilege of converting a part
of these into *Mayorazgos*, a species of fief, introduced into the Spanish system of feudal jurisprudence †, which can neither be divided nor
alienated. Thus a great portion of landed property, under this rigid form of entail, is withheld from circulation, and descends from father
to son unimproved, and of little value either to
the proprietor or to the community. In the
account which I have given of the reduction of
Peru, various examples occur of enormous tracks
of country occupied by some of the conquerors ‡.
The excesses in other provinces were similar; for
as the value of the lands which the Spaniards acquired was originally estimated according to the
number of Indians which lived upon them, America was in general so thinly peopled, that only
districts of great extent could afford such a number of labourers as might be employed in the
mines with any prospect of considerable gain.
The pernicious effects of those radical errors in
the distribution and nature of property in the
Spanish settlements, are felt through every department of industry, and may be considered as
one great cause of a progress in population so

---

* Dr. Smith's Inquiry. ii. 166.   † Recop. lib. iv.
tit. iii. L 24.   ‡ Book vi. vol. iii. p. 105.

much slower than that which has taken place in better constituted colonies *.

To this we may add, that the support of the enormous and expensive fabric of their ecclesiastical establishment, has been a burden on the Spanish colonies, which has greatly retarded the progress of population and industry. The payment of tithes is a heavy tax on industry ; and if the exaction of them be not regulated and circumscribed by the wisdom of the civil magistrate, it becomes intolerable and ruinous. But instead of any restraint on the claims of ecclesiastics, the inconsiderate zeal of the Spanish legislators admitted them into America in their full extent, and at once imposed on their infant colonies a burden which is in no slight degree oppressive to society, even in its most improved state. As early as the year 1501, the payment of tithes in the colonies was enjoined, and the mode of it regulated by law. Every article of primary necessity, towards which the attention of new settlers must naturally be turned, is subjected to that grievous exaction †. Nor were the demands of the clergy confined to articles of simple and easy culture. Its more artificial and operose productions, such as sugar, indigo, and cochineal, were soon declared to be tithable ‡ ; and thus the industry of the planter was taxed in every stage of its progress, from its rudest essay to its highest improvement. To the weight of this legal imposition, the bigotry of the American Spaniards has made many voluntary additions. From their fond delight in the external

* See Note CLXXIII.   † Recop. lib. i. tit. xir. l. 2.
‡ Recop. lib. i. tit. xiv. l. 3. and 4.

pomp and parade of religion, and from superstitious reverence for ecclesiastics of every denomination, they have bestowed profuse donatives on churches and monasteries, and have unprofitably wasted a large proportion of that wealth, which might have nourished and given vigour to productive labour in growing colonies.

But so fertile and inviting are the regions of America which the Spaniards have occupied, that notwithstanding all the circumstances which have checked and retarded population, it has gradually increased, and filled the colonies of Spain with citizens of various orders. Among these, the Spaniards who arrive from Europe, distinguished by the name of *Chapetones*, are the first in rank and power. From the jealous attention of the Spanish court to secure the dependence of the colonies on the parent state, all departments of consequence are filled by persons sent from Europe ; and, in order to prevent any of dubious fidelity from being employed, each must bring proof of a clear descent from a family of *Old Christians*, untainted with any mixture of Jewish or Mahometan blood, and never disgraced by any censure of the inquisition *. In such pure hands, power is deemed to be safely lodged, and almost every public function, from the viceroyalty downwards, is committed to them alone. Every person, who by his birth, or residence in America, may be suspected of any attachment or interest adverse to the mother country, is the object of distrust to such a degree, as amounts nearly to an exclusion from all offices of confidence or authority †. By

* Recopil. lib ix. tit. xxvi. l. 15, 16.
† See Note CLXXIV.

this conspicuous predilection of the court, the Chapetones are raised to such pre-eminence in America, that they look down with disdain on every other order of men.

The character and state of the *Creoles*, or descendants of Europeans settled in America, the second class of subjects in the Spanish colonies, have enabled the Chapetones to acquire other advantages, hardly less considerable than those which they derive from the partial favour of government. Though some of the Creolian race are descended from the conquerors of the New World; though others can trace up their pedigree to the noblest families in Spain; though many are possessed of ample fortunes, yet, by the enervating influence of a sultry climate, by the rigour of a jealous government, and by their despair of attaining that distinction to which mankind naturally aspire, the vigour of their minds is so entirely broken, that a great part of them waste life in luxurious indulgences, mingled with an illiberal superstition still more debasing. Languid and unenterprising, the operations of an active extended commerce would be to them so cumbersome and oppressive, that in almost every part of America they decline engaging in it. The interior traffic of every colony, as well as any trade which is permitted with the neighbouring provinces, and with Spain itself, are carried on chiefly by the Chapetones *, who, as the recompence of their industry, amass immense wealth, while the Creoles, sunk in sloth, are satisfied with the revenues of their paternal estates.

* Voy. de Ulloa, i. 27. 251.   Voy. de Frezier, 227.

From this stated competition for power and wealth between those two orders of citizens, and the various passions excited by a rivalship so interesting, their hatred is violent and implacable. On every occasion, symptoms of this aversion break out, and the common appellations which each bestows on the other, are as contemptuous as those which flow from the most deep-rooted national antipathy *. The court of Spain, from a refinement of distrustful policy, cherishes those seeds of discord, and foments this mutual jealousy, which not only prevents the two most powerful classes of its subjects in the New World from combining against the parent state, but prompts each, with the most vigilant zeal, to observe the motions and to counteract the schemes of the other.

The third class of inhabitants in the Spanish colonies is a mixed race, the offspring either of an European and a negro, or of an European and Indian, the former called *Mulattoes*, the latter *Mestizos*. As the court of Spain, solicitous to incorporate its new vassals with its ancient subjects, early encouraged the Spaniards settled in America to marry the natives of that country, several alliances of this kind were formed in their infant colonies †. But it has been more owing to licentious indulgence, than to compliance with this injunction of their sovereigns, that this mixed breed has multiplied so greatly, as to constitute a considerable part of the population in all the Spanish settlements. The several stages of descent in this race, and the gradual variations

* Gage's Survey, p. 9. Frezier, 226. † Recopil. lib. vi· tit. i. l. 2. Herrera, dec. 1. lib. v. c. 12. Dec. 3. lib. vii. c. 2.

of shade until the African black, or the copper colour of America, brighten into an European complexion are accurately marked by the Spaniards, and each distinguished by a peculiar name. Those of the first and second generations are considered and treated as mere Indians and Negroes; but in the third descent, the characteristic hue of the former disappears; and in the fifth, the deeper tint of the latter is so entirely effaced, that they can no longer be distinguished from Europeans, and become entitled to all their privileges *. It is chiefly by this mixed race, whose frame is remarkably robust and hardy, that the mechanic arts are carried on in the Spanish settlements, and other active functions in society are discharged, which the two higher classes of citizens, from pride or from indolence, disdain to exercise †.

The negroes hold the fourth rank among the inhabitants of the Spanish colonies. The introduction of that unhappy part of the human species into America, together with their services and sufferings there, shall be fully explained in another place; here they are mentioned chiefly, in order to point out a peculiarity in their situation under the Spanish dominion. In several of their settlements, particularly in New Spain, negroes are mostly employed in domestic service. They form a principal part in the train of luxury, and are cherished and caressed by their superiors, to whose vanity and pleasures they are equally subservient. Their dress and appearance are hardly less splendid than that of their masters,

* Voy. de Ulloa, i. p. 27. † Ibid. i. 29. Voy. de Bouguer, p. 104. Melendez, Tesoros Verdaderos, i. 354.

whose manners they imitate, and whose passions
they imbibe *. Elevated by this distinction,
they have assumed such a tone of superiority over
the Indians, and treat them with such insolence
and scorn, that the antipathy between the two
races has become implacable. Even in Peru,
where negroes seem to be more numerous, and
are employed in field-work as well as domestic
service, they maintain their ascendant over the
Indians, and the mutual hatred of one to the
other subsists with equal violence. The laws
have industriously fomented this aversion, to
which accident gave rise, and, by most rigorous
injunctions, have endeavoured to prevent every
intercourse that might form a bond of union be-
tweeen the two races. Thus by an artful policy,
the Spaniards derive strength from that circumstance in population which is the weakness of o-
ther European colonies, and have secured as associates and defenders, those very persons who
elsewhere are objects of jealousy and terror †.

The Indians form the last, and the most depressed order of men in the country which belonged to their ancestors. I have already traced
the progress of the Spanish ideas with respect to
the condition and treatment of that people, and
have mentioned the most important of their more
early regulations, concerning a matter of so much
consequence in the administration of their new
dominions. But since the period to which I have
brought down the history of America, the information and experience acquired during two

* Gage, p. 56. Voy. de Ulloa, i. 451.
† Recopil. lib. vii. tit. v. l. 7. Herrera, dec. 8. lib.
vii. c. 12. Frezier, 244.

centuries, have enabled the court of Spain to make such improvements in this part of its A-merican system, that a short view of the present condition of the Indians may prove both curious and interesting.

By the famous regulations of Charles V. in 1542, which have been so often mentioned, the high pretensions of the conquerors of the New World, who considered its inhabitants as slaves, to whose service they had acquired a full right of property, were finally abrogated. From that period, the Indians have been reputed freemen, and entitled to the privileges of subjects. When admitted into this rank, it was deemed just, that they should contribute towards the support and improvement of the society which had adopted them as members. But as no considerable bene-fit could be expected from the voluntary efforts of men unacquainted with regular industry, and averse to labour, the court of Spain found it ne-cessary to fix and secure, by proper regulations, what it thought reasonable to exact from them. With this view, an annual tax was imposed up-on every male, from the age of eighteen to fif-ty; and at the same time, the nature as well as the extent of the services which they might be required to perform, were ascertained with pre-cision. This tribute varies in different provin-ces ; but if we take that paid in New Spain as a medium, its annual amount is nearly four shil-lings a head ; no exorbitant sum in countries where, as at the source of wealth, the value of money is extremely low *. The right of levy-

* See Note CLXXV.　Recopil. lib. vi. tit. v. l. 42.
Hackluyt, vol. iii. p. 461.

ing this tribute likewise varies. In America, every Indian is either an immediate vassal of the crown, or depends upon some subject to whom the district in which he resides has been granted for a limited time, under the denomination of an *encomienda*. In the former case, about three-fourths of the tax is paid into the royal treasury; in the latter, the same proportion of it belongs to the holder of the grant. When Spain first took possession of America, the greater part of it was parcelled out among its conquerors, or those who first settled there, and but a small portion reserved for the crown. As those grants, which were made for two lives only *, reverted successively to the sovereign, he had it in his power either to diffuse his favours by grants to new proprietors, or to augment his own revenue by valuable annexations †. Of these, the latter has been frequently chosen ; the number of Indians now depending immediately on the crown, is much greater than in the first age after the conquest, and this branch of the royal revenue continues to extend.

The benefit arising from the services of the Indians accrues either to the crown, or to the holder of the *encomienda*, according to the same rule observed in the payment of tribute. Those services, however, which can now be legally exacted, are very different from the tasks originally imposed upon the Indians. The nature of the work which they must perform is defined, and an equitable recompence is granted for their labour. The stated services demanded of the

* Recopil. lib. vi. tit. viii. l. 48. Solorz. de Ind. Jure lib. ii. c. 61.   † See Note CLXXVI.

Indians may be divided into two branches. They are either employed in works of primary necessity, without which society cannot subsist comfortably, or are compelled to labour in the mines, from which the Spanish colonies derive their chief value and importance. In consequence of the former, they are obliged to assist in the culture of maize, and other grain of necessary consumption, in tending cattle, in erecting edifices of public utility, in building bridges, and in forming high roads *; but they cannot be constrained to labour in raising vines, olives, and sugar-canes, or any species of cultivation, which has for its object the gratification of luxury, or commercial profit †. In consequence of the latter, the Indians are compelled to undertake the more unpleasant task of extracting ore from the bowels of the earth, and of refining it by successive processes, no less unwholesome than operose ‡.

The mode of exacting both these services is the same, and is under regulations framed with a view of rendering it as little oppressive as possible to the Indians. They are called out successively in divisions, termed *Mitas*, and no person can be compelled to go but in his turn. In Peru, the number called out must not exceed the seventh part of the inhabitants in any district §. In New Spain, where the Indians are more numerous, it is fixed at four in the hundred ||. During what time the labour of such Indians as

* Recopil. lib. vi. tit. xiii. l. 19.   Solorz. de Ind. Jure, ii. lib i. c. 6, 7. 9.   † Recopil. lib. vi. tit. xiii. l. 8.   Solorz. lib. i. c. 7. N° 41, &c.   ‡ See Note CLXXVII. § Recop. lib. vi. tit. xii. l. 21. || Recopil. lib. vi. l. 22

are employed in agriculture continues, I have not been able to learn *. But in Peru, each mita, or division, destined for the mines, remains there six months; and while engaged in this service, a labourer never receives less than two shillings a day, and often earns more than double that sum †. No Indian residing at a greater distance than thirty miles from a mine, is included in the mita, or division, employed in working it ‡; nor are the inhabitants of the low country exposed now to certain destruction, as they were at first, when under the dominion of the conquerors, by compelling them to remove from that warm climate, to the cold elevated regions where minerals abound §.

The Indians who live in the principal towns, are entirely subject to the Spanish laws and magistrates; but in their own villages, they are governed by Caziques, some of whom are the descendants of their ancient lords, others are named by the Spanish viceroys. These regulate the petty affairs of the people under them, according to maxims of justice, transmitted to them by tradition from their ancestors. To the Indians, this jurisdiction, lodged in such friendly hands, affords some consolation; and so little formidable is this dignity to their new masters, that they often allow it to descend by hereditary right ‖. For the farther relief of men so much exposed to oppression, the Spanish court has appointed an officer in every district, with the title of Protector of

---

* See Note CLXXVIII.   † Ulloa Entreten. 265, 266.
‡ Recopil. lib. vi. tit. xii. l. 3.   § Ibid. l. 29. and tit. i. l. 13. See Note CLXXIX.   ‖ Solorz. de Jure Ind. lib. i. c. 26. Recop'l. lib. vi. tit. vii.

the Indians.   It is his function, as the name im-
plies, to assert the rights of the Indians; to appear as their defender in the courts of justice;
and, by the interposition of his authority, to set
bounds to the encroachments and exactions of
his countrymen *.   A certain portion of the reserved fourth of the annual tribute, is destined
for the salary of the caziques and protectors;
another is applied to the maintenance of the clergy employed in the instruction of the Indians †.
Another part seems to be appropriated for the benefit of the Indians themselves, and is applied for
the payment of their tribute in years of famine,
or when a particular district is affected by any
extraordinary local calamity ‡.   Besides this, provision is made by various laws, that hospitals shall
be founded in every new settlement for the reception of Indians §.   Such hospitals have accordingly
been erected, both for the indigent and infirm, in
Lima, in Cuzco, and in Mexico, where the Indi-
ans are treated with tenderness and humanity ||.

Such are the leading principles in the jurisprudence and policy by which the Indians are now
governed in the provinces belonging to Spain.
In those regulations of the Spanish monarchs, we
discover no traces of that cruel system of exter-
mination, which they have been charged with
adopting; and if we admit, that the necessity of
securing subsistence for their colonies, or the advantages derived from working the mines, give
them a right to avail themselves of the labour of

* Solorz. lib. i. c. 17. p. 201.   Recop. lib. vi. tit. vi.
† Recop. lib. vi. tit. v. l. 30. tit. xvi. l. 12—15.   ‡ Ibid.
lib. vi. tit. iv. l. 13.   § Ibid. lib. i. tit. iv. l. 1, &c.
|| Voy. de Ulloa, i. 429. 509.   Churchill, iv. 496.

X 3

the Indians, we must allow, that the attention
with which they regulate and recompence that
labour is provident and sagacious.   In no code
of laws is greater solicitude displayed, or precautions multiplied, with more prudent concern
for the preservation, the security, and the happiness of the subject, than we discover in the
collection of the Spanish laws for the Indies.
But those later regulations, like the more early
edicts which have been already mentioned, have
too often proved ineffectual remedies against the
evils which they were intended to prevent.   In
every age, if the same causes continue to operate,
the same effects must follow.   From the immense
distance between the power entrusted with the
execution of laws, and that by whose authority
they are enacted, the vigour even of the most
absolute government must relax, and the dread
of a superior, too remote to observe with accuracy, or to punish with dispatch, must insensibly
abate.   Notwithstanding the numerous injunctions of the Spanish monarch, the Indians still
suffer on many occasions, both from the avarice
of individuals, and from the exactions of the magistrates who ought to have protected them; un-
reasonable tasks are imposed; the term of their
labour is prolonged beyond the period fixed by
law, and they groan under many of the insults
and wrongs which are the lot of a dependent
people *.   From some information on which I
can depend, such oppression abounds more in Peru than in any other colony.   But it is not general.   According to the accounts even of those
authors who are most disposed to exaggerate the

* See Note CLXXX.

sufferings of the Indians, they in several provinces enjoy not only ease, but affluence; they possess large farms; they are masters of numerous herds and flocks; and, by the knowledge which they have acquired of European arts and industry, are supplied not only with the necessaries, but with many luxuries of life *.

After explaining the form of civil government in the Spanish colonies, and the state of the various orders of persons subject to it, the peculiarities in their ecclesiastical constitution merit consideration. Notwithstanding the superstitious veneration with which the Spaniards are devoted to the Holy See, the vigilant and jealous policy of Ferdinand early prompted him to take precautions against the introduction of the papal dominion into America. With this view, he solicited Alexander VI. for a grant to the crown of the tithes in all the newly discovered countries †, which he obtained on condition of his making provision for the religious instruction of the natives. Soon after, Julius II. conferred on him and his successors the right of patronage, and the absolute disposal of all ecclesiastical benefices there ‡. But these pontiffs, unacquainted with the value of what he demanded, bestowed those donations with an inconsiderate liberality, which their successors have often lamented, and wished to recal. In consequence of those grants, the Spanish monarchs have become in effect the heads of the American church. In them the administration of its revenues is vested. Their no-

* Gage's Survey, p. 85. 90. 104. 119, &c.　　† Bulla
Alex. VI. A D. 1501. ap. Solorz. de Jure Ind. ii. p. 498.
‡ Bulla Julii II. 1508, ap. Solorz. de Jure Ind. ii. 509.

mination of persons to supply vacant benefices is instantly confirmed by the pope. Thus, in all Spanish America, authority of every species centers in the Crown. There no collision is known between spiritual and temporal jurisdiction. The king is the only superior; his name alone is heard of, and no dependence upon any foreign power has been introduced. Papal bulls cannot be admitted into America, nor are they of any force there, until they have been previously examined and approved of by the royal council of the Indies * ; and if any bull should be surreptitiously introduced and circulated in America without obtaining that approbation, ecclesiastics are required not only to prevent it from taking effect, but to seize all the copies of it, and transmit them to the council of the Indies †. To this limitation of the papal jurisdiction, equally singular, whether we consider the age and nation in which it was devised, or the jealous attention with which Ferdinand and his successors have studied to maintain it in full force ‡, Spain is indebted, in a great measure, for the uniform tranquillity which has reigned in her American dominions.

The hierarchy is established in America in the same form as in Spain, with its full train of archbishops, bishops, deans, and other dignitaries. The inferior clergy are divided into three classes, under the denomination of *Curas, Doctrineros,* and *Missioneros.* The first are parish priests in those parts of the country where the Spaniards

* Recopil. lib. i. tit. ix. l. 2. and Autas del Consejo de las Indias, clxi.   † Recopil. lib. i. tit. vii. l. 55.
‡ Ibid. lib. i. tit. vii. l. 55. passim.

have settled. The second have the charge of such districts as are inhabited by Indians subjected to the Spanish government, and living under its protection. The third are employed in instructing and converting those fiercer tribes, which disdain submission to the Spanish yoke, and live in remote or inaccessible regions, to which the Spanish arms have not penetrated. So numerous are the ecclesiastics of all those various orders, and such the profuse liberality with which many of them are endowed, that the revenues of the church in America are immense. The Romish superstition appears with its utmost pomp in the New World. Churches and convents there are magnificent and richly adorned ; and on high festivals, the display of gold and silver, and precious stones, is such as exceeds the conception of an European *. An ecclesiastical establishment so splendid and expensive, is unfavourable, as has been formerly observed, to the progress of rising colonies ; but in countries where riches abound, and the people are so delighted with parade that religion must assume it in order to attract their veneration, this propensity to ostentation has been indulged, and becomes less pernicious.

The early institution of monasteries in the Spanish colonies, and the inconsiderate zeal in multiplying them, have been attended with consequences more fatal. In every new settlement, the first object should be to encourage population, and to incite every citizen to contribute towards augmenting the number and strength of the community. During the youth and vigour of society, while there is room to spread, and sustenance

* Voy. de Ulloa, i. 43*.

is procured with facility, mankind increase with
amazing rapidity. But the Spaniards had hardly taken possession of America, when, with a
most preposterous policy, they began to erect
convents, where persons of both sexes were shut
up, under a vow to defeat the purpose of nature,
and to counteract the first of her laws. Influenced by a misguided piety, which ascribes trans-
cendant merit to a state of celibacy, or allured
by the prospect of that listless ease, which, in
sultry climates, is deemed supreme felicity, numbers crowded into those mansions of sloth and
superstition, and are lost to society. As none
but persons of Spanish extract are admitted into
the monasteries of the New World, the evil is
more sensibly felt, and every monk or nun may
be considered as an active person withdrawn from
civil life.   The impropriety of such foundations,
in any situation where the extent of territory requires additional hands to improve it, is so obvious, that some catholic states have expressly prohibited any person in their colonies from taking
the monastic vows *.   Even the Spanish monarchs, on some occasions, seem to have been a-
larmed with the spreading of a spirit so adverse
to the increase and prosperity of their colonies,
that they have endeavoured to check it †.   But
the Spaniards in America, more thoroughly under the influence of superstition than their countrymen in Europe, and directed by ecclesiastics
more bigoted and illiterate, have conceived such
an high opinion of monastic sanctity, that no regulations can restrain their zeal ; and, by the

* Voy. de Ulloa, ii. 124.   † Herrera, dec. v. lib. ix.
c. 1, 2. Recop. lib. i. tit. iii. L 1, 2. tit. iv. c. 2. Solorz.
lib. iii. c. 23.

excess of their ill-judged bounty, religious houses have multiplied to a degree no less amazing
than pernicious to society *.

In viewing the state of colonies, where not
only the number but influence of ecclesiastics is
so great, the character of this powerful body is
an object that merits particular attention. A
considerable part of the secular clergy in Mexico
and Peru are natives of Spain. As persons long
accustomed, by their education, to the retirement and indolence of academic life, are more
incapable of active enterprise, and less disposed
to strike into new paths than any order of men,
the ecclesiastical adventurers by whom the American church is recruited, are commonly such as,
from merit or rank in life, have little prospect
of success in their own country. Accordingly,
the secular priests in the New World are still
less distinguished than their brethren in Spain
for literary accomplishments of any species; and
though, by the ample provision which has been
made for the American church, many of its
members enjoy the ease and independence which
are favourable to the cultivation of science, the
body of secular clergy has hardly, during two
centuries and a half, produced one author whose
works convey such useful information, or possess
such a degree of merit, as to be ranked among
those which attract the attention of enlightened
nations. But the greatest part of the ecclesiastics
in the Spanish settlements are regulars. On the
discovery of America, a new field opened to the
pious zeal of the monastic orders; and, with a
becoming alacrity, they immediately sent forth

* See Note CLXXXI.

missionaries to labour in it. The first attempt
to instruct and convert the Americans, was made
by monks ; and, as soon as the conquest of any
province was completed, and its ecclesiastical
establishment began to assume some form, the
popes permitted the missionaries of the four mendicant orders, as a reward for their services, to
accept of parochial charges in America, to perform all spiritual functions, and to receive the
tithes, and other emoluments of the benefice,
without depending on the jurisdiction of the
bishop of the diocese, or being subject to his
censures.   In consequence of this, a new career
of usefulness, as well as new objects of ambition,
presented themselves.   Whenever a call is made
for a fresh supply of missionaries, men of the most
ardent and aspiring minds, impatient under the
restraint of a cloister, weary of its insipid uni-
formity, and fatigued with the irksome repetition of its frivolous functions, offer their service
with eagerness, and repair to the New World in
quest of liberty and distinction.   Nor do they
pursue distinction without success.   The highest
ecclesiastical honours, as well as the most lucrative preferments in Mexico and Peru, are often
in the hands of regulars ; and it is chiefly to the
monastic orders that the Americans are indebted
for any portion of science which is cultivated
among them.   They are almost the only Spanish
ecclesiastics from whom we have received any
accounts, either of the civil or natural history of
the various provinces in America. Some of them,
though deeply tinged with the indelible superstition of their profession, have published books
which give a favourable idea of their abilities.

The natural and moral history of the New World, by the Jesuit Acosta, contains more accurate observations, perhaps, and more sound science, than are to be found in any description of remote countries published in the sixteenth century.

But the same disgust with monastic life, to which America is indebted for some instructors of worth and abilities, filled it with others of a very different character. The giddy, the profligate, the avaricious, to whom the poverty and rigid discipline of a convent are intolerable, consider a mission to America as a release from mortification and bondage. There they soon obtain some parochial charge, and far removed, by their situation, from the inspection of their monastic superiors, and exempt, by their character, from the jurisdiction of their diocesan *, they are hardly subject to any controul. According to the testimony of the most zealous catholics, many of the regular clergy in the Spanish settlements are not only destitute of the virtues becoming their profession, but regardless of that external decorum and respect for the opinion of mankind, which preserve a semblance of worth where the reality is wanting. Secure of impunity, some regulars, in contempt of their vow of poverty, engage openly in commerce ; and are so rapaciously eager in amassing wealth, that they become the most grievous oppressors of the Indians, whom it was their duty to have protected. Others, with no less flagrant violation of their vow of chastity, indulge with little disguise in the most dissolute licentiousness †.

* Avendano Thes. Indic. ii. 253.
† See Note CLXXXII.

Various schemes have been proposed for re-
dressing enormities so manifest and so offensive.
Several persons, no less eminent for piety than
discernment, have contended, that the regulars,
in conformity to the canons of the church, ought
to be confined within the walls of their cloisters,
and should no longer be permitted to encroach
on the functions of the secular clergy. Some
public-spirited magistrates, from conviction of
its being necessary to deprive the regulars of a
privilege bestowed at first with good intention,
but of which time and experience had discovered
the pernicious effects, openly countenanced the
secular clergy in their attempts to assert their
own rights. The prince D'Esquilache, viceroy
of Peru under Philip III. took measures so decisive and effectual for circumscribing the regulars within their proper sphere, as struck them
with general consternation *. They had recourse
to their usual arts. They alarmed the superstitious, by representing the proceedings of the
viceroy as innovations fatal to religion. They
employed all the refinements of intrigue, in order
to gain persons in power; and seconded by the
powerful influence of the Jesuits, who claimed
and enjoyed all the privileges which belonged to
the mendicant orders in America, they made a
deep impression on a bigoted prince, and a weak
ministry. The ancient practice was tolerated.
The abuses which it occasioned continued to increase, and the corruption of monks, exempt from
the restraints of discipline, and the inspection of
any superior, became a disgrace to religion. At
last, as the veneration of the Spaniards for the

* See Note CLXXXIII.

monastic orders began to abate, and the power
of the Jesuits was on the decline, Ferdinand VI.
ventured to apply the only effectual remedy, by
issuing an edict prohibiting regulars of every
denomination from taking the charge of any
parish with the cure of souls; and declaring,
that on the demise of the present incumbents,
none but secular priests, subject to the jurisdiction of their diocesans, shall be presented to vacant benefices *.   If this regulation is carried
into execution with steadiness in any degree proportional to the wisdom with which it is framed,
a very considerable reformation may take place
in the ecclesiastical state of Spanish America,
and the secular clergy may gradually become a
respectable body of men.   The deportment of
many ecclesiastics, even at present, seems to be
decent and exemplary, otherwise we can hardly
suppose that they would be held in such high
estimation, and possess such a wonderful ascendant over the minds of their countrymen throughout all the Spanish settlements.

But whatever merit the Spanish ecclesiastics in
America may possess, the success of their endeavours, in communicating the knowledge of true
religion to the Indians, has been more imperfect
than might have been expected, either from the
degree of their zeal, or from the dominion which
they had acquired over that people.   For this,
various reasons may be assigned.   The first missionaries, in their ardour to make proselytes, admitted the people of America into the Christian
church, without previous instruction in the doctrines of religion, and even before they them-

* Real Cedula MS. *penes me.*

Y 2

selves had acquired such knowledge of the Indian language, as to be able to explain to the natives the mysteries of faith, or the precepts of duty. Resting upon a subtle distinction in scholastic theology, between that degree of assent which is founded on a complete knowledge and conviction of duty, and that which may be yielded when both these are imperfect, they adopted this strange practice, no less inconsistent with the spirit of a religion which addresses itself to the understanding of men, than repugnant to the dictates of reason. As soon as any body of people, overawed by dread of the Spanish power, moved by the example of their own chiefs, incited by levity, or yielding from mere ignorance, expressed the slightest desire of embracing the religion of their conquerors, they were instantly baptized. While this rage of conversion continued, a single clergyman baptized in one day above five thousand Mexicans, and did not desist until he was so exhausted by fatigue that he was unable to lift his hands *. In the course of a few years after the reduction of the Mexican empire, the sacrament of baptism was administered to more than four millions †. Proselytes adopted with such inconsiderate haste, and who were neither instructed in the nature of the tenets to which it was supposed they had given assent, nor taught the absurdity of those which they were required to relinquish, retained their veneration for their ancient superstitions in full force, or mingled an attachment to its doctrines and rites with that slender knowledge of Christianity

---

* P. Torribio, MS. Torquem. Mond. Ind. lib. xvi. c. 6.
† Torribio, MS. Torquem. lib. xvi. c. 8

which they had acquired. These sentiments the new converts transmitted to their posterity, into whose minds they have sunk so deep, that the Spanish ecclesiastics, with all their industry, have not been able to eradicate them. The religious institutions of their ancestors are still remembered, and held in honour, by many of the Indians both in Mexico and Peru; and whenever they think themselves out of reach of inspection by the Spaniards, they assemble and celebrate their idolatrous rites *.

But this is not the most unsurmountable obstacle to the progress of Christianity among the Indians. The powers of their uncultivated understandings are so limited, their observations and reflections reach so little beyond the mere objects of sense, that they seem hardly to have the capacity of forming abstract ideas, and possess not language to express them. To such men, the sublime and spiritual doctrines of Christianity must be, in a great measure, incomprehensible. The numerous and splendid ceremonies of the popish worship catch the eye, please and interest them; but when their instructors attempt to explain the articles of faith, with which those external observances are connected, though the Indians may listen with patience, they so little conceive the meaning of what they hear, that their acquiescence does not merit the name of belief. Their indifference is still greater than their incapacity. Attentive only to the present moment, and ingrossed by the objects before them, the Indians so seldom reflect upon what

* Voy. de Ulloa, i. 341.   Torquem. lib. xv c. 23 lib. xvi. c. 28.   Gage, 171.

Y 3

is past, or take thought for what is to come, that neither the promises nor threats of religion make much impression upon them; and while their foresight rarely extends so far as the next day, it is almost impossible to inspire them with solicitude about the concerns of a future world. Astonished equally at their slowness of comprehension, and at their insensibility, some of the early missionaries pronounced them a race of men so brutish, as to be incapable of understanding the first principles of religion. A council held at Lima decreed, that, on account of this incapacity, they ought to be excluded from the sacrament of the Eucharist *. Though Paul III. by his famous bull, issued in the year 1537, declared them to be rational creatures, entitled to all the privileges of Christians † ; yet, after the lapse of two centuries, during which they have been members of the church, so imperfect are their attainments in knowledge, that very few possess such a portion of spiritual discernment, as to be deemed worthy of being admitted to the holy communion ‡. From this idea of their incapacity and imperfect knowledge of religion, when the zeal of Philip II. established the inquisition in America in the year 1570, the Indians were exempted from the jurisdiction of that severe tribunal ǁ, and still continue under the inspection of their diocesans. Even after the most perfect instruction, their faith is held to be feeble and dubious; and though some of them have been taught the learned languages, and

* Torquem. lib. xvi. c. 20. Garcia Origin. 311.   † Torquem. lib. xvi. c. 25.
‡ Voy. de Ulloa, i. 343.
ǁ Recop. lib. vi. tit. i. l. 35.

have gone through the ordinary course of academic education with applause, their frailty is still so much suspected, that few Indians are either ordained priests, or received into any religious order *.

From this brief survey, some idea may be formed of the interior state of the Spanish colonies. The various productions with which they supply and enrich the mother country, and the system of commercial intercourse between them, come next in order to be explained. If the dominions of Spain in the New World had been of such moderate extent, as bore a due proportion to the parent state, the progress of her colonizing might have been attended with the same benefit as that of other nations. But when, in less than half a century, her inconsiderate rapacity had seized on countries larger than all Europe, her inability to fill such vast regions with a number of inhabitants sufficient for the cultivation of them, was so obvious, as to give a wrong direction to all the efforts of the colonists. They did not form compact settlements, where industry, circumscribed within proper limits, both in its views and operations, is conducted with that sober persevering spirit, which gradually converts whatever is in its possession to a proper use, and derives thence the greatest advantage. Instead of this, the Spaniards, seduced by the boundless prospect which opened to them, divided their possessions in America into governments of great extent. As their number was too small to attempt the regular culture of the immense provinces which they occupied rather than peo-

* Torquem. lib. xvii. c. 13.   See Note CLXXXIV.

pled, they bent their attention to a few objects that allured them with hopes of sudden and exorbitant gain, and turned away with contempt from the humbler paths of industry, which lead more slowly, but with greater certainty, to wealth and increase of national strength.

Of all the methods by which riches may be acquired, that of searching for the precious metals is one of the most inviting, to men who are either unaccustomed to the regular assiduity with which the culture of the earth and the operations of commerce must be carried on, or who are so enterprising and rapacious as not to be satisfied with the gradual returns of profit which they yield. Accordingly, as soon as the several countries in America were subjected to the dominion of Spain, this was almost the only method of acquiring wealth which occurred to the adventurers by whom they were conquered. Such provinces of the continent as did not allure them to settle, by the prospect of their affording gold and silver, were totally neglected. Those in which they met with a disappointment of the sanguine expectations they had formed, were abandoned. Even the value of the islands, the first-fruits of their discoveries, and the first object of their attention, sunk so much in their estimation, when the mines which had been opened in them were exhausted, that they were deserted by many of the planters, and left to be occupied by more industrious possessors. All crowded to Mexico and Peru, where the quantities of gold and silver found among the natives, who searched for them with little industry and less skill, promised an unexhausted store, as the recompence of more intelligent and persevering efforts.

During several years, the ardour of their researches was kept up by hope, rather than success. At length, the rich silver mines of Potosi, in Peru, were accidentally discovered in the year 1545 [*], by an Indian, as he was clambering up the mountain, in pursuit of a Llama which had strayed from his flock. Soon after, the mines of Sacotecas, in New Spain, little inferior to the other in value, were opened. From that time, successive discoveries have been made in both colonies, and silver mines are now so numerous, that the working of them, and of some few mines of gold in the provinces of Tierra Firmé, and the New Kingdom Granada, has become the capital occupation of the Spaniards, and is reduced into a system no less complicated than interesting. To describe the nature of the various ores, the mode of extracting them from the bowels of the earth, and to explain the several processes by which the metals are separated from the substances with which they are mingled, either by the action of fire, or the attractive powers of mercury, is the province of the natural philosopher or chymist, rather than of the historian.

The exuberant profusion with which the mountains of the New World poured forth their treasures, astonished mankind, who had been accustomed hitherto to receive a penurious supply of the precious metals from the more scanty stores contained in the mines of the ancient hemisphere. According to principles of computation which

[*] Fernandez, p. i. lib. xi. c. 11.

appear to be extremely moderate, the quantity
of gold and silver that has been regularly entered
in the ports of Spain, is equal in value to four
millions sterling annually, reckoning from the
year 1492, in which America was discovered, to
the present time. This, in two hundred and
eighty-three years, amounts to eleven hundred
and thirty-two millions. Immense as this sum is,
the Spanish writers contend, that as much more
ought to be added to it, in consideration of
treasure which has been extracted from the
mines, and imported fraudulently into Spain,
without paying duty to the king. By this account, Spain has drawn from the New World a
supply of wealth, amounting at least to two
thousand millions of pounds sterling *.

The mines, which have yielded this amazing
quantity of treasure, are not worked at the expence of the crown, or of the public. In order
to encourage private adventurers, the person
who discovers and works a new vein, is entitled
to the property of it. Upon laying his claim to
such a discovery before the governor of the province, a certain extent of land is measured off,
and a certain number of Indians allotted him,
under the obligation of his opening the mine
within a limited time, and of his paying the cus-
tomary duty to the king for what it shall produce. Invited by the facility with which such
grants are obtained, and encouraged by some
striking examples of success in this line of adventure; not only the sanguine and the bold, but
the timid and diffident, enter upon it with astonish-

* Uztariz Theor. y Pract. de Commercia, c. 3. Herrera, dec. viii. lib. xi. c. 15. See Note CLXXXV.

ing ardour. With vast objects always in view, fed continually with hope, and expecting every moment that fortune will unveil her secret stores, and give up the wealth which they contain to their wishes, they deem every other occupation insipid and uninteresting. The charms of this pursuit, like the rage for deep play, are so bewitching, and take such full possession of the mind, as even to give a new bent to the natural temper. Under its influence, the cautious become enterprising, and the covetous profuse. Powerful as this charm naturally is, its force is augmented by the arts of an order of men known in Peru by the cant name of *searchers*. These are commonly persons of desperate fortunes, who, availing themselves of some skill in mineralogy, accompanied with the insinuating manner and confident pretensions peculiar to projectors, address the wealthy and the credulous. By plausible descriptions of the appearances which they have discovered of rich veins hitherto unexplored ; by producing, when requisite, specimens of promising ore ; by affirming, with an imposing assurance, that success is certain, and that the expence must be trifling, they seldom fail to persuade. An association is formed ; a small sum is advanced by each copartner ; the mine is opened ; the *searcher* is entrusted with the sole direction of every operation ; unforeseen difficulties occur ; new demands of money are made ; but, amidst a succession of disappointments and delays, hope is never extinguished, and the ardour of expectation hardly abates. For it is observed, that if any person once enter this seducing path, it is almost impossible to return ;

his ideas alter, he seems to be possessed with another spirit, visions of imaginary wealth are continually before his eyes, and he thinks and speaks, and dreams of nothing else *.

Such is the spirit that must be formed, wherever the active exertions of any society are chiefly employed in working mines of gold and silver. No spirit is more adverse to such improvements in agriculture and commerce, as render a nation really opulent. If the system of administration in the Spanish colonies had been founded upon principles of sound policy, the power and ingenuity of the legislature would have been exerted with as much ardour, in restraining its subjects from such pernicious industry, as is now employed in alluring them towards it. " Projects of mining," (says a good judge of the political conduct of nations,) " in-
" stead of replacing the capital employed in
" them, together with the ordinary profit of
" stock, commonly absorb both capital and pro-
" fit. They are the projects, therefore, to
" which, of all others, a prudent lawgiver, who
" desired to increase the capital of his nation,
" would least choose to give any extraordinary
" encouragement, or to turn towards them a
" greater share of that capital than would go to
" them of its own accord. Such, in reality, is
" the absurd confidence which all men have in
" their own good fortune, that wherever there
" is the least probability of success, too great a
" share of it is apt to go to them of its own ac-
" cord †." But in the Spanish colonies, go-

* Ulloa Entreten. p. 223. † Dr. Smith's Inquiry, &c. ii. 155.

vernment is studious to cherish a spirit which it should have laboured to depress, and, by the sanction of its approbation, augments that inconsiderate credulity, which has turned the active industry of Mexico and Peru into such an improper channel. To this may be imputed the slender progress which Spanish America has made during two centuries and a half, either in useful manufactures, or in those lucrative branches of cultivation, which furnish the colonies of other nations with their staple commodities. In comparison with the precious metals, every bounty of nature is so much despised, that this extravagant idea of their value has mingled with the idiom of language in America, and the Spaniards settled there denominate a country *rich*, not from the fertility of its soil, the abundance of its crops, or the exuberance of its pastures, but on account of the minerals which its mountains contain. In quest of these, they abandon the delightful plains of Peru and Mexico, and resort to barren and uncomfortable regions, where they have built some of the largest towns which they possess in the New World. As the activity and enterprise of the Spaniards originally took this direction, it is now so difficult to bend them a different way, that although, from various causes, the gain of working mines is much decreased, the fascination continues, and almost every person, who takes any active part in the commerce of New Spain or Peru, is still engaged in some adventure of this kind [*].

But though mines are the chief object of the Spaniards, and the precious metals which these

* See Note CLXXXVI.

yield form the principal article in their commerce with America; the fertile countries which they possess there, abound with other commodities of such value or scarcity, as to attract a considerable degree of attention. Cochineal is a production almost peculiar to New Spain, of such demand in commerce, that the sale is always certain, and it yields such profit, as amply rewards the labour and care employed in rearing the curious insects of which this valuable drug is composed, and preparing it for the market. Quinquina, or Jesuits Bark, the most salutary simple, perhaps, and of most restorative virtue, that Providence, in compassion to human infirmity, has made known unto man, is found only in Peru, to which it affords a lucrative branch of commerce. The Indigo of Guatimala is superior in quality to that of any province in America, and cultivated to a considerable extent. Cacao, though not peculiar to the Spanish colonies, attains to its highest state of perfection there, and from the great consumption of chocolate in Europe, as well as in America, is a valuable commodity. The Tobacco of Cuba, of more exquisite flavour than any brought from the New World; the Sugar raised in that island, in Hispaniola, and in New Spain, together with drugs of various kinds, may be mentioned among the natural productions of America, which enrich the Spanish commerce. To these must be added, an article of no inconsiderable account, the exportation of hides; for which, as well as for many of those which I have enumerated, the Spaniards are more indebted to the wonderful fertility of the country than to their own foresight and industry. The domestic animals of Europe, particularly horned cattle, have multiplied in the New World with a rapidity which almost exceeds belief. A few years after the Spaniards settled there, the herds of tame cattle became so numerous, that their proprietors reckoned them by thousands *. Less attention being paid to them, as they continued to increase, they were suffered to run wild, and spreading over a country of boundless extent, under a mild climate, and covered with rich pasture, their number became immense. They range over the vast plains which extend from Buenos-Ayres, towards the Andes, in herds of thirty or forty thousand; and the unlucky traveller who once falls in among them, may proceed several days before he can disentangle himself from among the crowd that covers the face of the earth, and seems to have no end. They are hardly less numerous in New Spain, and in several other provinces: they are killed merely for the sake of their hides; and the slaughter at certain seasons is so great, that the stench of their carcases, which are left in the field, would infect the air, if large packs of wild dogs, and vast flocks of *gallinazos*, or American valtures, the most voracious of all the feathered kind, did not instantly devour them. The number of those hides exported in every fleet to Europe is very great, and is a lucrative branch of commerce †.

* Oviedo ap. Ramus. iii. 101, B Hackluyt. iii. 466. 511.
† Acosta, lib. iii. c. 33. Ovallo Hist. of Chili. Church. Collect. iii. 47. sep. Ibid. v. p. 680. 692. Lettres Edif. xiii. 235. Feuillé, i. 242.

Almost all these may be considered as staple commodities peculiar to America, and different, if we except that last mentioned, from the productions of the mother country.

When the importation into Spain of those various articles from her colonies first became active and considerable, her interior industry and manufactures were in a state so prosperous, that with the product of these she was able both to purchase the commodities of the New World, and to answer it growing demands. Under the reigns of Ferdinand and Isabella, and Charles V. Spain was one of the most industrious countries in Europe. Her manufactures in wool, and flax, and silk, were so extensive, as not only to furnish what was sufficient for her own consumption, but to afford a surplus for exportation. When a market for them, formerly unknown, and to which she alone had access, opened in America, she had recourse to her domestic store, and found there an abundant supply *. This new employment must naturally have added vivacity to the spirit of industry. Nourished and envigorated by it, the manufactures, the population, and wealth of Spain might have gone on increasing in the same proportion with the growth of her colonies. Nor was the state of the Spanish marine at this period less flourishing than that of its manufactures. In the beginning of the sixteenth century, Spain is said to have possessed above a thousand merchant ships †, a number probably far superior to that of any nation in Europe in that age. By the aid which foreign trade and domestic industry give reciprocally to each other

* See Note CLXXXVII. † Campomanes, ii. 140.

in their progress, the augmentation of both must have been rapid and extensive, and Spain might have received the same accession of opulence and vigour from her acquisitions in the New World, that other powers have derived from their colonies there.

But various causes prevented this. The same thing happens to nations as to individuals. Wealth, which flows in gradually, and with moderate increase, feeds and nourishes that activity which is friendly to commerce, and calls it forth into vigorous and well-conducted exertions; but when opulence pours in suddenly, and with too full a stream, it overturns all sober plans of industry, and brings along with it a taste for what is wild and extravagant, and daring in business or in action. Such was the great and sudden augmentation of power and revenue that the possession of America brought into Spain; and some symptoms of its pernicious influence upon the political operations of that monarchy soon began to appear. For a considerable time, however, the supply of treasure from the New World was scanty and precarious, and the genius of Charles V. conducted public measures with such prudence, that the effects of this influence were little perceived. But when Philip II. ascended the Spanish throne, with talents far inferior to those of his father, and remittances from the colonies became a regular and considerable branch of revenue, the fatal operation of this rapid change in the state of the kingdom, both on the monarch and his people, was at once conspicuous. Philip, possessing that spirit of unceasing assiduity, which often characterises the ambition of men of moderate talents, entertained such an high opinion of his own resources, that he thought nothing too arduous for him to undertake: Shut up himself in the solitude of the Escurial, he troubled and annoyed all the nations around him. He waged open war with the Dutch and English; he encouraged and aided a rebellious faction in France; he conquered Portugal, and maintained armies and garrisons in Italy, Africa, and both the Indies. By such a multiplicity of great and complicated operations, pursued with ardour during the course of a long reign, Spain was drained both of men and money. Under the weak administration of his successor, Philip III. the vigour of the nation continued to decrease, and sunk into the lowest decline, [A. D. 1611] when the inconsiderate bigotry of that monarch expelled at once near a million of his most industrious subjects, at the very time when the exhausted state of the kingdom required some extraordinary exertion of political wisdom to augment its numbers, and to revive its strength. Early in the seventeenth century, Spain felt such a diminution in the number of her people, that, from inability to recruit her armies, she was obliged to contract her operations. Her flourishing manufactures were fallen into decay. Her fleets, which had been the terror of all Europe, were ruined. Her extensive foreign commerce was lost. The trade between different parts of her own dominions was interrupted, and the ships which attempted to carry it on, were taken and plundered by enemies whom she once despised. Even agriculture, the primary object of industry in every prosperous state, was neglected, and one of the most fertile countries in Europe hardly raised what was sufficient for the support of its own inhabitants.

In proportion as the population and manufactures of the parent state declined, the demands of her colonies continued to increase. The Spaniards, like their monarchs, intoxicated with the wealth which poured in annually upon them, deserted the paths of industry, to which they had been accustomed, and repaired with eagerness to those regions from which this opulence issued. By this rage of emigration, another drain was opened, and the strength of the colonies augmented by exhausting that of the mother country. All those emigrants, as well as the adventurers who had at first settled in America, depended absolutely upon Spain for almost every article of necessary consumption. Engaged in more alluring and lucrative pursuits, or prevented by restraints which government imposed, they could not turn their own attention towards establishing the manufactures requisite for comfortable subsistence. They received (as I have observed in another place) their clothing, their furniture, whatever ministers to the ease or luxury of life, and even their instruments of labour, from Europe. Spain, thinned of people, and decreasing in industry, was unable to supply their growing demands. She had recourse to her neighbours. The manufactures of the Low Countries, of England, of France, and of Italy, which her wants called into existence, or animated with new vivacity, furnished in abundance whatever she required. In vain did the fundamental law, concerning the exclusion of foreign-

ers from trade with America, oppose this innovation. Necessity, more powerful than any sta-
tute, defeated its operations, and constrained the
Spaniards themselves to concur in eluding it.
The English, the French, and Dutch, relying
on the fidelity and honour of Spanish merchants,
who lend their names to cover the deceit, send
out their manufactures to America, and receive
the exorbitant price for which they are sold
there, either in specie, or in the rich commódi-
ties of the New World. Neither the dread of
danger, nor the allurement of profit, ever induced a Spanish factor to betray or defraud the
person who confided in him * ; and that probity,
which is the pride and distinction of the nation,
contributes to its ruin. In a short time, not
above a twentieth part of the commodities exported to America was of Spanish growth or
fabric † ; all the rest was the property of foreign merchants, though entered in the name
of Spaniards. The treasure of the New World
may be said henceforward not have belonged
to Spain. Before it reached Europe, it was an-
ticipated as the price of goods purchased from
foreigners. That wealth which, by an internal
circulation, would have spread through each vein
of industry, and have conveyed life and move-
ment to every branch of manufacture, flowed
out of the kingdom with such a rapid course, as
neither enriched nor animated it. On the other
hand, the artisans of rival nations, encouraged
by this quick sale of their commodities, improved so much in skill and industry, as to be
able to afford them at a rate so low, that the

* Zavala Representacion, p. 226. † Campomanes, ii. 158.

manufactures of Spain, which could not vie with theirs, either in quality or cheapness of work, were still farther depressed. This destructive commerce drained off the riches of the nation faster, and more completely, than even the extravagant schemes of ambition carried on by its monarchs. Spain was so much astonished and distressed, at beholding her American treasures vanish almost as soon as they were imported, that Philip III. unable to supply what was requisite in circulation, issued an edict, by which he endeavoured to raise copper money to a value in currency nearly equal to that of silver * ; and the lord of the Peruvian and Mexican mines was reduced to a wretched expedient, which is the last resource of petty impoverished states.

Thus the possessions of Spain in America have not proved a source of population and of wealth to her, in the same manner as those of other nations. In the countries of Europe, where the spirit of industry subsists in full vigour, every person settled in such colonies as are similar in their situation to those of Spain, is supposed to give employment to three or four at home in supplying his wants †. But wherever the mother country cannot afford this supply, every emigrant may be considered as a citizen lost to the community, and strangers must reap all the benefit of answering his demands.

Such has been the internal state of Spain from the close of the sixteenth century, and such her inability to supply the growing wants of her colonies. The fatal effects of this disproportion

* Uztarez, c. 104.   † Child on Trade and Colonies.

between their demands, and her capacity of answering them, have been much increased by the mode in which Spain has endeavoured to regulate the intercourse between the mother country and the colonies. It is from her idea of monopolizing the trade with America, and debarring her subjects there from any communication with foreigners, that all her jealous and systematic arrangements have arisen. These are so singular in their nature and consequences as to merit a particular explanation. In order to secure the monopoly at which she aimed, Spain did not vest the trade with her colonies in an exclusive company, a plan which has been adopted by nations more commercial, and at a period when mercantile policy was an object of greater attention, and ought to have been better understood. The Dutch gave up the whole trade with their colonies, both in the East and West Indies, to exclusive companies. The English, the French, the Danes, have imitated their example with respect to the East Indian commerce; and the two former have laid a similar restraint upon some branches of their trade with the New World. The wit of man cannot, perhaps, devise a method for checking the progress of industry and population in a new colony more effectual than this. The interest of the colony, and of the exclusive company, must in every point be diametrically opposite; and as the latter possesses such advantages in this unequal contest, that it can prescribe at pleasure the terms of intercourse, the former must not only buy dear and sell cheap, but must suffer the mortification of having the increase of its surplus stock discouraged by those very persons to whom alone it can dispose of its productions *.

Spain, it is probable, was preserved from falling into this error in policy, by the high ideas which she early formed concerning the riches of the New World. Gold and silver were commodities of too high value to vest a monopoly of them in private hands. The crown wished to retain the direction of a commerce so inviting; and, in order to secure that, ordained the cargo of every ship fitted out for America, to be inspected by the officers of the *Casa de Contratacion* in Seville, before it could receive a licence to make the voyage; and that on its return, a report of the commodities which it brought should be made to the same board, before it could be permitted to land them. In consequence of this regulation, all the trade of Spain with the New World centered originally in the port of Seville, and was gradually brought into a form, in which it has been conducted, with little variation, from the middle of the sixteenth century almost to our own times. For the greater security of the valuable cargoes sent to America, as well as for the more easy prevention of fraud, the commerce of Spain with its colonies is carried on by fleets which sail under strong convoys. These fleets, consisting of two squadrons, one distinguished by the name of the *Galeons*, the other by that of the *Flota*, are equipped annually. Formerly they took their departure from Seville; but as the port of Cadiz has been found more commodious, they have sailed from it since the year 1720.

* Smith's Inquiry. ii. 171.

The galeons destined to supply Tierra Firmé, and the kingdoms of Peru and Chili, with almost every article of luxury or necessary consumption that an opulent people can demand, touch first at Carthagena, and then at Porto-Bello. To the former, the merchants of Santa Martha, Caraccas, the New Kingdom of Granada, and several other provinces, resort. The latter is the great mart for the rich commerce of Peru and Chili. At the season when the galeons are expected, the product of all the mines in these two kingdoms, together with their other valuable commodities, is transported by sea to Panama. From thence, as soon as the appearance of the fleet from Europe is announced, they are conveyed across the isthmus, partly on mules, and partly down the river Chagre to Porto-Bello. This paltry village, the climate of which, from the pernicious union of excessive heat, continual moisture, and the putrid exhalations arising from a rank soil, is more fatal to life than any perhaps in the known world, is immediately filled with people. From being the residence of a few negroes and mulattoes, and of a miserable garrison relieved every three months, Porto-Bello assumes suddenly a very different aspect, and its streets are crowded with opulent merchants from every corner of Peru and the adjacent provinces. A fair is opened, the wealth of America is exchanged for the manufactures of Europe; and, during its prescribed term of forty days, the richest traffic on the face of the earth is begun and finished, with that simplicity of transaction, and that unbounded confidence, which accom-

pany extensive commerce *.   The Flota holds
its course to Vera Cruz.   The treasures and
commodities of New Spain and the depending
provinces, which were deposited at Puebla de
los Angeles in expectation of its arrival, are carried thither, and the commercial operations of
Vera Cruz, conducted in the same manner with
those of Porto-Bello, are inferior to them only
in importance and value.   Both fleets, as soon
as they have completed their cargoes from America, rendezvous at the Havanna, and return in
company to Europe.

The trade of Spain with her colonies, while
thus fettered and restricted, came necessarily to
be conducted with the same spirit, and upon the
same principles, as that of an exclusive company.
Being confined to a single port, it was of course
thrown into a few hands, and almost the whole
of it was gradually engrossed by a small number
of wealthy houses, formerly in Seville, and now
in Cadiz.   These by combinations, which they
can easily form, may altogether prevent that
competition which preserves commodities at their
natural price; and by acting in concert, to which
they are prompted by their mutual interest, they
may raise or lower the value of them at pleasure.
In consequence of this, the price of European
goods in America is always high, and often exorbitant.   A hundred, two hundred, and even
three hundred per cent. are profits not uncommon in the commerce of Spain with her colonies †.   From the same engrossing spirit it frequently happens, that traders of the second

* See Note CLXXXVIII.   † B. Ulloa Retabliss.
part ii. p. 191.

order, whose warehouses do not contain a complete assortment of commodities for the American market, cannot purchase from the more opulent merchants such goods as they want at a lower price than that for which they are sold in the colonies. With the same vigilant jealousy that an exclusive company guards against the intrusion of the free trader, those overgrown monopolists endeavour to check the progress of every one whose encroachments they dread. This restraint of the American commerce to one port, not only affects its domestic state, but limits its foreign operations. A monopolist may acquire more, and certainly will hazard less, by a confined trade which yields exorbitant profit, than by an extensive commerce, in which he receives only a moderate return of gain. It is often his interest not to enlarge, but to circumscribe the sphere of his activity ; and, instead of calling forth more vigorous exertions of commercial industry, it may be the object of his attention to check and set bounds to them. By some such maxim, the mercantile policy of Spain seems to have regulated its intercourse with America. Instead of furnishing the colonies with European goods in such quantity as might render both the price and the profit moderate ; the merchants of Seville and Cadiz seem to have supplied them with a sparing hand, that the eagerness of competition amongst customers obliged to purchase in a scanty market, might enable the Spanish factors to dispose of their cargoes with exorbitant gain. About the mid-

* Smith's Inquiry, ii. 171.   Campomanes, Educ. Popul. i. 438.

dle of the last century, when the exclusive trade
to America from Seville was in its most flourishing state, the burden of the two united squadrons of the Galeons and Flota did not exceed
twenty-seven thousand five hundred tons *. The
supply which such a fleet could carry, must have
been very inadequate to the demands of those
populous and extensive colonies, which depended
upon it for all the luxuries, and many of the
necessaries of life.

Spain early became sensible of her declension
from her former prosperity, and many respectable and virtuous citizens employed their thoughts
in devising methods for reviving the decaying industry and commerce of their country. From
the violence of the remedies proposed, we may
judge how desperate and fatal the malady appeared. Some, confounding a violation of police
with criminality against the state, contended,
that in order to check illicit commerce, every
person convicted of carrying it on, should be
punished with death and confiscation of all his
effects †. Others, forgetting the distinction between civil offences and acts of impiety, insisted,
that contraband trade should be ranked among
the crimes reserved for the cognizance of the Inquisition, that such as were guilty of it might
be tried and punished, according to the secret
and summary form in which that dreadful tribunal exercises its jurisdiction ‡. Others, un-
instructed by observing the pernicious effects of
monopolies in every country where they have

* Campomanes, Educ. Popul. i. 435. ii. 110.
† M. de Santa Cruz Commercia Suelto, p. 142.
‡ Moncada Restauracion politica de Espagna, p. 41.

been established, have proposed to vest the trade
with America in exclusive companies, which interest would render the most vigilant guardians
of the Spanish commerce against the encroachment of the interlopers *.

Besides these wild projects, many schemes,
better digested and more beneficial, were suggested. But, under the feeble monarchs with
whom the reign of the Austrian line in Spain
closed, incapacity and indecision are conspicuous
in every department of government. Instead of
taking for their model the active administration
of Charles V. they affected to imitate the cautious procrastinating wisdom of Philip II. and
destitute of his talents, they deliberated perpetually, but determined nothing. No remedy
was applied to the evils under which the national
commerce, domestic as well as foreign, languished.
These evils continued to increase, and Spain,
with dominions more extensive and more opulent
than any European state, possessed neither vigour, nor money †, nor industry. At length, the
violence of a great national convulsion roused
the slumbering genius of Spain. The efforts of
the two contending parties in the civil war,
kindled by the dispute concerning the succession
of the crown at the beginning of this century,
called forth, in some degree, the ancient spirit
and vigour of the nation. While men were thus
forming, capable of adopting sentiments more
liberal than those which had influenced the
councils of the monarchy during the course of a
century, Spain derived from an unexpected

* Zavalla y Augnon Representacion, &c. p. 190.
† See Note CLXXXIX.

source the means of availing itself of their talents. The various powers who favoured the pretensions either of the Austrian or Bourbon candidate for the Spanish throne, sent formidable fleets and armies to their support; France, England, and Holland, remitted immense sums to Spain. These were spent in the provinces which became the theatre of war. Part of the American treasure, of which foreigners had drained the kingdom, flowed back thither. From this era, one of the most intelligent Spanish authors dates the revival of the monarchy; and, however humiliating the truth may be, he acknowledges, that it is to her enemies his country is indebted for the acquisition of a fund of circulating specie, in some measure adequate to the exigencies of the public *.

As soon as the Bourbons obtained quiet possession of the throne, they discerned this change in the spirit of the people, and in the state of the nation, and took advantage of it; for although that family has not given monarchs to Spain remarkable for superiority of genius, they have all been beneficent princes, attentive to the happiness of their subjects, and solicitous to promote it. It was, accordingly, the first object of Philip V. to suppress an innovation which had crept in during the course of the war, and had overturned the whole system of the Spanish commerce with America. The English and Dutch, by their superiority in naval power, having acquired such command of the sea as to cut off all intercourse between Spain and her colonies, Spain, in order to furnish her subjects

* Campomanes, i. 420.

A a 3

in America those necessaries of life, without
which they could not exist, and as the only
means of receiving from thence any part of
their treasure, departed so far from the usual
rigour of its maxims as to open the trade with
Peru to her allies the French. The merchants
of St. Malo, to whom Louis XIV. granted the
privilege of this lucrative commerce, engaged in
it with vigour, and carried it on upon principles
very different from those of the Spaniards. They
supplied Peru with European commodities at a
moderate price, and not in stinted quantity.
The goods which they imported were conveyed
to every province of Spanish America, in such
abundance as had never been known in any
former period. If this intercourse had been continued, the exportation of European commodities from Spain must have ceased, and the dependence of the colonies on the mother country
have been at an end. The most peremptory injunctions were therefore issued [1713], prohibiting the admission of foreign vessels into any port
of Peru or Chili *, and a Spanish squadron was
employed to clear the South Sea of intruders,
whose aid was no longer necessary.

But though, on the cessation of the war,
which was terminated by the treaty of Utrecht,
Spain obtained relief from one encroachment on
her commercial system, she was exposed to ano-
ther, which she deemed hardly less pernicious.
As an inducement that might prevail with Queen
Anne to conclude a peace, which France and
Spain desired with equal ardour, Philip V. not

* Frezier Voy. 256.   B. Ulloa Retab. ii 104, &c. Alcedo y Ferrera. Aviso, &c. 236.

only conveyed to Great Britain the *Assiento*, or contract for supplying the Spanish colonies with negroes, which had formerly been enjoyed by France, but granted it the more extraordinary privilege of sending annually to the fair of Porto-Bello, a ship of five hundred tons, laden with European commodities. In consequence of this, British factories were established at Carthagena, Panama, Vera Cruz, Buenos Ayres, and other Spanish settlements. The veil with which Spain had hitherto covered the state and transactions of her colonies was removed. The agents of a rival nation, residing in the towns of most extensive trade, and of chief resort, had the best opportunities of becoming acquainted with the interior condition of the American provinces, of observing their stated and occasional wants, and of knowing what commodities might be imported into them with the greatest advantage. In consequence of information so authentic and expeditious, the merchants of Jamaica and other English colonies who traded to the Spanish main, were enabled to assort and proportion their cargoes so exactly to the demands of the market, that the contraband commerce was carried on with a facility, and to an extent unknown in any former period. This however was not the most fatal consequence of the Assiento to the trade of Spain. The agents of the British South-Sea Company, under cover of the importation which they were authorised to make by the ship sent annually to Porto-Bello, poured in their commodities on the Spanish continent without limitation or restraint. Instead of a ship of five hundred tons, as stipulated in the treaty, they usually employed one which exceeded nine hundred tons in burden. She was accompanied by two or three smaller vessels, which, mooring in some neighbouring creek, supplied her clandestinely with fresh bales of goods, to replace such as were sold. The inspectors of the fair, and officers of the revenue, gained by exorbitant presents, connived at the fraud *. Thus, partly by the operations of the company, and partly by the activity of private interlopers, almost the whole trade of Spanish America was engrossed by foreigners. The immense commerce of the Galeons, formerly the pride of Spain, and the envy of other nations, sunk to nothing, [1737] and the squadron itself, reduced from fifteen thousand to two thousand tons †, served hardly any purpose but to fetch home the royal revenue arising from the fifth on silver.

While Spain observed those encroachments, and felt so sensibly their pernicious effects, it was impossible not to make some effort to restrain them. Her first expedient was to station ships of force, under the appellation of *Guarda Costas,* upon the coasts of those provinces to which interlopers most frequently resorted. As private interest concurred with the duty which they owed to the public, in rendering the officers who commanded those vessels vigilant and active, some check was given to the progress of the contraband trade, though in dominions so extensive, and so accessible by sea, hardly any number of cruisers was sufficient to guard against its inroads

* See Note CXC.   † Alcedo y Herrera, p. 359.
Campomanes, i. 436.

in every quarter. This interruption of an intercourse which had been carried on with so
much facility, that the merchants in the British
colonies were accustomed to consider it almost as
an allowed branch of commerce, excited mur-
murs and complaints. These authorised, in
some measure, and rendered more interesting, by
several unjustifiable acts of violence committed
by the captains of the Spanish Guarda Costas,
precipitated Great Britain into a war with Spain
[1739]; in consequence of which the latter obtained a final release from the Assiento, and was
left at liberty to regulate the commerce of her
colonies, without being restrained by any engagement with a foreign power.

As the formidable encroachments of the English on their American trade, had discovered to
the Spaniards the vast consumption of European
goods in their colonies, and taught them the
advantage of accommodating their importations
to the occasional demand of the various provinces, they perceived the necessity of devising
some method of supplying their colonies different from their ancient one, of sending thither
periodical fleets. That mode of communication
had been found not only to be uncertain, as the
departure of the Galeons and Flota was sometimes retarded by various accidents, and often
prevented by the wars which raged in Europe;
but long experience had shewn it to be ill adapted to afford America a regular and timely supply of what it wanted. The scarcity of European goods in the Spanish settlements frequently became excessive; their price rose to an
enormous height; the vigilant eye of mercantile

attention did not fail to observe this favourable opportunity; an ample supply was poured in by interlopers from the English, the French, and Dutch islands; and when the Galeons at length arrived, they found the markets so glutted by this illicit commerce, that there was no demand for the commodities with which they were loaded. In order to remedy this, Spain has permitted a considerable part of her commerce with America to be carried on by *register ships*. These are fitted out, during the intervals between the stated seasons when the Galeons and Flota sail, by merchants in Seville or Cadiz, upon obtaining a licence from the council of the Indies, for which they pay a very high premium, and are destined for those ports in America where any extraordinary demand is foreseen or expected. By this expedient, such a regular supply of the commodities for which there is the greatest demand is conveyed to the American market, that the interloper is no longer allured by the same prospect of excessive gain, or the people in the colonies urged by the same necessity, to engage in the hazardous adventures of contraband trade.

In proportion as experience manifested the advantages of carrying on trade in this mode, the number of register ships increased; and at length, in the year 1748, the Galeons, after having been employed upwards of two centuries, were finally laid aside. From that period there has been no intercourse with Chili and Peru but by single ships, dispatched from time to time as occasion requires, and when the merchants expect a profitable market will open. These ships sail round Cape Horn, and convey directly to the ports of the South Sea the productions and manufactures of Europe, for which the people settled in those countries were formerly obliged to repair to Porto-Bello or Panama. These towns, as has been formerly observed, must gradually decline, when deprived of that commerce to which they owed their prosperity. This disadvantage however is more than compensated by the beneficial effects of this new arrangement, as the whole continent of South America receives new supplies of European commodities, with so much regularity, and in such abundance, as must not only contribute greatly to the happiness, but increase the population of all the colonies settled there. But as all the register ships destined for the South Sea, must still take their departure from Cadiz, and are obliged to return thither *, this branch of the American commerce, even in its new and improved form, continues subject to the restraints of a species of monopoly, and feels those pernicious effects of it, which I have already described.

Nor has the attention of Spain been confined to regulating the trade with its more flourishing colonies; it has extended likewise to the reviving commerce in those settlements where it was neglected, or had decayed. Among the new tastes which the people of Europe have acquired, in consequence of importing the productions of those countries which they conquered in America, that for chocolate is one of the most universal. The use of this liquor made with a paste, formed of the nut or almond of

* Campomanes, i. 43. 44.

the cacao-tree, compounded with various in-
gredients, the Spaniards first learned from the
Mexicans; and it has appeared to them, and to
the other European nations, so palatable, so
nourishing, and so wholesome, that it has become a commercial article of considerable importance.   The cacao tree grows spontaneously
in several parts of the torrid zone; but the nuts
of the best quality, next to those of Guatimala
on the South Sea, are produced in the rich plains
of Caraccas, a province of Tierra Firmè.   In
consequence of this acknowledged superiority in
the quality of cacao in that province, and its
communication with the Atlantic, which facili-
tates the conveyance to Europe, the culture of
the cacao there is more extensive than in any
district of America.   But the Dutch, by the
vicinity of their settlements in the small islands
of Curazoa and Buen-Ayre to the coast of Caraccas, gradually engrossed the greatest part of
the cacao trade.   The traffic with the mother
country for this valuable commodity ceased almost entirely; and such was the supine negli-
gence of the Spaniards, or the defects of their
commercial arrangements, that they were obliged
to receive from the hands of foreigners this production of their own colonies at an exorbitant
price.   In order to remedy an evil no less disgraceful than pernicious to his subjects, Philip V.
in the year 1728, granted to a body of merchants, an exclusive right to the commerce with
Caraccas and Cumana, on condition of their
employing, at their own expence, a sufficient
number of armed vessels to clear the coast of interlopers.   This society, distinguished sometimes

by the name of the Company of Guipuscoa,
from the province of Spain in which it is established, and sometimes by that of the Company
of Caraccas, from the district of America to
which it trades, has carried on its operations
with such vigour and success, that Spain has recovered an important branch of commerce, which
she had suffered to be wrested from her, and is
plentifully supplied with an article of extensive
consumption at a moderate price. Not only the
parent state, but the colony of Caraccas, has derived great advantages from this institution; for
although, at the first aspect, it may appear to
be one of those monopolies whose tendency is
to check the spirit of industry, instead of calling it forth to new exertions, it has been prevented from operating in this manner by several
salutary regulations, framed upon foresight of
such bad effects, and of purpose to obviate them.
The planters in the Caraccas are not left to depend entirely on the company, either for the
importation of European commodities, or the
sale of their own productions. The inhabitants
of the Canary islands have the privilege of sending thither annually a register ship of considerable burden; and from Vera Cruz in New
Spain, a free trade is permitted in every port
comprehended in the charter of the company.
In consequence of this, there is such a competition, that both with respect to what the colonies
purchase, and what they sell, the price seems
to be fixed at its natural and equitable rate.
The company has not the power of raising the
former, or of degrading the latter at pleasure;
and accordingly, since it was established, the

increase of culture, of population, and of live stock, in the province of Caraccas, has been very considerable *.

But as it is slowly that nations relinquish any system which time has rendered venerable, and as it is still more slowly that commerce can be diverted from the channel in which it has long been accustomed to flow; Philip V. in his new regulations concerning the American trade, paid such deference to the ancient maxim of Spain, concerning the limitation of all importation from the New World to one harbour, as to oblige both the register ships which returned from Peru, and those of the Guipuscoan Company from Caraccas, to deliver their cargoes in the port of Cadiz. Since his reign, sentiments more liberal and enlarged begin to spread in Spain. The spirit of philosophical inquiry, which it is the glory of the present age to have turned from frivolous or abstruse speculations to the business and affairs of men, has extended its influence beyond the Pyrenees. In the researches of ingenious authors, concerning the police or commerce of nations, the errors and defects of the Spanish system with respect to both met every eye, and have not only been exposed with severity, but are held up as a warning to other states. The Spaniards, stung with the reproaches of these authors, or convinced by their arguments, and admonished by several enlightened writers of their own country, seem at length to have discovered the destructive tendency of those narrow maxims, which, by cramping commerce in all its operations, have so long retarded its progress.

* See Note CXCI.

It is to the monarch now on the throne, that Spain is indebted for the first public regulation formed in consequence of such enlarged ideas.

While Spain adhered with rigour to her ancient maxims concerning her commerce with America, she was so much afraid of opening any channel by which an illicit trade might find admission into the colonies, that she almost shut herself out from any intercourse with them, but that which was carried on by her annual fleets. There was no establishment for a regular communication of either public or private intelligence between the mother country and its American settlements. From the want of this necessary institution, the operations of the state, as well as the business of individuals, were retarded or conducted unskilfully, and Spain often received from foreigners her first information with respect to very interesting events in her own colonies. But though this defect in police was sensibly felt, and the remedy for it was obvious, that jealous spirit with which the Spanish monarchs guarded the exclusive trade, restrained them from applying it. At length Charles III. surmounted those considerations which had deterred his predecessors, and in the year 1764 appointed packet-boats to be dispatched on the first day of each month, from Corugna to the Havanna or Porto-Rico. From thence letters are conveyed in smaller vessels to Vera Cruz and Porto-Bello, and transmitted by post through the kingdoms of Tierra Firmè, Granada, Peru, and New Spain. With no less regularity packet-boats sail once in two months to Rio de la Plata, for the accommodation of the provinces to the

Bb 2

east of the Andes. Thus provision is made for a speedy and certain circulation of intelligence throughout the vast dominions of Spain, from which equal advantages must redound to the political and mercantile interest of the kingdom *. With this new arrangement, a scheme of extending commerce has been more immediately connected. Each of the packet-boats, which are vessels of some considerable burden, is allowed to take in half a loading of such commodities as are the product of Spain, and most in demand in the ports whither they are bound. In return for these, they may bring home to Corugna an equal quantity of American productions †. This may be considered as the first relaxation of those rigid laws which confined the trade with the New World to a single port, and the first attempt to admit the rest of the kingdom to some share in it.

It was soon followed by one more decisive. In the year 1765, Charles III. laid open the trade to the windward islands, Cuba, Hispaniola, Porto-Rico, Margarita, and Trinidad, to his subjects in every province of Spain. He permitted them to sail from certain ports in each province, which are specified in the edict, at any season, and with whatever cargo they deemed most proper, without any other warrant than a simple clearance from the customhouse of the place whence they took their departure. He released them from the numerous and oppressive duties imposed on goods exported to America, and in place of the whole, substituted a moderate

* Ponz Viage de Espagna, vi. Prol. p. 15.
† Append. ii. a la Educ. Pop. p. 31.

tax of six in the hundred on the commodities sent from Spain. He allowed them to return either to the same port, or to any other where they might hope for a more advantageous market, and there to enter the homeward cargo, on payment of the usual duties. This ample privilege, which at once broke through all the fences which the jealous policy of Spain had been labouring, for two centuries and a half, to throw round its commercial intercourse with the New World, was soon after extended to Louisiana, and to the provinces of Yucatan and Campeachy *.

The propriety of this innovation, which may be considered as the most liberal effort of Spanish legislation, has appeared from its effects. Prior to the edict in favour of the free trade, Spain derived hardly any benefit from its neglected colonies in Hispaniola, Porto-Rico, Margarita, and Trinidad. Its commerce with Cuba was inconsiderable, and that of Yucatan and Campeachy was engrossed almost entirely by interlopers. But as soon as a general liberty of trade was permitted, the intercourse with those provinces revived, and has gone on with a rapidity of progression, of which there are few examples in the history of nations. In less than ten years, the trade of Cuba has been more than trebled. Even in those settlements where, from the languishing state of industry, greater efforts were requisite to restore its activity, their commerce has been doubled. It is computed, that such a number of ships is already employed in the free trade, that the tonnage of them far exceeds that

* Append. iL a la Educ. Pop. 37. 44. 91.

of the Galeons and Flota, at the most flourishing
era of their commerce.   The benefits of this arrangement are not confined to a few merchants,
established in a favourite port.   They are diffused through every province of the kingdom; and
by opening a new market for their various productions and manufactures, must encourage and
add vivacity to the industry of the farmer and
artificer.   Nor does the kingdom profit only by
what it exports; it derives advantage likewise
from what it receives in return, and has the prospect of being soon able to supply itself with several commodities of extensive consumption, for
which it formerly depended on foreigners.   The
consumption of sugar in Spain is perhaps as great
in proportion to the number of its inhabitants,
as that of any European kingdom.   But though
possessed of countries in the New World, whose
soil and climate are most proper for rearing the
sugar cane; though the domestic culture of that
valuable plant in the kingdom of Granada was
once considerable; such has been the fatal tendency of ill-judged institutions in America, and
such the pressure of improper taxes in Europe,
that Spain has lost almost entirely this branch of
industry, which has enriched other nations.
This commodity, which has now become an article of primary necessity in Europe, the Spaniards were obliged to purchase of foreigners,
and had the mortification to see their country
drained annually of great sums on that account *.
But if that spirit, which the permission of free
trade has put in motion, shall persevere in its
efforts with the same vigour, the cultivation of

* Uztariz, c. 94.

sugar in Cuba and Porto-Rico may increase so much, that in a few years, it is probable, that their growth of sugars may be equal to the demand of the kingdom.

Spain has been induced, by her experience of the beneficial consequences resulting from having relaxed somewhat of the rigour of her ancient laws with respect to the commerce of the mother country with the colonies, to permit a more liberal intercourse of one colony with another. By one of the jealous maxims of the old system, all the provinces situated on the South Seas were prohibited, under the most severe penalties, from holding any communication with one another. Though each of these yield peculiar productions, the reciprocal exchange of which might have added to the happiness of their respective inhabitants, or have facilitated their progress in industry, so solicitous was the Council of the Indies to prevent their receiving any supply of their wants but by the periodical fleets from Europe, that in order to guard against this, it cruelly debarred the Spaniards in Peru, in the southern provinces of New Spain, in Guatimala, and the New Kingdom of Granada, from such a correspondence with their fellow-subjects as tended manifestly to their mutual prosperity. Of all the numerous restrictions devised by Spain for securing the exclusive trade with her American settlements, none perhaps was more illiberal, none seems to have been more sensibly felt, or to have produced more hurtful effects. This grievance, coeval with the settlements of Spain in the countries situated on the Pacific Ocean, is at last redressed. In the year 1774, Charles III. published an edict, granting to the four great provinces which I have mentioned, the privilege of a free trade with each other *. What may be the effects of opening this communication between countries destined by their situation for reciprocal intercourse, cannot yet be determined by experience. They can hardly fail of being beneficial and extensive. The motives for granting this permission are manifestly no less laudable, than the principle on which it is founded is liberal ; and both discover the progress of a spirit in Spain, far elevated above the narrow prejudices and maxims on which her system for regulating the trade, and conducting the government of her colonies, was originally founded.

At the same time that Spain has been intent on introducing regulations, suggested by more enlarged views of policy, into her system of American commerce, she has not been inattentive to the interior government of her colonies. Here too there was much room for reformation and improvement ; and Don Joseph Galvez, who has now the direction of the department for Indian affairs in Spain, has enjoyed the best opportunities, not only of observing the defects and corruption in the political frame of the colonies, but of discovering the scources of those evils. After being employed seven years in the New World on an extraordinary mission, and with very extensive powers, as inspector-general of New Spain ; after visiting in person the remote provinces of Cinaloa, Sonora, and California, and making several important alterations

* Real Cedula. *penes me.* Ponz Viage de Espagna, vi· Prologo. p. 2. Note CXCII.

in the state of the police and revenue ; he began his ministry with a general reformation of the tribunals of justice in America.   In consequence of the progress of population and wealth in the colonies, the business of the Courts of Audience has increased so much, that the number of judges of which they were originally composed has been found inadequate to the growing labours and duties of the office, and the salaries settled upon them have been deemed inferior to the dignity of the station.   As a remedy for both, he obtained a royal edict, establishing an additional number of judges in each court of Audience, with higher titles, and more ample appointments *.

To the same intelligent minister Spain is indebted for a new distribution of government in its American provinces.   Even since the establishment of a third viceroyalty in the New Kingdom of Granada, so great is the extent of the Spanish dominions in the New World, that several places subject to the jurisdiction of each viceroy, were at such an enormous distance from the capitals in which they resided, that neither their attention, nor their authority, could reach so far.   Some provinces subordinate to the viceroy of New Spain, lay above two thousand miles from Mexico.   There were countries subject to the viceroy of Peru still farther from Lima. The people in those remote districts could hardly be said to enjoy the benefit of civil government. The oppression and insolence of its inferior ministers they often feel, and rather submit to these

* Gazeta de Madrid, 19th March 1776.

in silence, than involve themselves in the expence and trouble of resorting to the distant capitals, where alone they can find redress.   As a remedy for this, a fourth viceroyalty has been erected [Aug. 1776], to the jurisdiction of which are subjected the provinces of Rio de la Plata, Buenos-Ayres, Paraguay, Tucuman, Potosi, St. Cruz de la Sierra, Charcas, and the towns of Mendoza and St Juan.   By this well-judged arrangement two advantages are gained.   All the inconveniences occasioned by the remote situation of those provinces, which had been long felt, and long complained of, are, in a great measure, removed.   The countries most distant from Lima are separated from the viceroyalty of Peru, and united under a superior, whose seat of government at Buenos-Ayres will be commodious and accessible.   The contraband trade with the Portuguese, which was become so extensive as must have put a final stop to the exportation of commodities from Spain to her southern colonies, may be checked more thoroughly, and with greater facility, when the supreme magistrate, by his vicinity to the places in which it is carried on, can view its progress and effects with his own eyes.   Don Pedro Zevallos, who has been raised to this new dignity, with appointments equal to those of the other viceroys, is well acquainted both with the state and the interest of the countries over which he is to preside, having served in them long, and with distinction.   By this dismemberment, succeeding that which took place at the erection of the viceroyalty of the New Kingdom of Granada, almost two third parts of the territories, originally subject to the viceroys of Peru, are now lopped off from their jurisdiction.

The limits of the viceroyalty of New Spain have likewise been considerably circumscribed, and with no less propriety and discernment. Four of its most remote provinces, Sonora, Cinaloa, California, and New Navarre, have been formed into a separate government. The Chevalier de Croix, who is entrusted with this command, is not dignified with the title of viceroy, nor does he enjoy the appointments belonging to that rank, but his jurisdiction is altogether independent on the viceroyalty of New Spain. The erection of this last government seems to have been suggested, not only by the consideration of the remote situation of those provinces from Mexico, but by attention to the late discoveries made there, which I have mentioned *. Countries containing the richest mines of gold that have hitherto been discovered in the New World, and which probably may arise into great importance, required the immediate inspection of a governor, to whom they should be specially committed. As every consideration of duty, of interest, and of vanity, must concur in prompting those new governors to encourage such exertions as tend to diffuse opulence and prosperity through the provinces committed to their charge, the beneficial effects of this arrangement may be considerable. Many districts in America, long depressed by the languor and feebleness natural to the provinces which compose the extremities of an overgrown empire, may be animated with vigour and activity, when brought so near the

* Book vii. vol. iii. p. 186.

seat of power as to feel its invigorating influence.

Such, since the accession of the princes of the House of Bourbon to the throne of Spain, has been the progress of their regulations, and the gradual expansion of their views, with respect to the commerce and government of their American colonies. Nor has their attention been so entirely engrossed by what related to the more remote parts of their dominions, as to render them neglectful of what was still more important, the reformation of domestic errors and defects in policy. Fully sensible of the causes to which the declension of Spain from her former prosperity ought to be imputed, they have made it a great object of their policy to revive a spirit of industry among their subjects, and to give such extent and perfection to their manufactures, as may enable them to supply the demands of America from their own stock, and to exclude foreigners from a branch of commerce which has been so fatal to the kingdom. This they have endeavoured to accomplish, by a variety of edicts issued since the peace of Utrecht. They have granted bounties for the encouragement of some branches of industry; they have lowered the taxes on others; they have either entirely prohibited, or have loaded with additional duties, such foreign manufactures as come in competition with their own; they have instituted societies for the improvement of trade and agriculture; they have planted colonies of husbandmen in some uncultivated districts of Spain, and divided among them the waste fields; they have had recourse to every expedient, de-

vised by commercial wisdom, or commercial jealousy, for reviving their own industry, and dis-
countenancing that of other nations. These,
however, it is not my province to explain, or to
inquire into their propriety and effects. There
is no effort of legislation more arduous, no experiment in policy more uncertain, than an attempt to revive the spirit of industry where it
has declined, or to introduce it where it is unknown. Nations already possessed of extensive
commerce, enter into competition with such advantages, derived from the large capitals and
extensive credit of their merchants, the dexterity
of their manufacturers, the alertness acquired by
habit in every department of business, that the
state which aims at rivalling or supplanting
them, must expect to struggle with many difficulties, and be content to advance slowly. If
the quantity of productive industry, now in
Spain, be compared with that of the kingdom
under the last listless monarchs of the Austrian
line, its progress must appear considerable, and
is sufficient to alarm the jealousy, and to call
forth the most vigorous efforts, of the nations
now in possession of the lucrative trade which
the Spaniards aim at wresting from them. One
circumstance may render those exertions of Spain
an object of more serious attention to the other
European powers. They are not to be ascribed
wholly to the influence of the crown and its
ministers. The sentiments and spirit of the people seem to second the provident care of their
monarchs, and to give it greater effect. The
nation has adopted more liberal ideas, not only
with respect to commerce, but domestic policy.

In all the later Spanish writers, defects in the arrangements of their country concerning both are acknowledged, and remedies proposed, which ignorance rendered their ancestors incapable of discerning, and pride would not have allowed them to confess *. But after all that the Spaniards have done, much remains to do. Many pernicious institutions and abuses, deeply incorporated with the system of internal policy and taxation which has been long established in Spain, must be abolished, before industry and manufactures can recover an extensive activity.

Still, however, the commercial regulations of Spain with respect to her colonies, are too rigid and systematical to be carried into complete execution. The legislature that loads trade with impositions too heavy, or fetters it by restrictions too severe, defeats its own intention, and is only multiplying the inducements to violate its statutes, and proposing an high premium to encourage illicit traffic. The Spaniards, both in Europe and America, being circumscribed in their mutual intercourse by the jealousy of the crown, or oppressed by its exactions, have their invention continually on the stretch how to elude its edicts. The vigilance and ingenuity of private interest discover means of effecting this, which public wisdom cannot foresee, nor public authority prevent. This spirit counteracting that of the laws, pervades the commerce of Spain with America in all its branches ; and from the highest departments in government, descends to the lowest. The very officers appointed to check contraband trade, are often employed as instru-

* See Note CXCIII.

ments in carrying it on; and the boards instituted to restrain and punish it, are the channels
through which it flows.   The king is supposed,
by the most intelligent Spanish writers, to be de-
frauded, by various artifices, of more than one
half of the revenue which he ought to receive
from America * ; and as long as it is the interest
of so many persons to screen those artifices from
detection, the knowledge of them will never
reach the throne.   " How many ordinances,"
says Corita, " how many instructions, how many
" letters from our sovereign, are sent in orde
" to correct abuses, and how little are they ob
" served, and what small advantage is derived
" from them.   To me the old observation ap-
" pears just, that where there are many physi-
" cians, and many medicines, there is a want
" of health ; where there are many laws, and
" many judges, there is want of justice.   We
" have viceroys, presidents, governors, oydors,
" corrigidors, alcaldes, and thousands of algua-
" zils abound everywhere ; but notwithstanding
" all these, public abuses continue to multi-
" ply †."   Time has increased the evils which
he lamented as early as the reign of Philip II.
A spirit of corruption has infected all the colonies of Spain in America.   Men far removed
from the seat of government ; impatient to acquire wealth, that they may return speedily from
what they are apt to consider as a state of exile
in a remote unhealthful country ; allured by opportunities too tempting to be resisted, and seduced by the example of those around them ;
find their sentiments of honour and of duty gra-

* Solorz. de Ind. Jure, ii. lib. v.   † MS. penes me.

dually relax. In private life, they give themselves up to a dissolute luxury, while in their public conduct they become unmindful of what they owe to their sovereign and to their country.

Before I close this account of the Spanish trade in America, there remains one detached, but important branch of it, to be mentioned. Soon after his accession to the throne, Philip II. formed a scheme of planting a colony in the Philippine islands, which had been neglected since the time of their discovery; and he accomplished it by means of an armament fitted out from New Spain *, [1564]. Manila, in the island of Luconia, was the station chosen for the capital of this new establishment. From it an active commercial intercourse began with the Chinese, and a considerable number of that industrious people, allured by the prospect of gain, settled in the Philippine islands under the Spanish protection. They supplied the colony so amply with all the valuable productions and manufactures of the East, as enabled it to open a trade with America, by a course of navigation the longest from land to land on our globe. In the infancy of this trade, it was carried on with Callao, on the coast of Peru; but experience having discovered the impropriety of fixing upon that as the port of communication with Manila, the staple of the commerce between the east and west was removed from Callao to Acapulco, on the coast of New Spain.

After various arrangements, it has been brought into a regular form. One or two ships depart annually from Acapulco, which are per-

* Torquem. i. lib. v. c. 14.

mitted to carry out silver to the amount of five
hundred thousand pesos *, but they have hardly
any thing else of value on board ; in return for
which, they bring back spices, drugs, china,
and japan wares, calicoes, chintz, muslins, silks,
and every precious article, with which the benignity of the climate, or the ingenuity of its
people, has enabled the East to supply the rest
of the world.   For some time the merchants of
Peru were admitted to participate in this traffic,
and might send annually a ship to Acapulco, to
wait the arrival of the vessels from Manila, and
receive a proportional share of the commodities
which they imported. At length, the Peruvians
were excluded from this trade by most rigorous
edicts, and all the commodities from the East
reserved solely for the consumption of New
Spain.

In consequence of this indulgence, the inhabitants of that country enjoy advantages unknown
in the other Spanish colonies.   The manufactures
of the East are not only more suited to a warm
climate, and more showy than those of Europe,
but can-be sold at a lower price ; while, at the
same time, the profits upon them are so considerable, as to enrich all those who are employed
either in bringing them from Manila, or vending
them in New Spain.   As the interest both of
the buyer and seller concurred in favouring this
branch of commerce, it has continued to extend,
in spite of regulations concerted with the most
anxious jealousy to circumscribe it.   Under cover
of what the laws permit to be imported, great
quantities of India goods are poured into the

* Recop. lib. ix. c. 45. l. 6.

markets of New Spain * ; and when the flota arrives at Vera Cruz from Europe, it often finds the wants of the people already supplied by cheaper and more acceptable commodities.

There is not, in the commercial arrangements of Spain, any circumstance more inexplicable than the permission of this trade between New Spain and the Philippines, or more repugnant to its fundamental maxim of holding the colonies in perpetual dependence on the mother country, by prohibiting any commercial intercourse that might suggest to them the idea of receiving a supply of their wants from any other quarter. This permission must appear still more extraordinary, from considering that Spain herself carries on no direct trade with her settlements in the Philippines, and grants a privilege to one of her American colonies which she denies to her subjects in Europe. It is probable, that the colonists, who originally took possession of the Philippines, having been sent out from New Spain, begun this intercourse with a country which they considered, in some measure, as their parent state, before the court of Madrid was aware of its consequences, or could establish regulations in order to prevent it. Many remonstrances have been presented against this trade, as detrimental to Spain, by diverting into another channel a large portion of that treasure which ought to flow into the kingdom, as tending to give rise to a spirit of independence in the colonies, and to encourage innumerable frauds, against which it is impossible to guard, in transactions so far removed from the inspection of

* See Note CXCIV.

government.   But as it requires no slight effort
of political wisdom and vigour to abolish any
practice which numbers are interested in supporting, and to which time has added the sanction of its authority, the commerce between
New Spain and Manila seems to be as considerable as ever, and may be considered as one chief
cause of the elegance and splendour conspicuous
in this part of the Spanish dominions.

But notwithstanding this general corruption
in the colonies of Spain, and the diminution of
the income belonging to the public, occasioned
by the illicit importations made by foreigners
as well as by the various frauds of which the colonists themselves are guilty in their commerce
with the parent state, the Spanish monarchs receive a very considerable revenue from their
American dominions.   This arises from taxes of
various kinds, which may be divided into three
capital branches.   The first contains what is
paid to the king, as sovereign, or superior lord
of the New World : to this class belongs the
duty on the gold and silver raised from the mines,
and the tribute exacted from the Indians ; the
former is termed by the Spaniards the *right of
signiory*, the latter is the *duty on vassalage*.   The
second branch comprehends the numerous duties
upon commerce, which accompany and oppress
it in every step of its progress, from the greatest
transactions of the wholesale merchant to the
petty traffic of the vender by retail.   The third
includes what accrues to the king, as head of the
church, and administrator of ecclesiastical funds
in the New World.   In consequence of this, he
receives the first-fruits, annates, spoils, and other

spiritual revenues, levied by the apostolic chamber in Europe ; and is entitled, likewise, to the profit arising from the sale of the bull of Cruzado.   This bull, which is published every two years, contains an absolution from past offences by the pope, and, among other immunities, a permission to eat several kinds of prohibited food, during Lent, and on meagre days.   The monks employed in dispersing those bulls, extol their virtues with all the fervour of interested eloquence ; the people, ignorant and credulous, listen with implicit assent ; and every person in the Spanish colonies, of European, Creolian, or mixed race, purchases a bull, which is deemed essential to his salvation, at the rate set upon it by government *.

What may be the amount of those various funds, it is almost impossible to determine with precision.   The extent of the Spanish dominions in America, the jealousy of government, which renders them inaccessible to foreigners, the mysterious silence which the Spaniards are accustomed to observe with respect to the interior state of their colonies, combine in covering this subject with a veil which it is not easy to remove. But an account, apparently no less accurate than it is curious, has lately been published of the royal revenue in New Spain, from which we may form some idea with respect to what is collected in the other provinces.   According to that account, the crown does not receive from all the departments of taxation in New Spain above a million of our money, from which one half must be deducted as the expence of the provincial

* See Note CXCV.

establishment *. Peru, it is probable, yields a sum not inferior to this ; and if we suppose that all the other regions of America, including the islands, furnish a third share of equal value, we shall not perhaps be far wide from the truth, if we conclude, that the net public revenue of Spain, raised in America, does not exceed a million and a half sterling. This falls far short of the immense sums to which suppositions, founded upon conjecture, have raised the Spanish revenue in America †. It is remarkable, however, upon one account. Spain and Portugal are the only European powers who derive a direct revenue from their colonies. All the advantage that accrues to other nations from their American dominions, arises from the exclusive enjoyment of their trade ; but beside this, Spain has brought her colonies to contribute towards increasing the power of the state ; and in return for protection, to bear a proportional share of the common burden.

Accordingly, the sum which I have computed to be the amount of the Spanish revenue from America, arises wholly from the taxes collected there, and is far from being the whole of what accrues to the king from his dominions in the New World. The heavy duties imposed on the commodities exported from Spain to America ‡, as well as what is paid by those which she sends home in return ; the tax upon the negro slaves, with which Africa supplies the New World, together with several smaller branches of finance, bring large sums into the treasury, the precise

* See Note CXCVI.   † See Note CXCVII.
‡ See Note CXCVIII.

extent of which I cannot pretend to ascertain.

But if the revenue which Spain draws from America be great, the expence of administration in her colonies bears proportion to it. In every department, even of her domestic police and finances, Spain has adopted a system more complex, and more encumbered with a variety of tribunals, and a multitude of officers, than that of any European nation, in which the sovereign possesses such extensive power. From the jealous spirit with which Spain watches over her American settlements, and her endeavours to guard against fraud in provinces so remote from inspection, boards and officers have been multiplied there with still more anxious attention. In a country where the expence of living is great, the salaries allotted to every person in public office must be high, and must load the revenue with an immense burden. The parade of government greatly augments the weight of it. The viceroys of Mexico, Peru, and the New Kingdom of Granada, as representatives of the king's person, among people fond of ostentation, maintain all the state and dignity of royalty. Their courts are formed upon the model of that at Madrid, with horse and foot guards, a household regularly established, numerous attendants, and ensigns of power, displaying such pomp as hardly retains the appearance of a delegated authority. All the expence incurred by supporting the external and permanent order of government is defrayed by the crown. The viceroys have besides peculiar appointments suited to their exalted station. The salaries fixed by law are indeed extremely moderate; that of the viceroy of Peru is only thirty thousand ducats; and that of the viceroy of Mexico, twenty thousand ducats *. Of late they have been raised to forty thousand.

These salaries, however, constitute but a small part of the revenue enjoyed by the viceroys. The exercise of an absolute authority extending to every department of government, and the power of disposing of many lucrative offices, afford them many opportunities of accumulating wealth. To these, which may be considered as legal and allowed emoluments, large sums are often added by exactions, which, in countries so far removed from the seat of government, it is not easy to discover, and impossible to restrain. By monopolizing some branches of commerce, by a lucrative concern in others, by conniving at the frauds of merchants, a viceroy may raise such an annual revenue, as no subject of any European monarch enjoys †. From the single article of presents made to him on the anniversary of his *Name day* (which is always observed as an high festival), I am informed that a viceroy has been known to receive sixty thousand pesos. According to a Spanish saying, the legal revenues of a viceroy are known, his real profits depend upon his opportunities and his conscience. Sensible of this, the kings of Spain, as I have formerly observed, grant a commission to their viceroys only for a few years. This circumstance, however, renders them often more rapacious, and adds to the ingenuity and ardour wherewith they labour to improve every moment of power, which they know is hastening fast to a

* Recop. lib. iii. tit. iii. c. 72.   † See Note CXCIX.

period; and short as its duration is, it usually affords sufficient time for repairing a shattered fortune, or for creating a new one.   But even in situations so trying to human frailty, there are instances of virtue that remain unseduced: In the year 1772, the Marquis de Croix finished the term of his viceroyalty in New Spain with unsuspected integrity ; and instead of bringing home exorbitant wealth, returned with the admiration and applause of a grateful people, whom his government had rendered happy.

NOTES

AND

ILLUSTRATIONS.

NOTE CXXVIII. p. 5.

By this time horses had multiplied greatly in the Spanish settlements on the continent. When Cortes began his expedition in the year 1518, though his armament was more considerable than that of Pizarro, and composed of persons superior in rank to those who invaded Peru, he could procure no more than sixteen horses.

NOTE CXXIX. p. 6.

In the year 1740, D. Ant. Ulloa and D. George Juan travelled from Guayquil to Motupe, by the same route which Pizarro took. From the description of their journey, one may form an idea of the difficulty of his march. The sandy plains between St. Michael de Pieura and Motupe extend 90 miles, without water, without a tree, a plant, or any green thing, on a dreary stretch of burning sand. Voyage, tom. ii p. 399, &c.

NOTE CXXX. p. 12.

This extravagant and unseasonable discourse of Valverde has been censured by all historians, and with justice. But though he seems to have been an illiterate and bigoted monk, nowise resembling the good Olmedo, who accompanied Cortes, the absurdity of his address to Atahualpa must not be charged wholly upon him. His harangue is evidently a translation or paraphrase of that form, concerted by a junto of Spanish divines and lawyers, in the year 1509, for explaining the right of their king to the sovereignty of the New World, and for directing the officers employed in America how they

should take possession of any new country.   See Vol. i.
Note xxiii.   The sentiments contained in Valverde's
harangue must not then be imputed to the bigoted imbe-
cility of a particular man, but to that of the age.   But
Gomara and Benzoni relate one circumstance concerning Valverde, which, if authentic, renders him an object, not of contempt only, but of horror.   They assert,
that during the whole action, Valverde continued to excite the soldiers to slaughter, calling to them to strike
the enemy, not with the edge, but with the points of their
swords.   Gom. Cron. c. 113.   Benz. Histor. Nov. Orbis,
lib. iii. c. 3.   Such behaviour was very different from
that of the Roman Catholic clergy in other parts of A-
merica, where they uniformly exerted their influence to
protect the Indians, and to moderate the ferocity of
their countrymen.

NOTE XXXI. p. 13.

Two different systems have been formed concerning
the conduct of Atahualpa.   The Spanish writers, in order to justify the violence of their countrymen, contend,
that all the Inca's professions of friendship were feigned;
and that his intention in agreeing to an interview with
Pizarro at Caxamalca, was to cut off him and his followers at one blow; that for this purpose he advanced
with such a numerous body of attendants who had arms
concealed under their garments, to execute this scheme.
This is the account given by Xerez and Zarate, and a-
dopted by Herrera.   But if it had been the plan of the
Inca to destroy the Spaniards, one can hardly imagine
that he would have permitted them to march unmolested through the desert of Motupe, or have neglected to
defend the passes in the mountains, where they might
have been attacked with so much advantage.   If the Peruvians marched to Caxamalca with an intention to fall
upon the Spaniards, it is inconceivable, that of so great
a body of men prepared for action, not one should attempt to make resistance, but all tamely suffer themselves to be butchered by an enemy whom they were
armed to attack.   Atahualpa's mode of advancing to
the interview, has the aspect of a peaceable procession,
not of a military enterprise.   He himself and his followers were, in their habits of ceremony, preceded, as

on days of solemnity, by unarmed harbingers. Though rude nations are frequently cunning and false, yet, it a scheme of deception and treachery must be imputed, either to a monarch that had no great reason to be alarmed at a visit from strangers who solicited admission into his presence as friends, or to an adventurer so daring and so little scrupulous as Pizarro, one cannot hesitate in determining where to fix the presumption of guilt. Even amidst the endeavours of the Spanish writers to palliate the proceedings of Pizarro, one plainly perceives, that it was his intention, as well as his interest, to seize the Inca, and that he had taken measures for that purpose, previous to any suspicion of that monarch's designs.

Garcilasso de la Vega, extremely solicitous to vindicate his countrymen, the Peruvians, from the crime of having concerted the destruction of Pizarro and his followers, and no less afraid to charge the Spaniards with improper conduct towards the Inca, has framed another system. He relates, that a man of majestic form, with a long beard, and garments reaching to the ground, having appeared in a vision to Viracocha, the eighth Inca, and declared that he was a child of the Sun, that monarch built a temple in honour of his person, and erected an image of him, resembling as nearly as possible the singular form in which he had exhibited himself to his view. In this temple, divine honours were paid to him by the name of Viracocha. P. i. lib. iv. c. 21. lib. v. c. 22. When the Spaniards first appeared in Peru, the length of their beards, and the dress they wore, struck every person so much with their likeness to the image of Viracocha, that they supposed them to be children of the Sun, who had descended from heaven to earth. All concluded, that the fatal period of the Peruvian empire was now approaching, and that the throne would be occupied by new possessors. Atahualpa himself considering the Spaniards as messengers from heaven, was so far from entertaining any thoughts of resisting them, that he determined to yield implicit obedience to their commands. From those sentiments flowed his professions of love and respect. To those were owing the cordial reception of Soto and Ferdinand Pizarro in his camp, and the submissive reverence with which he himself advanced to visit the Spanish general in his quarters; but from the gross ignorance of Philippillo the interpreter, the declaration of the Spaniards, and his answer to it, were so ill explained, that by their mutual inability to comprehend each other's intentions, the fatal rencounter at Caxamalca, with all its dreadful consequences, was occasioned.

It is remarkable, that no traces of this superstitious veneration of the Peruvians for the Spaniards, are to be found either in Xerez, or Sancho, or Zarate, previous to the interview at Caxamalca; and yet the two former served under Pizarro at that time, and the latter visited Peru soon after the conquest. If either the Inca himself, or his messengers, had addressed the Spaniards in the words which Garcilasso puts in their mouths, they must have been struck with such submissive declarations; and they would certainly have availed themselves of them to accomplish their own designs with greater facility. Garcilasso himself, though his narrative of the intercourse between the Inca and Spaniards, preceding the rencounter at Caxamalca, is founded on the supposition of his believing them to be Viracochas, or divine beings, p. 2. lib. i. c. 17, &c. yet with his usual inattention and inaccuracy he admits, in another place, that the Peruvians did not recollect the resemblance between them and the god Viracocha, until the fatal disasters subsequent to the defeat at Caxamalca, and then only began to call them Viracochas. P. i. lib. v. c. 21. This is confirmed by Herrera, dec. 5. lib. ii. c. 12. In many different parts of America, if we may believe the Spanish writers, their countrymen were considered as divine beings who had descended from heaven. But in this instance, as in many which occur in the intercourse between nations whose progress in refinement is very unequal, the ideas of those who used the expression were different from the ideas of those who heard it. For such is the idiom of the Indian languages, or such is the simplicity of those who speak them, that when they see any thing with which they were formerly unacquainted, and of which they do not know the origin, they say, that it came down from heaven. Nugnez, Ram. iii. 327, C.

The account which I have given of the sentiments and proceedings of the Peruvians, appears to be more natural and consistent than either of the two preceding, and is better supported by the facts related by the contemporary historians.

According to Xerez, p. 200, two thousand Peruvians were killed. Sancho makes the number of the slain six or seven thousand. Ram. iii. 274. D. By Garcilasso's account, five thousand were massacred. P. ii. lib. i. c. 25. The number which I have mentioned. being the medium between the extremes, may probably be nearest the truth.

NOTE CXXXII. p. 14.

NOTHING can be a more striking proof of this, than that three Spaniards travelled from Caxamalça to Cuzco. The distance between them is six hundred miles. In every place throughout this great extent of country, they were treated with all the honours which the Peruvians paid to their sovereigns, and even to their divinities. Under pretext of amassing what was wanting for the ransom of the Inca, they demanded the plates of gold with which the walls of the Temple of the Sun in Cuzco were adorned; and though the priests were unwilling to alienate those sacred ornaments, and the people refused to violate the shrine of their god, the three Spaniards, with their own hands, robbed the temple, of part of this valuable treasure: and such was the reverence of the natives for their persons, that though they beheld this act of sacrilege with astonishment, they did not attempt to prevent or disturb the commission of it. Zarate, lib. ii. c. 6. Sancho ap. Ramus. iii. 373. D.

NOTE CXXXIII. p. 26.

ACCORDING to Herrera, the spoil of Cuzco, after setting apart the king's *fifth*, was divided among 480 persons. Each received 4000 pesos. This amounts to 1,920,000 pesos. Dec. 5. lib. vi. c 3. But as the general, and other officers, were entitled to a share far greater than that of the private men, the sum total must have risen much beyond what I have mentioned. Gomara, c. 123, and Zarate, lib. ii. c. 8. satisfy themselves with asserting in general, that the plunder of Cuzco was of greater value than the ransom of Atahualpa.

NOTE CXXXIV. p. 28.

No expedition in the New World was conducted with more persevering courage than that of Alvarado, and in none were greater hardships endured. Many of the persons engaged in it were, like their leader, veterans who had served under Cortes, inured to all the rigour of American war. Such of my readers as have not an opportunity of perusing the striking description of their sufferings by Zarate or Herrera, may form some idea of the nature of their march from the sea-coast to Quito, by consulting the account which D. Ant. Ulloa gives of his own journey in 1736, nearly in the same route. Voy. tom. i. p. 178. &c. or that of M. Bouguer, who proceeded from Puerto Viejo to Quito, by the same road which Alvarado took. He compares his own journey with that of the Spanish leader, and by the comparison gives a most striking idea of the boldness and patience of Alvarado, in forcing his way through so many obstacles. Voyage du Perou, p. 28, &c.

NOTE CXXXV. p. 29.

According to Herrera, there were entered on account of the king in gold, 155,300 pesos, and 5400 marks, (each 8 ounces) of silver, besides several vessels and ornaments, some of gold, and others of silver; on account of private persons, in gold, 499,000 pesos, and 54,000 marks of silver. Dec. 5. lib. vi. c. 13.

NOTE CXXXVI. p. 37.

The Peruvians not only imitated the military arts of the Spaniards, but had recourse to devices of their own. As the cavalry were the chief object of their terror, they endeavoured to render them incapable of acting, by means of a long thong with a stone fastened to each end. This, when thrown by a skilful hand, twisted about the horse and its rider, and entangled them so as to obstruct their motions. Herrera mentions this as an invention of their own. Dec. 5. lib. viii. c. 4. But as I have observed, vol. ii. book iv. this weapon is common among several barbarous tribes towards the extremity of South America; and it is more probable, that the Peruvians had observed the dexterity with which they used it in hunting, and on this occasion adopted it themselves. The Spaniards were considerably annoyed by it, Herrera. ibid. Another instance of the ingenuity of the Peruvians deserves mention: By turning a river out of its channel, they overflowed a valley, in which a body of the enemy was posted, so suddenly, that it was with the utmost difficulty the Spaniards made their escape. Herrera, dec. 5. lib. viii. c. 5.

NOTE CXXXVII. p. 56.

Herrera's account of Orellana's voyage is the most minute, and apparently the most accurate. It was probably taken from the journal of Orellana himself. But the dates are not distinctly marked. His navigation down the Coca, or Napo, begun early in February 1541; and he arrived at the mouth of the river on the 26th of August, having spent near seven months in the voyage. M. de la Condamine, in the year 1743, sailed from Cuenca to Para, a settlement of the Portuguese at the mouth of the river, a navigation much longer than that of Orellana, in less than four months. Voyage, p. 179. But the two adventurers were very differently provided for the voyage. This hazardous undertaking, to which ambition prompted Orellana, and to which the love of science led M. de la Condamine, was undertaken in the year 1769, by Madame Godin des Odonais, from conjugal affection. The narrative of the hardships which she suffered, of the dangers to which she was exposed, and of the disasters which befel her, is one of the most singular and affecting stories in any language, exhibiting in her conduct a striking picture of the fortitude which distinguishes the one sex, mingled with the sensibility and tenderness peculiar to the other. Lettre de M. Godin, à M. de la Condamine.

NOTE CXXXVIII. p. 59.

Herrera gives a striking picture of their indigence. Twelve gentlemen who had been officers of distinction under Almagro, lodged in the same house, and having but one cloak among them, it was worn alternately by him who had occasion to appear in public, while the rest, from the want of a decent dress, were obliged to keep within doors. Their former friends and companions were so much afraid of giving offence to Pizarro, that they durst not entertain or even converse with them. One may conceive what was the condition and what the indignation of men once accustomed to power and opulence, when they felt themselves poor and despised, without a roof under which to shelter their heads, while they beheld others, whose merit and services were not equal to theirs, living with splendour in sumptuous edifices.   Dec 6 lib. viii. c. 6.

NOTE CXXXIX.   p. 71.

HERRERA, whose accuracy entitles him to great credit, asserts, that Gonzalo Pizarro possessed domains in the neighbourhood of Chuquesaca de la Plata, which yielded him an annual revenue greater than that of the archbishop of Toledo, the best endowed see in Europe. Dec. 7. lib. vi. c. 3.

NOTE CXL.   p. 81.

ALL the Spanish writers describe his march, and the distresses of both parties, very minutely.   Zarate observes, that hardly any parallel to it occurs in history, either with respect to the length of the retreat, or the ardour of the pursuit.   Pizarro, according to his computation, followed the viceroy upwards of three thousand miles.   Lib. v. c. 16. 26.

NOTE CXLI.   p. 99.

IT amounted, according to Fernandez, the best informed historian of that period, to one million four hundred thousand pesos.   Lib. ii. c 79.

NOTE CXLII.   p. 101.

CARVAJAL, from the beginning, had been an advocate for an accommodation with Gasca.   Finding Pizarro incapable of holding that bold course which he originally suggested, he recommended to him a timely submission to his sovereign as the safest measure.   When the president's offers were first communicated to Carvajal, " by our Lady (said he, in that strain of buffoonery which was familiar to him), the priest issues gracious bulls.   He gives them both good and cheap; let us not only accept them, but wear them as relics about our necks." Fernandez, lib. ii. c. 63.

NOTE CXLIII. p. 106.

DURING the rebellion of Gonzalo Pizarro, seven hundred men were killed in battle, and three hundred and eighty were hanged or beheaded. Herrera, dec. 8, lib. iv. c. 1. Above three hundred of these were cut off by Carvajal. Fernandez, lib. ii. c. 91. Zarate makes the number of those put to a violent death five hundred. Lib. vii. c. 1.

NOTE CXLIV. p. 113.

IN my inquiries concerning the manners and policy of the Mexicans, I have received much information from a large manuscript of Don Alonso de Corita, one of the judges in the Court of Audience of Mexico. In the year 1553, Philip II. in order to discover the mode of levying tribute from his Indian subjects, that would be most beneficial to the crown, and least oppressive to them, addressed a mandate to all the Courts of Audience in America, enjoining them to answer certain queries which he proposed to them, concerning the ancient form of government established among the various nations of Indians, and the mode in which they had been accustomed to pay taxes to their kings or chiefs. In obedience to this mandate, Corita, who had resided nineteen years in America, fourteen of which he passed in New Spain, composed the work of which I have a copy. He acquaints his sovereign, that he had made it an object during his residence in America, and in all its provinces which he had visited, to inquire diligently into the manners and customs of the natives; that he had conversed for this purpose with many aged and intelligent Indians, and consulted several of the Spanish ecclesiastics, who understood the Indian languages most perfectly, particularly some of those who landed in New Spain soon after the conquest. Corita appears to be a man of some learning, and to have carried on his inquiries with the diligence and accuracy to which he pretends. Greater credit is due to his testimony from one circumstance. His work was not composed with a view to publication, or in support of any particular theory, but contains simple, though full answers to queries proposed to him officially. Though Herrera does not mention him among the authors whom he had followed as guides in his history,

I should suppose, from several facts of which he takes notice, as well as from several expressions which he uses, that this memorial of Corita was not unknown to him.

NOTE CXLV. p. 124.

THE early Spanish writers were so hasty and inaccurate in estimating the numbers of people in the provinces and towns of America, that it is impossible to ascertain that of Mexico itself with any degree of precision. Cortes describes the extent and populousness of Mexico in general terms, which imply that it was not inferior to the greatest cities in Europe. Gomara is more explicit, and affirms, that there were 60,000 houses or families in Mexico. Cron. c. 78. Herrera adopts his opinion, Dec. 2. lib. vii. c. 13. and the generality of writers follow them implicitly without inquiry or scruple. According to this account, the inhabitants of Mexico must have been about 300,000. Torquemada, with his usual propensity to the marvellous, asserts, that there were a hundred and twenty thousand houses or families in Mexico, and consequently about six hundred thousand inhabitants. Lib. iii. c. 23. But in a very judicious account of the Mexican empire, by one of Cortes's officers, the population is fixed at 60,000 people. Ramusio, iii. 309. A. Even by this account, which probably is much nearer the truth than any of the foregoing, Mexico was a great city.

NOTE CXLVI. p. 128.

IT is to P. Torribio de Benavente, that I am indebted for this curious observation. Palafox, bishop of Ciudad de la Puebla los Angeles, confirms and illustrates it more fully. The Mexican (says he) is the only language in which a termination indicating respect *filavas reverentiales y de cortesia*, may be affixed to every word. By adding the final syllable *zin* or *azin* to any word, it becomes a proper expression of veneration in the mouth of an inferior. If, in speaking to an equal, the word Father is to be used, it is *Tatl*, but an inferior says Tatzin. One priest speaking to another, calls him *Teopixque*; a person of inferior rank calls him *Teopixcatzin*. The name of the emperor who reigned when Cortes invaded Mexico, was *Montezuma*, but his vassals, from

reverence, pronounced it *Montezumazin*. Torribio, MS.
Palaf. Virtudes del Indio. p. 65. The Mexicans had
not only reverential nouns, but reverential verbs. The
manner in which these are formed from the verbs in
common use, is explained by D. Jos. Aug. Aldama y Gue-
vara, in his Mexican grammar, N° 188.

NOTE CXLVII. p. 133.

FROM comparing several passages in Corita and Herrera, we may collect, with some degree of accuracy,
the various modes in which the Mexicans contributed
towards the support of government. Some persons of
the first order seem to have been exempted from the
payment of any tribute, and, as their only duty to the
public, were bound to personal service in war, and to
follow the banner of their sovereign with their vassals.
2. The immediate vassals of the crown were bound not
only to personal military service, but paid a certain proportion of the produce of their lands in kind. 3. Those
who held offices of honour or trust, paid a certain share
of what they received in consequence of holding these.
4. Each *Capullæ*, or association, cultivated some part of
the common field allotted to it, for the behoof of the
crown, and deposited the produce in the royal grana-
ries. 5. Some part of whatever was brought to the public markets, whether fruits of the earth, or the various
productions of their artists and manufacturers, was demanded for the public use, and the merchants who paid
this were exempted from every other tax. 6. The *Mayeques*, or *adscripti glebæ*, were bound to cultivate certain
districts in every province, which may be considered as
crown lands, and brought the increase into public storehouses. Thus the sovereign received some part of whatever was useful or valuable in the country, whether it
was the natural production of the soil, or acquired by
the industry of the people. What each contributed towards the support of government, seems to have been
inconsiderable. Corita, in answer to one of the queries
put to the Audience of Mexico by Philip II. endeavours
to estimate in money the value of what each citizen
might be supposed to pay, and does not reckon it at more
than three or four *reals*, about eighteen pence, or two
shillings a head.

NOTE CXLVIII. p. 133.

CORTES, who seems to have been as much astonished with this, as with any instance of Mexican ingenuity, gives a particular description of it. Along one of the causeways, says he, by which they enter the city, are conducted two conduits, composed of clay tempered with mortar, about two paces in breadth, and raised about six feet. In one of them is conveyed a stream of excellent water, as large as the body of a man, into the centre of the city, and it supplies all the inhabitants plentifully. The other is empty, that when it is necessary to clean or repair the former, the stream of water may be turned into it. As this conduit passes along two of the bridges, where there are breaches in the causeway, through which the salt water of the lake flows, it is conveyed over them in pipes as large as the body of an ox, then carried from the conduit to the remote quarters of the city in canoes, and sold to the inhabitants. Relat. ap. Ramus. 241, A.

NOTE CXLIX. p. 135.

IN the armoury of the royal palace of Madrid, are shewn suits of armour, which are called Montezuma's. They are composed of thin lacquered copper-plates. In the opinion of very intelligent judges, they are evidently eastern. The forms of the silver ornaments upon them, representing dragons, &c. may be considered as a confirmation of this. They are infinitely superior in point of workmanship to any effort of American art. The Spaniards probably received them from the Philippine islands. The only unquestionable specimen of Mexican art that I know of in Great Britain, is a cup of very fine gold, which is said to have belonged to Montezuma. It weighs 5 oz. 12 dwt. Three drawings of it were exhibited to the Society of Antiquaries, June 10, 1765. A man's head is represented on this cup. On one side the full face, on the other the profile, on the third the back parts of the head. The relievo is said to have been produced by punching the inside of the cup, so as to make the representation of a face on the outside. The features are gross, but represented with some degree of art, and certainly too rude for Spanish workmanship. This cup was purchased by Edward Earl of Orford.

while he lay in the harbour of Cadiz with the fleet under his command, and is now in the possession of his grandson, Lord Archer. I am indebted for this information to my respectable and ingenious friend Mr. Barrington.—In the sixth volume of the Archæologia, p. 107, is published an account of some masks of Terra Cotta, brought from a burying-ground on the American continent, about seventy miles from the British settlement on the Mosquito shore. They are said to be likenesses of chiefs, or other eminent persons. From the description and engravings of them, we have additional proof of the imperfect state of arts among the Americans.

NOTE CL. p. 141.

THE learned reader will perceive how much I have been indebted, in this part of my work, to the guidance of the Bishop of Gloucester, who has traced the successive steps by which the human mind advanced in this line of its progress, with much erudition, and greater ingenuity. He is the first, as far as I know, who formed a rational and consistent theory concerning the various modes of writing practised by nations, according to the various degrees of their improvement. Div. Legation of Moses, iii. 69, &c. Some important observations have been added by M. le President de Brosses, the learned and intelligent author of the Traité de la Formation Mechanique des Langues, tom. i. 295, &c.

As the Mexican paintings are the most curious monuments extant of the earliest mode of writing, it will not be improper to give some account of the means by which they were preserved from the general wreck of every work of art in America, and communicated to the Public. For the most early and complete collection of these published by Purchas, we are indebted to the attention of that curious inquirer, Hakluyt. Don Antonio Mendoza, viceroy of New Spain, having deemed those paintings a proper present for Charles V. the ship in which they were sent to Spain was taken by a French cruizer, and they came into the possession of Thevet, the king's geographer, who having travelled himself into the New World, and described one of its provinces, was a curious observer of whatever tended to illustrate the manners of the Americans. On his death they were purchased by Hakluyt, at that time chaplain of the English

ambassador to the French court; and, being left by him
to Purchas, were published at the desire of the learned
antiquary Sir Henry Spelman. Purchas, iii. 1065. They
were translated from English into French by Melchize-
deck Thevenot, and published in his collection of voya-
ges. A. D. 1683.

The second specimen of Mexican picture-writing was
published by Dr. Francis Gemelli Carreri, in two copper-
plates.   The first is a map, or representation of the progress of the ancient Mexicans on their first arrival in
the country, and of the various stations in which they
settled, before they founded the capital of their empire
in the lake of Mexico.   The second is a Chronological
Wheel, or Circle, representing the manner in which
they computed and marked their cycle of fifty-two years.
He received both from Don Carlos de Siguenza y Congor-
ra, a diligent collector of ancient Mexican documents.
But as it seems now to be a received opinion (founded,
as far as I know, on no good evidence) that Carreri was
never out of Italy, and that his famous *Giro del Mundo*
is an account of a fictitious voyage, I have not mentioned
these paintings in the text.   They have, however, manifestly the appearance of being Mexican productions,
and are allowed to be so by Boturini, who was well qualified to determine whether they were genuine or sup-
posititious.   M. Clavigero, likewise, admits them to be
genuine paintings of the ancient Mexicans.   To me they
always appeared to be so, though, from my desire to
rest no part of my narrative upon questionable authority,
I did not refer to them.   The style of painting in the
former is considerably more perfect than any other specimen of Mexican design; but as the original is said to
have been much defaced by time, I suspect that it has
been improved by some touches from the hand of an
European artist. Carreri, Churchill, iv. p. 487. The
Chronological Wheel is a just delineation of the Mexican
mode of computing time, as described by Acosta, lib. vi.
c. 2.   It seems to resemble one which that learned Jesuit had seen; and if it be admitted as a genuine monument, it proves that the Mexicans had artificial or arbitrary characters, which represented several things besides numbers. Each month is there represented by a
symbol expressive of some work or rite peculiar to it.

The third specimen of Mexican painting was discovered by another Italian. In 1736, Lorenzo Boturini Benaduci set out for New Spain, and was led by several incidents to study the language of the Mexicans, and to collect the remains of their historical monuments. He persisted nine years in his researches, with the enthusiasm of a projector, and the patience of an antiquary. In 1746, he published at Madrid, *Idea de una Nueva Historia General de la America Septentrional*, containing an account of the result of his inquiries; and he added to it a catalogue of his American Historical Museum, arranged under thirty-six different heads. His idea of a New History appears to me the work of a whimsical credulous man. But his catalogue of Mexican maps, paintings, tribute-rolls, calendars, &c. is much larger than one could have expected. Unfortunately a ship, in which he had sent a considerable part of them to Europe, was taken by an English privateer during the war between Great Britain and Spain which commenced in the year 1739; and it is probable that they perished by falling into the hands of ignorant captors. Boturini himself incurred the displeasure of the Spanish court, and died in an hospital at Madrid. The History, of which the *Idea*, &c. was only a *prospectus*, was never published. The remainder of his Museum seems to have been dispersed. Some part of it came into the possession of the present archbishop of Toledo, when he was primate of New Spain, and he published from it that curious tribute-roll which I have mentioned.

The only other collection of Mexican paintings, as far as I can learn, is in the Imperial Library at Vienna. By order of their Imperial Majesties, I have obtained such a specimen of these as I desired, in eight paintings, made with so much fidelity, that I am informed the copies could hardly be distinguished from the originals. According to a note in this *Codex Mexicanus*, it appears to have been a present from Emanuel king of Portugal to Pope Clement VII. who died A. D. 1523. After passing through the hands of several illustrious proprietors, it fell into those of the cardinal of Saxe-Eisenach, who presented it to the emperor Leopold. These paintings are manifestly Mexican, but they are in a style very different from any of the former. An engraving has been made of one of them, in order to gratify such of my readers as may deem this an object worthy of their attention. Were it an object of sufficient importance, it might, perhaps, be possible, by recourse to the plates of Purchas, and the archbishop of Toledo, as a key, to form plausible conjectures concerning the meaning of this picture. Many of the figures are evidently similar. A A are targets and darts, almost in the same form with those published by Purchas, p. 1070, 1071, &c. B B are figures of temples, nearly resembling those in Purchas, p. 1109. and 1113; and in Lorenzana, Plate II. C. is a bale of mantles, or cotton cloths, the figure of which occurs in almost every plate of Purchas and Lorenzana. E E E seems to be Mexican captains in their war dress, the fantastic ornaments of which resemble the figures in Purchas, p. 1110, 1111, 2113. I should suppose this picture to be a tribute-roll, as their mode of noting numbers occurs frequently, D D D, &c. According to Boturini, the mode of computation by the number of knots, was known to the Mexicans as well as to the Peruvians, p. 85. and the manner in which the number of units is represented in the Mexican paintings in my possession, seems to confirm this opinion. They plainly resemble a string of knots on a cord or slender rope.

Since I published the former edition, Mr. Waddilove, who is still pleased to continue his friendly attention to procure me information, has discovered, in the Library of the Escurial, a volume in folio, consisting of forty sheets of a kind of pasteboard, each the size of a common sheet of writing paper, with great variety of uncouth and whimsical figures of Mexican painting, in very fresh colours, and with an explanation in Spanish to most of them. The first twenty-two sheets are the signs of the months, days, &c. About the middle of each sheet are two or more large figures for the month, surrounded by the signs of the days. The last eighteen sheets are not so filled with figures. They seem to be the signs of deities, and images of various objects. According to this Calendar in the Escurial, the Mexican year contained 286 days, divided into 22 months of 13 days. Each day is represented by a different sign, taken from some natural object, a serpent, a dog, a lizard, a reed, a house. &c. The signs of days in the Calendar of the Escurial are precisely the same with those mentioned by Boturini. Idea, &c. p. 45. But, if we may give credit to that author, the Mexican year contained 360 days, divided into 18 months of 20 days. The order of days in every month was computed, according to him, first by what he calls a *tridecennary* progression of days from one to thirteen, in the same manner as in the Calendar of the Escurial, and then by a *septennary* progression of days from one to seven, making in all twenty. In this Calendar, not only the signs which distinguish each day, but the qualities supposed to be peculiar to each month, are marked. There are certain weaknesses which seem to accompany the human mind through every stage of its progress in observation and science. Slender as was the knowledge of the Mexicans in astronomy, it appears to have been already connected with judicial astrology. The fortune and character of persons born in each month are supposed to be decided by some superior influence predominant at the time of nativity. Hence it is foretold in the Calendar, that all who are born in one month will be rich, in another warlike, in a third luxurious, &c. The pasteboard, or whatever substance it may be on which the Calendar in the Escurial is painted, seems, by Mr. Waddilove's description of it, to resemble nearly that in the Imperial Library at Vienna. In several particulars, the figures bear some likeness to those in the plate which I have published. The figures marked D, which induce me to conjecture that this painting might be a tribute-roll similar to those published by Purchas and the archbishop of Toledo, Mr. Waddilove supposes to be signs of days; and I have such confidence in the accuracy of his observations, as to conclude his opinion to be well founded. It appears from the characters in which the explanations of the figures are written, that this curious monument of Mexican art has been obtained soon after the conquest of the empire. It is singular that it should never have been mentioned by any Spanish author.

NOTE CLI. p. 143.

The first was called, the Prince of the Deathful Lance; the second, the Divider of Men; the third, the Shedder of Blood; the fourth, the Lord of the Dark-house. Acosta, lib. vi. c. 25.

NOTE CLII   p. 149.

The Temple of Cholula, which was deemed more holy than any in New Spain, was likewise the most considerable. But it was nothing more than a mount of solid earth. According to Torquemada, it was above a quarter of a league in circuit at the base, and rose to the height of forty fathom. Mond. Ind. lib. iii. c. 19. Even M. Clavigero acknowledges, that all the Mexican temples were solid structures, or earthen mounts, and of consequence cannot be considered as any evidence of their having made any considerable progress in the art of building. Clavig. II. 207.

From inspecting various figures of temples in the paintings engraved by Purchas, there seems to be some reason for suspecting that all their temples were constructed in the same manner. See vol. iii. p. 1109, 1110. 1113.

NOTE CLIII. p. 151.

Not only in Tlascala, and Tepeaca, but even in Mexico itself, the houses of the people were mere huts built with turf, or mud, or the branches of trees. They were extremely low and slight, and without any furniture but a few earthen vessels. Like the rudest Indians, several families resided under the same roof, without having any separate apartments. Herrera, dec. 2. lib. vii. c. 13. lib. x. c. 22. Dec. 3. lib. iv. c. 17. Torquem. lib. iii. c. 23.

NOTE CLIV. p. 151.

I am informed by a person who resided long in New Spain, and visited almost every province of it, that there is not, in all the extent of that vast empire, any monument or vestige of any building more ancient than the conquest, nor of any bridge or highway, except some remains of the causeway from Guadaloupe to that gate of Mexico by which Cortes entered the city. MS. penes me. The author of another account in manuscript observes, " That at this day there does not remain even the smallest vestige of the existence of any ancient Indian building public or private, either in Mexico or in any province of New Spain. I have travelled, says he, through all the countries adjacent to them, viz. New Galicia, New Biscay, New Mexico, Sonora, Cinaloa, the New Kingdom of Leon, and New Santandero, without having observed any monument worth notice, except some ruins near an ancient village in the valley *de Casas Grandes*, in lat. N. 30°. 46′. longit. 248°. 24′, from the island of Teneriffe, or 460 leagues N. N. W. from Mexico." He describes these ruins minutely, and they appear to be the remains of a paltry building in turf and stone, plastered over with white earth or lime. A missionary informed that gentleman, that he had discovered the ruins of another edifice similar to the former, about an hundred leagues towards N. W. on the banks of the river St. Pedro. MS. *penes me*.

These testimonies derive great credit from one circumstance, that they were not given in support of any particular system or theory, but as simple answers to queries which I had proposed. It is probable, however, that when these gentlemen assert, that no ruins or monuments of any ancient work whatever are now to be discovered in the Mexican empire, they meant that there were no such ruins or monuments as conveyed any idea of grandeur or magnificence in the works of its ancient inhabitants. For it appears from the testimony of several Spanish authors, that in Otumba, Tlascala, Cholula, &c. some vestiges of ancient buildings are still visible. Villa Segnor Theatro Amer. p. 143. 308. 353. D. Fran. Ant. Lorenzana, formerly archbishop of Mexico, and now of Toledo, in his introduction to that edition of the Cartas de Relacion of Cortes, which he published at Mexico, mentions some ruins which are still visible in several of the towns through which Cortes passed in his way to the capital, p. 4, &c. But neither of these authors give any description of them; and they seem to be so very inconsiderable, as to shew only that some buildings had once been there. The large mount of earth at Cholula, which the Spaniards dignified with the name of temple, still remains, but without any steps by which to ascend, or any facing of stone. It appears now like a natural mount, covered with grass and shrubs, and possibly it was never any thing more. Torquem. lib. iii. c. 19. I have received a minute description of the remains of a temple near Cuernavaca, on the road from Mexico to Acapulco. It is composed of large stones, fitted to each other as nicely as those in the buildings of the Peruvians, which are hereafter mentioned. At the foundation it forms a square of 25 yards: but as it rises in height, it diminishes in extent, not gradually, but by being contracted suddenly at regular distances, so that it must have resembled the figure B in the plate. It terminated, it is said, in a spire.

NOTE CLV. p. 156.

The exaggeration of the Spanish historians, with respect to the number of human victims sacrificed in Mexico, appears to be very great. According to Gomara, there was no year in which twenty thousand human victims were not offered to the Mexican divinities, and in some years they amounted to fifty thousand. Cron. c. 229. The skulls of those unhappy persons were ranged in order in a building erected for that purpose, and two of Cortes's officers, who had counted them, informed Gomara that their number was an hundred and thirty-six thousand. Ibid. c. 82. Herrera's account is still more incredible, that the number of victims was so great, that five thousand had been sacrificed in one day, nay, on some occasions, no less than twenty thousand. Dec. 3. lib. ii. c. 16. Torquemada goes beyond both in extravagance, for he asserts, that twenty thousand children, exclusive of other victims, were slaughtered annually. Mond. Ind. lib. vii. c. 21. The most respectable authority in favour of such high numbers is that of Zumurraga, the first bishop of Mexico, who, in a letter to the chapter-general of his order, A. D 1631, asserts that the Mexicans sacrificed annually twenty thousand victims. Davila, Teatro Eccles. 125. In opposition to all these accounts, B. de las Casas observes, that if there had been such an annual waste of the human species, the country could never have arrived at that degree of populousness for which it was remarkable when the Spaniards first landed there. This reasoning is just. If the number of victims in all the provinces of New Spain had been so great, not only must population have been prevented from increasing, but the human race must have been exterminated in a short time; for besides the waste of the species by such numerous sacrifices, it is observable, that wherever the fate of captives taken in war is either certain death or perpetual slavery, as men can gain nothing by submitting speedily to an enemy, they always resist to the uttermost, and war becomes bloody and destructive to the last degree. Las Casas positively asserts, that the Mexicans never sacrificed more than fifty or a hundred persons in a year. See his dispute with Sepulveda, subjoined to his Brevissima Relacion, p. 105. Cortes does not specify what number of victims was sacrificed annually; but B. Diaz del Castello relates, that an inquiry having been made, with respect to this, by the Franciscan monks, who were sent into New Spain immediately after the conquest, it was found that about two thousand five hundred were sacrificed every year in Mexico. C. 207.

NOTE CLVI. p. 157.

It is hardly necessary to observe, that the Peruvian Chronology is not only obscure, but repugnant to conclusions deduced from the most accurate and extensive observations, concerning the time that elapses during each reign, in any given succession of princes. The medium has been found not to exceed twenty years. According to Acosta and Garcilasso de la Vega, Huana Capac, who died about the year 1527, was the twelfth Inca. According to this rule of computing, the duration of the Peruvian monarchy ought not to have been reckoned above two hundred and forty years; but they affirm that it had subsisted four hundred years. Acosta, lib. vi. c. 19. Vega, lib. i. c. 9. By this account each reign is extended at a medium to thirty-three years, instead of twenty, the number ascertained by Sir Isaac Newton's observations; but so imperfect were the Peruvian traditions, that though the total is boldly marked, the number of years in each reign is unknown.

NOTE CLVII. p. 164.

Many of the early Spanish writers assert, that the Peruvians offered human sacrifices. Xerez. p. 190. Zarate, lib. i. c. 11. Acosta, lib. v. c. 19. But Garcilasso de la Vega contends, that though this barbarous practice prevailed among their uncivilized ancestors, it was totally abolished by the Incas, and that no human victim was ever offered in any temple of the Sun. This assertion, and the plausible reasons with which he confirms it, are sufficient to refute the Spanish writers, whose accounts seem to be founded entirely upon report, not upon what they themselves had observed. Vega, lib. ii. c. 4. In one of their festivals, the Peruvians offered cakes of bread moistened with blood drawn from the arms, the eye-brows, and noses of their children. Id. lib. vii. c. 6 This rite may have been derived from their ancient practice, in their uncivilized state, of sacrificing human victims.

NOTE CLVIII. p. 169.

THE Spaniards have adopted both those customs of the ancient Peruvians. They have preserved some of the aqueducts or canals, made in the days of the Incas, and have made new ones, by which they water every field that they cultivate. Ulloa Voyage, tom. i. 422. 477. They likewise continue to use *guano*, or the dung of sea-fowl, as manure. Ulloa gives a description of the almost incredible quantity of it in the small islands near the coast. Ibid. 481.

NOTE CLIX. p. 171.

THE temple of Cayambo, the palace of the Inca at Callo, in the plain of Lacatunga, and that of Atun-Cannar, are described by Ulloa, tom. i. 286, &c. who inspected them with great care. M. de Condamine published a curious memoir concerning the ruins of Atun Cannar. Mem. de l'Academie de Berlin, A. D. 1746, p. 435. Acosta describes the ruins of Cuzco, which he had examined, lib. vi. c. 14. Garcilasso, in his usual style, gives pompous and confused descriptions of several temples, and other public edifices. Lib. iii. c. 1. c. 21. lib. vi. c. iv. Don —— Zapata, in a large treatise concerning Peru, which has not hitherto been published, communicates some information with respect to several monuments of the ancient Peruvians, which have not been mentioned by other authors. MS. *penes me.* Articulo xx. Ulloa describes some of the ancient Peruvian fortifications, which were likewise works of great extent and solidity. Tom. i. 391. Three circumstances struck all those observers: the vast size of the stones which the Peruvians employed in some of their buildings. Acosta measured one, which was thirty feet long, eighteen broad, and six in thickness; and yet, he sails, that in the fortress at Cuzco, there were stones considerably larger. It is difficult to conceive how the Peruvians could move these, and raise them to the height even of twelve feet. The second circumstance is, the imperfection of the Peruvian art, when applied to working in timber. By the patience and perseverance natural to Americans, stones may be formed into any shape, merely by rubbing one against another, or by the use of hatchets or other instruments made of stone; but with such rude tools, little progress can be made in carpentry. The Peruvians could not mortize two beams together, or give any degree of union or stability to any work composed of timber. As they could not form a centre, they were totally unacquainted with the use of arches in building, nor can Spanish authors conceive how they were able to frame a roof for those ample structures which they raised.

The third circumstance is a striking proof, which all the monuments of the Peruvians furnish, of their want of ingenuity and invention, accompanied with patience no less astonishing. None of the stones employed in those works were formed into any particular or uniform shape, which could render them fit for being compacted together in building. The Indians took them as they fell from the mountains, or were raised out of the quarries. Some were square, some triangular, some convex, some concave. Their art and industry were employed in joining them together, by forming such hollows in the one as perfectly corresponded to the projections or risings in the other. This tedious operation, which might have been so easily abridged, by adapting the surface of the stones to each other, either by rubbing, or by their hatchets of copper, would be deemed incredible, if it were not put beyond doubt by inspecting the remains of those buildings. It gives them a very singular appearance to an European eye. There is no regular layer or stratum of building, and no one stone resembles another in dimensions or form. At the same time, by the persevering, but ill-directed industry of the Indians, they are all joined with that minute nicety which I have mentioned. Ulloa made this observation concerning the form of the stones in the fortress of Atun-Cannar. Voy. i. p. 387. Pineto gives a similar description of the fortress of Cuzco, the most perfect of all the Peruvian works. Zapata MS. *penes me*. According to M de Condamine, there were regular strata of building in some parts of Atun-Cannar, which he remarks as singular, and as a proof of some progress in improvement.

NOTE CLX. p. 174.

THE appearance of those bridges, which bend with their own weight, wave with the wind, and are considerably agitated by the motion of every person who passes along them, is very frightful at first. But the Spaniards have found them to be the easiest mode of passing the torrents in Peru, over which it would be difficult to throw more solid structures either of stone or timber. They form those hanging bridges so strong and broad, that loaded mules pass along them. All the trade of Cuzco is carried on by means of such a bridge over the river Apurimac. Ulloa, tom. i. 358. A more simple contrivance was employed in passing smaller streams : A basket, in which the traveller was placed, being suspended from a strong rope stretched across the stream, it was pushed or drawn from one side to the other. Ibid.

NOTE CLXI. p. 185.

MY information with respect to those events is taken from *Noticia breve* de la expedicion militar de Sonora y Cinaloa, su exito feliz, y vantojoso estado, en que por consecuentia de ello, se han puesto ambas provincias, published at Mexico, June 7th 1771, in order to satisfy the curiosity of the merchants, who had furnished the viceroy with money for defraying the expence of the armament. The copies of this *Noticia* are very rare in Madrid ; but I have obtained one, which has enabled me to communicate these curious facts to the public. According to this account, there was found in the mine Yecorato in Cinaloa, a grain of gold of twenty-two carats, which weighed sixteen marks four ounces four ochavas; this was sent to Spain as a present fit for the king, and is now deposited in the royal cabinet at Madrid.

NOTE CLXII. p. 185.

THE uncertainty of geographers with respect to this point is remarkable for Cortes seems to have surveyed its coasts with great accuracy. The archbishop of Toledo has published, from the original, in the possession of the marquis del Valle, the descendant of Cortes, a map drawn in 1541, by the pilot Domingo Castillo, in which California is laid down as a peninsula, stretching out nearly in the same direction which is now given to it in the best maps, and the point where Rio Colorado enters the gulf is marked with precision. Hist. de Nueva Espagna, 327.

NOTE CLXIII. p. 188.

I AM indebted for this fact to M. L'Abbé Raynal, tom. iii. 103. and upon consulting an intelligent person, long settled on the Mosquito shore, and who has been engaged in the logwood trade, I find that ingenious author has been well informed. The logwood cut near the town of St. Francis of Campeachy, is of much better quality than that on the other side of Yucatan, and the English trade in the Bay of Honduras is almost at an end.

NOTE CLXIV. p. 204.

P. TORRIBIO de Benevente, or Motolinea, has enumerated ten causes of the rapid depopulation of Mexico, to which he gives the name of the Ten Plagues. Many of these are not peculiar to that province. 1. The introduction of the small-pox. This disease was first brought into New Spain in the year 1520, by a negroe slave who attended Narvaez in his expedition against Cortes. Torribio affirms, that one half of the people in the provinces visited with this distemper died. To this mortality occasioned by the small-pox, Torqemada adds the destructive effects of two contagious distempers which raged in the years 1545 and 1576. In the former 800,000 : in the latter, above two millions perished, according to an exact account taken by order of the viceroys. Mond. Ind. i. 642. The small-pox was not introduced into Peru for several years after the invasion of the Spaniards; but there too that distemper proved very fatal to the natives. Garcia Origen, p. 88. 2. The numbers who were killed or died of famine in their war with the Spaniards, particulary during the siege of Mexico. 3. The great famine that followed after the reduction of Mexico, as all the people engaged, either on one side or the other, had neglected the cultivation of their lands. Something similar to this happened in all the other countries conquered by the Spaniards.   4. The grievous tasks imposed by the Spaniards upon the people belonging to their Repartimientos.   5. The oppressive burden of taxes which they were unable to pay, and from which they could hope for no exemption.   6. The numbers employed in collecting the gold, carried down by the torrents from the mountains, who were forced from their own habitations, without any provision made for their subsistence, and subjected to all the rigour of cold in those elevated regions.   7. The immense labour of rebuilding Mexico, which Cortes urged on with such precipitate ardour, as destroyed an incredible number of people.   8. The number of people condemned to servitude, under various pretexts, and employed in working the silver mines.   These, marked by each proprietor with a hot iron, like his cattle, were driven in herds to the mountains.   The nature of the labour to which they were subjected there, the noxious vapours of the mines, the coldness of the climate, and scarcity of food, were so fatal, that Torribio affirms, the country round several of those mines, particularly near Guaxago, was covered with dead bodies, the air corrupted with their stench, and so many vultures, and other voracious birds, hovered about for their prey, that the sun was darkened with their flight.   10. The Spaniards, in the different expeditions which they undertook, and by the civil wars which they carried on, destroyed many of the natives, whom they compelled to serve them as *Tamemes*, or carriers of burdens.   This last mode of oppression was particularly ruinous to the Peruvians. From the number of Indians who perished in Gonzalo Pizarro's expedition into the countries to the east of the Andes, one may form some idea of what they suffered in similar services, and how fast they were wasted by them.   Torribio, MS.   Corita, in his breve y Summaria Relacion, illustrates and confirms several of Torribio's observations, to which he refers.   MS. *penes me.*

NOTE CLXV. p. 205.

EVEN Montesquieu has adopted this idea, lib. viii. c. 18.   But the passion of that great man for system, sometimes rendered him inattentive to research; and from his capacity to refine, he was apt, in some instances, to overlook obvious and just causes.

NOTE CLXVI. p. 205.

A STRONG proof of this occurs in the testament of Isabella, where she discovers the most tender concern for the humane and mild usage of the Indians. Those laudable sentiments of the queen have been adopted into the public law of Spain, and serve as the introduction to the regulations contained under the title *of the good treatment of the Indians.* Recopil. lib. vi. tit x.

NOTE CLXVII. p. 207.

IN the seventh *Title* of the first book of the *Recopilation*, which contains the laws concerning the powers and functions of archbishops and bishops, almost a third part of them relates to what is incumbent upon them as guardians of the Indians, and points out the various methods in which it is their duty to interpose, in order to defend them from oppression, either with respect to their persons or property. Not only do the laws commit to them this honourable and humane office, but the ecclesiastics of America actually exercise it.

Innumerable proofs of this might be produced from Spanish authors. But I rather refer to Gage, as he was not disposed to ascribe any merit to the popish clergy, to which they were not fully entitled., Survey, p. 14. 192, &c. Henry Hawks, an English merchant, who resided five years in New Spain previous to the year 1572, gives the same favourable account of the popish clergy. Hakluyt, iii. 466. By a law of Charles V. not only bishops, but other ecclesiastics are empowered to inform and admonish the civil magistrates, if any Indian is deprived of his just liberty and rights. Recopilac. lib. vi. tit. vi. ley 14.; and thus were constituted legal protectors of the Indians. Some of the Spanish ecclesiastics refused to grant absolution to such of their countrymen as possessed *Encomiendas,* and considered the Indians as slaves, or employed them in working their mines. Gonz. Davil. Teatro. Eccles. i. 157.

NOTE CLXVIII. p. 208.

ACCORDING to Gage, Chiapa dos Indos contains 4000 families, and he mentions it only as one of the largest Indian towns in America, p. 104.

NOTE CLXIX. p. 208.

IT is very difficult to obtain an accurate account of the state of population in those kingdoms of Europe where the police is most perfect, and where science has made the greatest progress. In Spanish America, where knowledge is still in its infancy, and few men have leisure to engage in researches merely speculative, little attention has been paid to this curious inquiry. But in the year 1741, Philip V. enjoined the viceroys and governors of the several provinces in America, to make an actual survey of the people under their jurisdiction, and to transmit a report concerning their number and occupations. In consequence of this order, the Conde de Fuen-Clara, viceroy of New Spain, appointed D. Jos. Antonio de Villa Segnor y Sanchez, to execute that commission in New Spain. From the reports of the magistrates in the several districts, as well as from his own observations and long acquaintance with most of the provinces, Villa Segnor published the result of his inquiries in his *Teatro Americano*. His report, however, is imperfect. Of the nine dioceses into which the Mexican empire has been divided, he has published an account of five only, viz. the archbishopric of Mexico, the bishoprics of Puebla de los Angeles, Mechoacan, Oaxaca, and Nova Galicia. The bishoprics of Yocatan, Verapaz, Chiapa, and Guatimala, are entirely omitted, though the two latter comprehend countries in which the Indian race is more numerous than in any part of New Spain. In his survey of the extensive diocese of Nova Galicia, the situation of the different Indian villages is described, but he specifies the number of people only in a small part of it. The Indians of that extensive province, in which the Spanish dominion is imperfectly established, are not registered with the same accuracy as in other parts of New Spain. According to Villa Segnor, the actual state of population in the five dioceses above mentioned, is of Spaniards, negroes, mulattoes, and mestizos, in the dioceses of

				Families.
Mexico	—	—	—	105,202
Los Angeles	—	—	—	30,600
Mechoacan	—	—	—	30,840
Oaxaca	—	—	—	7,296
Nova Galicia	—	—	—	16,770
				190,708
At the rate of five to a family, the total number is }				953,540

Indian families in the diocese of Mexico				119,511
Los Angeles	—	—	—	88,240
Mechoacan	—	—	—	36,196
Oaxaca	—	—	—	44,222
Nova Galicia	—	—	—	6,222
				294,391
At the rate of five to a family, the total number is }				1,471,955

We may rely with greater certainty on this computation of the number of Indians, as it is taken from the *Matricula*, or register, according to which the tribute paid by them is collected. As four dioceses of nine are totally omitted, and in that of Nova Galicia the numbers are imperfectly recorded, we may conclude, that the number of Indians in the Mexican empire exceeds two millions.

The account of the number of Spaniards, &c. seems not to be equally complete. Of many places, Villa Segnor observes in general terms, that several Spaniards, negroes, and people of mixed race, reside there, without specifying their number. If, therefore, we make allowance for these, and for all who reside in the four dioceses omitted, the number of Spaniards, and of those of a mixed race, may probably amount to a million and a half. In some places, Villa Segnor distinguishes between Spaniards and the three interior races of negroes, mulattoes, and mestizos, and marks their number separately. But he generally blends them together. But from the proportion observable in those places, where the number of each is marked, as well as from the ac.

E e 3

count of the state of population in New Spain by other authors, it is manifest that the number of negroes and persons of a mixed race far exceeds that of Spaniards. Perhaps the latter ought not to be reckoned above 500,000 to a million of the former.

Defective as this account may be, I have not been able to procure such intelligence concerning the number of people in Peru, as might enable me to form any conjecture equally satisfying with respect to the degree of its population. I have been informed, that in the year 1761, the protector of the Indians in the viceroyalty of Peru computed that 612,780 paid tribute to the king. As all females, and persons under age, are exempted from this tax in Peru, the total number of Indians ought by that account to be 2,449,120. MS. *penes me.*

I shall mention another mode, by which one may compute, or at least form a guess, concerning the state of population in New Spain and Peru. According to an account which I have reason to consider as accurate, the number of copies of the bull of Cruzada, exported to Peru on each new publication, is 1,171,953; to New Spain 2,649,326. I am informed, that but few Indians purchase bulls, and that they are sold chiefly to the Spanish inhabitants and those of mixed race, so that the number of Spaniards, and people of a mixed race, will amount by this mode of computation to at least three millions.

The number of inhabitants in many of the towns in Spanish America, may give us some idea of the extent of population, and correct the inaccurate but popular notion entertained in Great Britain, concerning the weak and desolate state of their colonies. The city of Mexico contains at least 150,000 people. It is remarkable that Torquemada, who wrote his *Monarquia Indiana* about the year 1612, reckons the inhabitants of Mexico at that time to be only 7000 Spaniards and 8000 Indians. Lib. iii. c. 26. Puebla de los Angeles contains above 60,000 Spaniards and people of a mixed race. Villa Segnor. p. 247. Guadalaxara contains above 30,000, exclusive of Indians. Id. ii. 206. Lima contains 54,000. D. Cosme Bueno Descr. de Peru, 1764. Carthagena contains 25,000. Potosi contains 25,000. Bueno, 1767. Popayan contains above 20,000. Ulloa, i. 287. Towns of a second class are still more numerous. The cities in the most thriving settlements of other European nations in America cannot be compared with these.

Such are the detached accounts of the number of people in several towns, which I found scattered in authors whom I thought worthy of credit. But I have obtained an enumeration of the inhabitants of the towns in the province of Quito, on the accuracy of which I can rely; and I communicate it to the public, both to gratify curiosity, and to rectify the mistaken notion which I have mentioned. St. Francisco de Quito, contains between 50 and 60,000 people of all the different races. Besides the city, there are in the *Corregimiento* 29 *curas* or parishes established in the principal villages, each of which has smaller hamlets depending upon it. The inhabitants of these are mostly Indians and mestizos. St. Joan de Pasto has between 6 and 8000 inhabitants, besides 27 dependent villages. St. Miguel de Ibarra 7000 citizens, and ten villages. The district of Havala between 18 and 20,000 people. The district of Tacunna between 10 and 12,000. The district of Ambato between 8 and 10,000, besides 16 depending villages. The city of Riobamba between 16 and 20,000 inhabitants, and 9 depending villages. The district of Chimbo between 6 and 8000. The city of Guayaquil from 16 to 20,000 inhabitants, and 14 depending villages. The district of Atrasi between 5 and 6000, and 4 depending villages. The city of Cuenza between 25 and 30,000 inhabitants, and 9 populous depending villages. The town of Laxa from 8 to 10,000 inhabitants, and 14 depending villages. This degree of population, though slender, if we consider the vast extent of the country, is far beyond what is commonly supposed. I have omitted to mention, in its proper place, that Quito is the only province in Spanish America that can be denominated a manufacturing country; hats, cotton stuffs, and coarse woollen cloths, are made there in such quantities, as to be sufficient not only for the consumption of the province, but to furnish a considerable article for exportation into other parts of Spanish America. I know not whether the uncommon industry of this province should be considered as the cause or the effects of its populousness. But among the ostentatious inhabitants of the New World, the passion for every thing that comes from Europe is so violent, that I am informed the manufactures of Quito are so much undervalued, as to be on the decline.

NOTE CLXX. p. 213.

These are established at the following places. St. Domingo in the island of Hispaniola, Mexico in New Spain, Lima in Peru, Panama in Tierra Firmé, Santiago in Guatimala, Guadalaxara in New Galicia, Santa Fé in the New Kingdom of Granada, La Plata in the country of Los Charcas, St. Francisco de Quito, St. Jago de Chili, Buenos Ayres. To each of these are subjected several large provinces, and some so far removed from the cities where the courts are fixed, that they can derive little benefit from their jurisdiction. The Spanish writers commonly reckon up twelve courts of Audience, but they include that of Manila in the Philippine Islands.

NOTE CLXXI. p. 219.

On account of the distance of Peru and Chili from Spain, and the difficulty of carrying commodities of such bulk as wine and oil across the isthmus of Panama, the Spaniards in those provinces have been permitted to plant vines and olives. But they are strictly prohibited from exporting wine or oil to any of the provinces on the Pacific Ocean, which are in such a situation as to receive them from Spain. Recop. lib. i. tit. xvii. l. 15—18.

NOTE CLXXIII. p. 221.

This computation was made by Benzoni, A. D. 1550, fifty-eight years after the discovery of America. Hist. Novi Orbis, lib. iii. c. 21. But as Benzoni wrote with the spirit of a malecontent, disposed to detract from the Spaniards in every particular, it is probable that his calculation is considerably too low.

NOTE CLXXIII. p. 223.

My information with respect to the division and transmission of property in the Spanish colonies, is imperfect. The Spanish authors do not explain this fully, and have not perhaps attended sufficiently to the effects of their own institutions and laws. Solorzano de Jure Ind. vol. ii. lib. ii. l. 16. explains in some measure the introduction of the tenure of *Mayorasgo*, and mentions some of its effects. Villa Segnor takes notice of a singular

lar consequence of it. He observes, that in some of the best situations in the city of Mexico, a good deal of ground is unoccupied, or covered only with the ruins of the houses once erected upon it; and adds, that as this ground is held by right of *Mayorazgo*, and cannot be alienated, that desolation and those ruins become perpetual. Theatr. Amer. vol. i. p. 34.

NOTE CLXXIV. p. 224.

THERE is no law that excludes Creoles from offices either civil or ecclesiastic. On the contrary, there are many *Cedulas* which recommend the conferring places of trust indiscriminately on the natives of Spain and America. Betancurt y Figueroa Derecho, &c. p. 5, 6. But notwithstanding such repeated recommendations, preferment in almost every line is conferred on native Spaniards. A remarkable proof of this is produced by the author last quoted. From the discovery of America to the year 1637, three hundred and sixty-nine bishops, or archbishops, have been appointed to the different dioceses in that country, and of all that number only twelve were Creoles, p. 40. This predilection for Europeans seems still to continue. By a royal mandate, issued in 1776, the chapter of the cathedral of Mexico is directed to nominate European ecclesiastics of known merit and abilities, that the king may appoint them to supply vacant benefices. MS. *penes me.*

NOTE CLXXV. p. 229.

MODERATE as this tribute may appear, such is the extreme poverty of the Indians in many provinces of America, that the exacting of it is intolerably oppressive. Pegna Itiner. par Parochos de Indios, p. 192.

NOTE CLXXVI. p. 230.

IN New Spain, on account of the extraordinary merit and services of the first conquerors, as well as the small revenue arising from the country previous to the discovery of the mines of Sacatecas, the *encomiendas* were granted for three, and sometimes for four lives. Recopil. lib. vi. tit. ii. c. 14. &c.

NOTE CLXXVII. p. 231.

D. ANT. ULLOA contends, that working in mines is not noxious, and as a proof of this informs us, that many mestizos and Indians, who do not belong to any Repartimiento, voluntarily hire themselves as miners; and several of the Indians, when the legal term of their service expires, continue to work in the mines of choice. *Entreten.* p. 265.   But his opinion concerning the wholesomeness of this occupation is contrary to the experience of all ages; and wherever men are allured by high wages, they will engage in any species of labour, however fatiguing or pernicious it may be.   D. Hern. Carillo Altemirano relates a curious fact incompatible with this opinion.   Wherever mines are wrought, says he, the number of Indians decreases; but in the province of Campeachy, where there are no mines, the number of Indians has increased more than a third since the conquest of America, though neither the soil nor climate be so favourable as in Peru or Mexico. Colbert Collect. In another memorial presented to Philip III. in the year 1609, Captain Juan Gonzalez de Azevedo asserts, that in every district of Peru, where the Indians are compelled to labour in the mines, their numbers were reduced to the half, and in some places to the third, of what it was under the viceroyalty of Don Fran. Toledo, in 1581.   Colb. Collect.

NOTE CLXXVIII. p. 232.

As labour of this kind cannot be prescribed with legal accuracy, the tasks seem to be in a great measure arbitrary, and, like the services exacted by feudal superiors, *in vinea prato aut messe*, from their vassals, are extremely burdensome, and often wantonly oppressive. Pegna Itiner. par Parochos de Indios.

NOTE CLXXIX. p. 232.

The turn of service known in Peru by the name of *Mita*, is called *Tapda* in New Spain.   There it continues no longer than a week at a time.   No person is called to serve at a greater distance from his habitation than 24 miles.   This arrangement is less oppressive to the Indians than that established in Peru.   Memorial of Hern. Carillo Altamirano. Colbert Collect.

NOTE CLXXX. p. 234.

The strongest proof of this may be deduced from the laws themselves. By the multitude and variety of rs-

gulations to prevent abuses, we may form an idea of
the number of abuses that prevail. Though the laws
Have wisely provided, that no Indian shall be obliged to
serve in any mine at a greater distance from his place
of residence than thirty miles; we are informed in a
memorial of D. Hernan Carillo Altamirano, presented to
the king, that the Indians of Peru are often compelled
to serve in mines at the distance of a hundred, a hundred and fifty, and even two hundred leagues from their
habitation.   Colbert Collect.   Many mines are situated
in parts of the country so barren, and so distant from
the ordinary habitations of the Indians, that the necessity of procuring labourers to work there, has obliged
the Spanish monarchs to dispense with their own regulations in several instances, and to permit the viceroys to
compel the people of more remote provinces to resort to
those mines.   Escalona Gazophyl. Peruv. lib. i. c. 16.
But in justice to them it should be observed, that they
have been studious to alleviate this oppression as much
as possible, by enjoining the viceroys to employ every
method in order to induce the Indians to settle in some
part of the country adjacent to the mines.   Id. ibid.

NOTE CLXXXI. p. 239.

TORQUEMADA, after a long enumeration, which has
the appearance of accuracy, concludes the number of
monasteries in New Spain to be four hundred. Mond.
Ind. lib. xix. c. 32. The number of monasteries in the
city of Mexico alone, was, in the year 1745. fifty-five.
Villa Segnor. Theat. Amer. i. 34. Ulloa reckons up
forty convents in Lima; and mentioning those for nuns,
he says, that a small town might be peopled out of them,
the number of persons shut up there is so great. Voy. i.
429. Philip III. in a letter to the viceroy of Peru,
A. D. 1620, observes, that the number of convents in
Lima was so great, that they covered more ground than
all the rest of the city. Solorz. lib. iii. c. 22. n. 57.
Lib. iii. c. 16. Torquem. lib. xv. c. 3. The first monastery in New Spain was founded A. D. 1525, four
years only after the conquest. Torq. lib. xv. c. 16.
    According to Gil Gonzalez Davila, the complete e-
stablishment of the American church in all the Spanish
settlements, was, in the year 1649, 1 patriarch, 6 archbishops, 32 bishops, 346 prebends, 2 abbots, 5 royal

chaplains, 840 convents.   Teatro Ecclesiastico de las Ind. Occident. vol. i. Pref.   When the order of Jesuits was expelled from all the Spanish dominions, the colleges, *professed* houses, and residences, which it possessed in the province of New Spain, were thirty, in Quito sixteen, in the New Kingdom of Granada thirteen, in Peru seventeen, in Chili eighteen, in Paraguay eighteen : in all a hundred and twelve.   Colleccion General de Providencias hasta acqui tomadas sobre estranamento, &c. de la Compagnia, part i. p. 19.   The number of Jesuits, priests, and novices in all these, amounted to 2245. MS. *penes me.*

In the year 1644, the city of Mexico presented a petition to the king, praying that no new monastery might be founded, and that the revenues of those already established might be circumscribed, otherwise the religious houses would soon acquire the property of the whole country.   The petitioners request likewise, that the bishops might be laid under restrictions in conferring holy orders, as there were at that time in New Spain above six thousand clergymen without any living.   Id. p. 16. These abuses must have been enormous indeed, when the superstition of American Spaniards was shocked, and induced to remonstrate against them.

NOTE CLXXXII. p. 241.

This description of the manners of the Spanish clergy, I should not have ventured to give upon the testimony of protestant authors alone, as they may be suspected of prejudice or exaggeration.   Gage, in particular, who had a better opportunity than any protestant, to view the interior state of Spanish America, describes the corruption of the church which he had forsaken, with so much of the acrimony of a new convert, that I should have distrusted his evidence, though it communicates some very curious and striking facts.   But Benzoni mentions the profligacy of ecclesiastics in America at a very early period after their settlement there.   Hist. lib. ii. c. 19, 20.   M. Frezier, an intelligent observer, and zealous for his own religion, paints the dissolute manners of the Spanish ecclesiastics in Peru, particularly the regulars, in stronger colours than I have employed.   Voy. p. 51, 215, &c.   M. Gentil confirms this account. Voy. t. 34.   Correal concurs with both, and adds many se-markable circumstances, Voy. i. 61. 155. 161. I have good reason to believe, that the manners of the regular clergy, particularly in Peru, are still extremely indecent. Acosta himself acknowledges that great corruption of manners had been the consequence of permitting monks to forsake the retirement and discipline of the cloister, and to mingle again with the world, by undertaking the charge of the Indian parishes. De procur. Ind. Salute, lib. iv. c. 11, &c. He mentions particularly those vices, of which I have taken notice, and considers the temptations to them as so formidable, that he leans to the opinion of those who hold that the regular clergy should not be employed as parish priests. Lib. v. c. 20. Even the advocates for the regulars admit, that many and great enormities abounded among the monks of different orders, when set free from the restraint of monastic discipline; and from the tone of their defence, one may conclude that the charge brought against them was not destitute of truth. In the French colonies, the state of the regular clergy is nearly the same as in the Spanish settlements, and the same consequences have followed. M. Biet, superior of the secular priests in Cayenne, inquires, with no less appearance of piety than of candour, into the causes of this corruption, and imputes it chiefly to the exemption of regulars from the jurisdiction and censures of their diocesans; to the temptations to which they are exposed; and to their engaging in commerce. Voy. p. 320. It is remarkable that all the authors, who censure the licentiousness of the Spanish regulars with the greatest severity, concur in vindicating the conduct of the Jesuits. Formed under a discipline more perfect than that of the other monastic orders, or animated by that concern for the honour of the society, which takes such full possession of every member of the order, the Jesuits, both in Mexico and Peru, it is allowed, maintained a most irreproachable decency of manners. Frezier, 223. Gentil, i. 34. The same praise is likewise due to the bishops and most of the dignified clergy. Frez. ibid.

A volume of the Gazette de Mexico for the years 1728, 1729, 1730, having been communicated to me, I find there a striking confirmation of what I have advanced concerning the spirit of low illiberal superstition prevalent in Spanish America. From the Newspapers of any nation, one may learn what are the objects which chiefly engross its attention, and which appear to it most interesting. The Gazette of Mexico is filled almost entirely with accounts of religious functions, with descriptions of processions, consecrations of churches, beatifications of saints, festivals, autos de fè, &c. Civil or commercial affairs, and even the transactions of Europe, occupy but a small corner in this magazine of monthly intelligence. From the titles of new books, which are regularly inserted in this Gazette, it appears that two thirds of them are treatises of scholastic theology, or of monkish devotion.

NOTE CLXXXIII. p. 242.

Solorzano, after mentioning the corrupt morals of some of the regular clergy with that cautious reserve which became a Spanish layman in touching on a subject so delicate, gives his opinion very explicitly, and with much firmness, against committing parochial charges to monks. He produces the testimony of several respectable authors of his country, both divines and lawyers, in confirmation of his opinion. De Jure Ind. ii. lib. iii. c. 16. A striking proof of the alarm excited by the attempt of the prince d'Esquilache to exclude the regulars from parochial cures, is contained in the Colbert collection of papers. Several memorials were presented to the king by the procurators for the monastic orders, and replies were made to these in name of the secular clergy. An eager, and even rancorous spirit, is manifest on both sides, in the conduct of this dispute.

NOTE CLXXXIV. p. 247.

Not only the native Indians, but the *Mestizos*, or children of a Spaniard and Indian, were originally excluded from the priesthood, and refused admission into any religious order. But, by a law issued September 28, 1588, Philip II. required the prelates of America to ordain such mestizos born in lawful wedlock, as they should find to be properly qualified, and to permit them to take the vows in any monastery where they had gone through a regular noviciate. Recopil. lib. i. tit. vii. l. 7. Some regard seems to have been paid to this law in New Spain; but none in Peru. Upon a representation of this to Charles II. in the year 1697, he issued a new edict en-

forcing the observation 'of it, and professing his desire
to have all his subjects, Indians and mestizos as well as
Spaniards, admitted to the enjoyment of the same privileges. Such, however, was the aversion of the Spaniards in America to the Indians and their race, that this
seems to have produced little effect; for, in the year
1725, Philip V. was obliged to renew the injunction in
a more peremptory tone. But so insurmountable are
the hatred and contempt of the Indians among the Peruvian Spaniards, that the present king has been constrained
to enforce the former edicts anew by a law, published
September 11, 1774. Real Cedula, MS. *penes me.*.

M. Clavigero has contradicted what I have related
concerning the ecclesiastical state of the Indians, particularly their exclusion from the sacrament of the Eucharist, and from holy orders, either as Seculars or Regulars, in such a manner as cannot fail to make a deep impression. He, from his own knowledge, asserts, " that
in New Spain not only are Indians permitted to partake
of the sacrament of the altar, but that Indian priests
are so numerous that they may be counted by hundreds;
and among these have been many hundreds of rectors,
canons, and doctors, and, as report goes, even a very
learned bishop. At present, there are many priests,
and not a few rectors, among whom there have been
three or four our own pupils." Vol. II. 348. &c. I
owe it therefore as a duty to the public, as well as to
myself, to consider each of these points with care, and
to explain the reasons which induced me to adopt the
opinion which I have published.

I knew that in the Christian church there is no distinction of persons, but that men of every nation who
embrace the religion of Jesus, are equally entitled to
every Christian privilege which they are qualified to receive. I knew, likewise, that an opinion prevailed, not
only among most of the Spanish laity settled in America,
but among " many ecclesiastics, (I use the words of
Herrera, Dec. 2. lib. ii. c. 15.) that the Indians were
not perfect or rational men, and were not possessed of
such capacity as qualified them to partake of the sacrament of the altar, or of any other benefit of our religion." It was against this opinion that Las Casas contended with the laudable zeal which I have described in
Books III. and VI. But as the Bishop of Darien, Doctor

F f 2

Sepulvida, and other respectable ecclesiastics, vigorously supported the common opinion concerning the incapacity of the Indians, it became necessary, in order to determine the point, that the authority of the Holy See should be interposed; and accordingly Paul III. issued a bull, A. D. 1537, in which, after condemning the opinion of those who held that the Indians, as being on a level with brute beasts, should be reduced to servitude, he declares, that they were really men, and as such were capable of embracing the Christian religion, and participating of all its blessings. My account of this bull, notwithstanding the cavils of M. Clavigero, must appear just to every person who takes the trouble of perusing it; and my account is the same with that adopted by Torquemada, lib xvi. c. 2? and by Garcia, Orig. p. 311 But even after this decis n, so low did the Spaniards residing in America rate the capacity of the natives, that the first council of Lima (I call it by that name on the authority of the best Spanish authors) discou enanced the admission of Indians to the holy communion. Torquem. lib. xvi. c. 20. In New Spain, the exclusion of Indians from the sacrament was still more explicit. Ibid After two centuries have elapsed, and notwithstanding all the improvement that the Indians may be supposed to have derived from their intercourse with the Spaniards during that period, we are informed by D. Ant. Ulloa, that in Peru. where, as will appear in the sequel of this note, they are supposed to be better instructed than in New Spain, their ignorance is so prodigious that very few are permitted to communicate, as being altogether destitute of the requisite capacity. Voy. I. 341, &c. Solorz. Polit. Ind. I. 203.

With respect to the exclusion of Indians from the priesthood, either as seculars or regulars, we may observe, that while it continued to be the common opinion that the natives of America, on account of their incapacity, should not be permitted to partake of the holy sacrament, we cannot suppose that they would be clothed with that sacred character, which entitled them to consecrate and to dispense it. When Torquemada composed his *Monarquia Indiana*, it was almost a century after the conquest of New Spain; and yet in his time, it was still the general practice to exclude Indians from holy orders. Of this we have the most satisfying evidence. Torquemada having celebrated the virtues and graces of the Indians at great length, and with all the complacency of a missionary, he starts as an objection to what he had asserted, " If the Indians really possess all the excellent qualities which you have described, why are they not permitted to assume the religious habit? Why are they not ordained priests and bishops, as the Jewish and Gentile converts were in the primitive church, especially as they might be employed with such superior advantage to other persons in the instruction of their countrymen?" Lib. xvii. c. 13.

In answer to this objection, which establishes, in the most unequivocal manner, what was the general practice at that period, Torquemada observes, that although by their natural dispositions the Indians are well fitted for a subordinate situation, they are destitute of all the qualities requisite in any station of dignity and authority; and that they are in general so addicted to drunkenness, that, upon the slightest temptation, one cannot promise on their behaving with the decency suitable to the clerical character. The propriety of excluding them from it, on these accounts, was, he observed, so well justified by experience, that when a foreigner of great erudition, who came from Spain, condemned the practice of the Mexican church, he was convinced of his mistake in a public disputation with the learned and most religious Father D. Juan de Gaona, and his retractation is still extant. Torquemada, indeed, acknowledges, as M. Clavigero observes, with a degree of exultation, that, in his time, some Indians had been admitted into monasteries; but, with the art of a disputant, he forgets to mention that Torquemada specifies only two examples of this, and takes notice that in both instances those Indians had been admitted by mistake. Relying upon the authority of Torquemada with regard to New Spain, and of Ulloa with regard to Peru, and considering the humiliating depression of the Indians in all the Spanish settlements, I concluded that they were not admitted into the ecclesiastical order, which is held in the highest veneration all over the New World.

But when M. Clavigero, upon his own knowledge, asserted facts so repugnant to the conclusion I had formed, I began to distrust it, and to wish for further information. In order to obtain this, I applied to a Spanish nobleman, high in office, and eminent for his abilities, who on different occasions has permitted me to have the honour and benefit of corresponding with him. I have been favoured with the following answer : " What you have written concerning the admission of Indians into holy orders, or into monasteries, in Book VIII. especially as it is explained and limited in Note LXXXVIII, of the quarto edition, is in general accurate, and conformable to the authorities which you quote. And although the congregation of the council resolved and declared, Feb. 13, A. D. 1682, that the circumstance of being an Indian, a mulatto, or mestizo, did not disqualify any person from being admitted into holy orders, if he was possessed of what is required by the canons to entitle him to that privilege ; this only proves such ordinations to be legal and valid (of which Solorzano, and the Spanish lawyers and historians quoted by him, Pol. Ind. lib. ii. c. 29. were persuaded), but it neither proves the propriety of admitting Indians into holy orders, nor what was then the common practice with respect to this ; but, on the contrary, it snews that there was some doubt concerning the ordaining of Indians, and some repugnance to it.

" Since that time, there have been some examples of admitting Indians into holy orders. We have now at Madrid an aged priest, a native of Tlascala. His name is D. Juan Cerilo de Castilla Aquihual catehutle, descended of a cazique converted to Christianity soon after the conquest. He studied the ecclesiastical sciences in a seminary of Puebla de los Angeles. He was a candidate, nevertheless, for ten years, and it required much interest before Bishop Abreu would consent to ordain him. This ecclesiastic is a man of unexceptionable character, modest, self-denied, and with a competent knowledge of what relates to his clerical functions. He came to Madrid above thirty-four years ago, with the sole view of soliciting admission for the Indians into the colleges and seminaries in New Spain, that if, after being well instructed and tried, they should find an inclination to enter into the ecclesiastical state, they might embrace it, and perform its functions with the greatest benefit to their countrymen, whom they could address in their native tongue. He has obtained various regulations favourable to his scheme, particularly that

the first college which became vacant in consequence of
the exclusion of the Jesuits, should be set apart for this
purpose. But neither these regulations, nor any similar
ones inserted in the laws of the Indies, has produced
any effect, on account of objections and representations
from the greater part of persons of chief consideration
employed in New Spain. Whether their opposition be
well founded or not, is a problem difficult to resolve,
and towards the solution of which, several distinctions
and modifications are requisite.

" According to the accounts of this ecclesiastic, and
the information of other persons who have resided in
the Spanish dominions in America, you may rest assured
that in the kingdom of Tierra Firmé no such thing is
known as either an Indian secular priest or monk; and
that in New Spain there are very few ecclesiastics of
Indian race. In Peru, perhaps, the number may be
greater, as in that country there are more Indians who
possess the means of acquiring such a learned education
as is necessary for persons who aspire to the clerical
character."

NOTE CLXXXV. p. 250.

Uztariz, an accurate and cautious calculator, seems
to admit, that the quantity of silver which does not
pay duty may be stated thus high. According to Herrera, there was not above a third of what was extracted
from Potosi that paid the king's fifth. Dec. 8. lib. ii.
c. 15. Solorzano asserts likewise, that the quantity of
silver which is fraudulently circulated, is far greater
than that which is regularly stamped, after paying the
fifth. De Ind. Jure, vol. ii. lib. v. p. 846.

NOTE CLXXXVI. p. 253.

When the mines of Potosi were discovered in the
year 1545, the veins were so near the surface, that the
ore was easily extracted, and so rich that it was refined
with little trouble and at a small expence, merely by
the action of fire. The simple mode of refining by
fusion alone continued until the year 1574, when the
use of mercury in refining silver, as well as gold, was
discovered. Those mines having been wrought without
interruption for two centuries, the veins are now sunk
so deep, that the expence of extracting the ore is greatly

increased. Besides this, the richness of the ore, contrary to what happens in most other mines, has become less, as the vein continued to dip. The vein has likewise diminished to such a degree, that one is amazed that the Spaniards should persist in working it. Other rich mines have been successively discovered, but in general the value of the ores has decreased so much, while the expence of extracting them has augmented, that the court of Spain, in the year 1736, reduced the duty payable to the king from a *fifth* to a *tenth*. All the quick-silver used in Peru, is extracted from the famous mine of Guancabelica, discovered in the year 1563. The crown has reserved the property of this mine to itself; and the persons who purchase the quicksilver, pay not only the price of it, but likewise a *fifth*, as a duty to the king. But, in the year 1761, this duty on quicksilver was abolished, on account of the increase of expence in working mines. Ulloa, Entretenimientos, xii—xv. Voyage, i. p. 505 523. In consequence of this abolition of the *fifth*, and some subsequent abatements of price, which became necessary on account of the increasing expence of working mines, quicksilver, which was formerly sold at eighty pesos the quintal, is now delivered by the king at the rate of sixty pesos. Campomanes Educ. Popul. ii. 132, Note. The duty on gold is reduced to a *twentieth*, or five per cent. Any of my readers, who are desirous of being acquainted with the mode in which the Spaniards conduct the working of their mines, and the refinement of the ore, will find an accurate description of the ancient method by Acosta, lib. iv. c. 1—13. And of the more recent improvements in the metallurgic art, by Gamboa Comment a las ordenanz. de minas, c. 22.

NOTE CLXXXVII. p. 256.

MANY remarkable proofs occur of the advanced state of industry in Spain, at the beginning of the sixteenth century. The number of cities in Spain was considerable, and they were peopled far beyond the proportion that was common in other parts of Europe. The causes of this I have explained, Hist. of Cha. V i. 158. Wherever cities are populous, that species of industry which is peculiar to them increases, artificers and manufacturers abound. The effect of the American trade in giving activity to these is manifest, from a singular fact. In the year 1545, while Spain continued to depend on its own industry for the supply of its colonies, so much work was bespoke from the manufacturers, that it was supposed they could hardly finish it in less than six years. Campom. i. 406. Such a demand must have put much industry in motion, and have excited extraordinary efforts. Accordingly, we are informed, that in the beginning of Philip II.'s reign, the city of Seville alone, where the trade with America centered, gave employment to no fewer than 16,000 looms in silk or woollen work, and that above 130,000 persons had occupation in carrying on these manufactures. Campom. ii. 472. But so rapid and pernicious was the operation of the causes which I shall enumerate, that before Philip III. ended his reign, the looms in Seville were reduced to 400, Uztariz, c. 7.

Since the publication of the first edition, I have the satisfaction to find my ideas concerning the early commercial intercourse between Spain and her colonies confirmed and illustrated by D. Bernardo Ward, of the Junta de Comercio at Madrid, in his *Proyecto Economico,* Part ii. c. i. " Under the reigns of Charles V. and Philip II." says he, " the manufactures of Spain and of the Low Countries subject to her dominion were in a most flourishing state. Those of France and England were in their infancy. The republic of the United Provinces did not then exist. No European power but Spain had colonies of any value in the New World. Spain could supply her settlements there with the productions of her own soil, the fabrics wrought by the hands of her own artizans, and all she received in return for these belonged to herself alone. Then the exclusion of foreign manufactures was proper, because it might be rendered effectual. Then Spain might lay heavy duties upon goods exported to America, or imported from it, and might impose what restraints she deemed proper upon a commerce entirely in her own hands. But when time and successive revolutions had occasioned an alteration in all those circumstances; when the manufactures of Spain began to decline, and the demands of America were supplied by foreign fabrics, the original maxims and regulations of Spain should have been accommodated to the change in her situation. The policy that was wise at one period, became absurd in the other."

NOTE CLXXXVIII. p. 265.

No bale of goods is ever opened, no chest of treasure is examined. Both are received on the credit of the persons to whom they belong; and only one instance of fraud is recorded, during the long period in which trade was carried on with this liberal confidence. All the coined silver which was brought from Peru to Porto-bello, in the year 1654, was found to be adulterated, and to be mingled with a fifth part of base metal. The Spanish merchants, with sentiments suitable to their usual integrity, sustained the whole loss, and indemnified the foreigners by whom they were employed. The fraud was detected, and the treasurer of the revenue in Peru, the author of it, was publicly burnt. B. Ulloa Retablis. de Manuf. &c. liv. ii. p. 102.

NOTE CLXXXIX. p. 268.

Many striking proofs occur of the scarcity of money in Spain. Of all the immense sums which have been imported from America, the amount of which I shall afterwards have occasion to mention, Moncada asserts, that there did not remain in Spain, in 1619, above two hundred millions of *pesos*, one half in coined money, the other in plate and jewels. Restaur. de Espagna, Disc. iii. c. 1. Uztariz, who published his valuable work in 1724, contends, that in money, plate, and jewels, there did not remain an hundred million. Theor. &c. c. 3. Campomanes, on the authority of a remonstrance from the community of merchants in Toledo to Philip III relates, as a certain proof how scarce cash had become, that persons who lent money, received a third part of the sum which they advanced as interest and premium. Educ. Popul. i. 417.

NOTE CXC. p. 272.

The account of the mode in which the factors of the South Sea Company conducted the trade in the fair of Porto-Bello, which was opened to them by the Assiento, I have taken from Don Dion. Alcedo y Herrera, president of the court of audience in Quito, and governor of that province. Don Dionysia was a person of such respectable character for probity and discernment, that his testimony, in any point, would be of much weight; but greater credit is due to it in this case, as he was an eye-witness of the transactions which he relates, and was often employed in detecting and authenticating the frauds which he describes. It is probable, however, that his representation, being composed at the commencement of the war which broke out between Great Britain and Spain in the year 1739, may, in some instances, discover a portion of the acrimonious spirit natural at that juncture His detail of facts is curious; and even English authors confirm it in some degree, by admitting both that various frauds were practised in the transactions of the annual ship, and that the contraband trade from Jamaica, and other British colonies, was become enormously great. But for the credit of the English nation it may be observed, that those fraudulent operations are not to be considered as deeds of the company, but as the dishonourable arts of their factors and agents. The company itself sustained a considerable loss by the Assiento trade. Many of its servants acquired immense fortunes. Anderson Chronol. deduct. ii. 388.

NOTE CXLI. p 278.

SEVERAL facts with respect to the institution, the progress, and the effects, of this company, are curious, and but little known to English readers. Though the province of Venezuela, or Caraccas, extends four hundred miles along the coast, and is one of the most fertile in America; it was so much neglected by the Spaniards, that during the twenty years prior to the establishment of the company, only five ships sailed from Spain to that province; and during sixteen years, from 1706 to 1722, not a single ship arrived from the Caraccas in Spain. Noticias de Real Compania de Caraccas, p. 28. During this period, Spain must have been supplied almost entirely with the large quantity of cacao, which it consumes, by foreigners. Before the erection of the company, neither tobacco nor hides were imported from Caraccas into Spain. Id. p 117. Since the commercial operations of the company began in the year 1731, the importation of cacao into Spain has increased amazingly. During thirty years subsequent to 1701, the number of *fanegas* of cacao (each a hundred and ten pounds) imported from Caraccas, was 643,215. During eighteen years subsequent to 1731, the number of *fanegas* imported was 869,247; and if we suppose the importation to be continued in the same proportion during the remainder of thirty years, it will amount to 1,448,746 *fanegas*, which is an increase of 805,531 *fanegas*. Id. p. 148. During eight years subsequent to 1756, there has been imported into Spain by the company 88.482 *arrobas* (each twenty-five pounds) of tobacco, and hides to the number of 177,354. Id. 161. Since the publication of the Noticias de Campania, in 1765, its trade seems to be on the increase. During five years subsequent to 1769, it has imported 179,156 *fanegas* of cacao into Spain, 36,208 arrobas of tobacco, 75,496 hides, and 221,432 pesos in specie. Campomanes, ii. 162 The last article is a proof of the growing wealth of the colony. It receives cash from Mexico in return for the cacao with which it supplies that province, and this it remits to Spain, or lays out in purchasing European goods. But besides this, the most explicit evidence is produced, that the quantity of cacao raised in the province is double to what it yielded in 1731; the number of its live stock is more than treble, and its inhabitants much augmented. The revenue of the bishop, which arises wholly from tithes, has increased from eight to twenty thousand pesos. Notic. p. 69. In consequence of the augmentation of the quantity of cacao imported into Spain, its price has decreased from eighty pesos for the *fanega* to forty. Id. 61. Since the publication of the first edition, I have learned that Guyana, including all the extensive provinces situated on the banks of the Orinoco, the islands of Trinidad and Margarita are added to the countries with which the company of Caraccas had liberty of trade by their former charters. Real Cedula, Nov. 19, 1776. But I have likewise been informed, that the institution of this company has not been attended with all the beneficial effects which I have ascribed to it. In many of its operations the illiberal and oppressive spirit of monopoly is still conspicuous. But in order to explain this, it would be necessary to enter into minute details, which are not suited to the nature of this work.

NOTE CXCII. p. 284.

THIS first experiment made by Spain of opening a free trade with any of her colonies, has produced effects so remarkable, as to merit some farther illustration.

The towns to which this liberty has been granted, are Cadiz and Seville, for the province of Andalusia; Alicant and Carthagena, for Valencia and Murcia; Barcelona, for Catalonia and Aragon; Santander, for Castile; Corugna, for Galicia; and Gijon, for Asturias. Append. ii. à la Educ. Popul. p. 41. These are either the ports of chief trade in their respective districts, or those most conveniently situated for the exportation of their respective productions. The following facts give a view of the increase of trade in the settlements to which the new regulations extend. Prior to the allowance of free trade, the duties collected in the custom-house at the Havannah were computed to be 104,208 pesos annually. During the five years preceding 1774, they rose at a medium to 308,000 pesos a year. In Yucatan, the duties have risen from 8000 to 15,000. In Hispaniola, from 2500 to 5600. In Porto-Rico, from 1200 to 7000. The total value of goods imported from Cuba into Spain, was reckoned, in 1774, to be 1,500,000 pesos. Educ. Popul. i. 450, &c.

NOTE CXCIII. p. 290.

The two Treatises of Don Pedro Rodriguez Campomanes, *Fiscal del real consejo y Supremo* (an office in rank and power nearly similar to that of Attorney-General in England), and Director of the Royal Academy of History, the one intitled Discurso sobre el Fomento de la Industria Popular; the other, Discurso sobre la Educacion Popular de los Artesanos y su Fomento; the former published in 1774, and the latter in 1775, afford a striking proof of this. Almost every point of importance with respect to interior police, taxation, agriculture, manufactures, and trade, domestic as well as foreign, is examined in the course of these works; and there are not many authors, even in the nations most eminent for commercial knowledge, who have carried on their inquiries with a more thorough knowledge of those various subjects, and a more perfect freedom from vulgar and national prejudices, or who have united more happily the calm researches of philosophy, with the ardent zeal of a public-spirited citizen. These books are in high estimation among the Spaniards, and it is a decisive evidence of the progress of their own ideas, that they are capable of relishing an author whose sentiments are so liberal,

NOTE CXCIV. p. 294.

THE galeon employed in that trade, instead of the six hundred tons, to which it is limited by law, Recop. lib. xlv. l. 15. is commonly from twelve hundred to two thousand tons burden. The ship from Acapulco, taken by Lord Anson, instead of the 500,000 pesos permitted by law, had on board 1,313,843 pesos, besides uncoined silver equal in value to 43,611 pesos more. Anson's Voyage, 384.

NOTE CXCV. p. 296.

THE price paid for the bull varies according to the rank of different persons. Those in the lowest order, who are servants or slaves, pay two reals of plate, or one shilling; other Spaniards pay eight reals, and those in public office, or who hold encomiendas, sixteen reals. Solorz. de Jure Ind. vol. ii. lib. iii. c. 25. According to Chilton, an English merchant who resided long in the Spanish settlements, the bull of Cruzado bore an higher price in the year 1570, being then sold for four reals at the lowest. Hakluyt, iii. 461. The price seems to have varied at different periods. That exacted for the bulls issued in the last *Predicacion*, will appear from the ensuing table, which will give some idea of the proportional numbers of the different classes of citizens in New Spain and Peru.

There were issued for New Spain,

Bulls at 10 pesos each	- - -	4
at 2 pesos each	- - -	22,601
at 1 peso each	- -	164,220
at 2 reals each	- - -	2,462,500
		2,649,325

For Peru,

at 16 pesos 4½ reals each	-	3
at 3 pesos 3 reals each	- -	14,202
at 1 peso 5½ reals	- -	78,822
at 4 reals	- - -	410,325
at 3 reals	- - -	668,601
		1,171,953

NOTE CXCVI. p. 297.

As Villa Segnor, to whom we are indebted for this information, contained in his Theatro Americano, published in Mexico, A. D. 1746, was accomptant-general in one of the most considerable departments of the royal revenue, and by that means had access to proper information, his testimony with respect to this point merits great credit. No such accurate detail of the Spanish revenues in any part of America has hitherto been published in the English language, and the particulars of it may appear curious and interesting to some of my readers.

From the bull of Cruzado, published every two years, there arises an annual revenue in pesos,	140,000
From the duty on silver	700,000
From the duty on gold	60,000
From tax on cards	70,000
From tax on Pulque, a drink used by the Indians	161,000
From tax on stamped paper	41,000
From ditto on ice	15,522
From ditto on leather	2,500
From ditto on gunpowder	71,550
From ditto on salt	32,000
From ditto on copper of Mechocan	1,000
From ditto on alum	6,500
From ditto on Juega de los gallos	21,100
From the half of ecclesiastical annats	49,000
From royal ninths of bishoprics, &c.	68,800
From the tribute of Indians	650,000
From Alcavala, or duty on sale of goods	721,875
From the Almajorifasgo, customhouse	373,333
From the mint	357,500
	3,552,680

This sum amounts to 819,161l. Sterling; and if we add to it the profit accruing from the sale of 5000 quintals of quicksilver, imported from the mines of Almaden, in Spain, on the king's account, and what accrues from the Averia, and some other taxes which Villa Segnor does not estimate, the public revenue in New Spain may well be reckoned above a million pounds Sterling money. Theat. Mex. vol. i. p. 38, &c. According to Villa Seg-

G g 2

nor, the total produce of the Mexican mines amounts at
a medium to eight millions of pesos in siver annually,
and to 5912 marks of gold. Ib. p. 44. Several branches
of the revenue have been explained in the course of the
history : some, which there was no occasion of mentioning, require a particular illustration. The right to the
titbes in the New World is vested in the crown of Spain,
by a bull of Alexander VI. Charles V. appointed them
to be applied in the following manner : One fourth is allotted to the bishop of the diocese, another fourth to the
dean and chapter, and other officers of the cathedral. The
remaining half is divided into nine equal parts. Two of
these, under the denomination of *los dos Novenos reales*, are
paid to the crown, and constitute a branch of the royal revenue. The other seven parts are applied to the maintenance of the parochial clergy, the building and support of
churches, and other pious uses. Recopil. lib. i. tit. xvi.
Ley. 23, &c. Avendano Thesaur. Indic. vol. i. p. 184.

The *Alcavala* is a duty levied by an excise on the sale
of goods. In Spain it amounts to ten per cent. In
America, to four per cent. Solorzano Polit. Indiana,
lib. vi. c. 8. Avendano, vol. i. 186.

The *Almajorifasgo*, or custom paid in America on
goods imported and exported, may amount on an ave-
rage to fifteen per cent. Recopil. lib. viii. tit. xiv.
Ley. 1. Avendano, vol. i. 188.

The *Averia*, or tax paid on account of convoys to guard
the ships sailing to and from America, was first imposed
when Sir Francis Drake filled the New World with terror by his expedition to the South Sea. It amounts to
two per cent. on the value of goods. Avendano, vol. i.
p. 189. Recopil. lib. ix. tit. ix. Ley. 43, 44.

I have not been able to procure any accurate detail of
the several branches of revenue in Peru, later than the
year 1614. From a curious manuscript, containing a
state of that viceroyalty in all its departments, presented to the Marquis of Montes Clares by Fran. Lopes Caravantes, accomptant-general in the tribunal of Lima,
it appears that the public revenue, as nearly as I can
compute the value of the money in which Caravantes
states his accounts, amounted in ducats at 4s. 11d.

to	2,372,768
Expences of government	1,242,992
Net free revenue (Carry over)	1,129,776

Net free revenue　(Brought over)　1,129,776

The total in Sterling money　-	£. 583,303
Expences of government　-　-	305,568

Net free revenue　-　£. 277,735

But several articles appear to be omitted in this computation, such as the duty on stamped paper, leather, ecclesiastical annats, &c. so that the revenue of Peru may be well supposed equal to that of Mexico.

In computing the expence of government in New Spain, I may take that of Peru as a standard. There the annual establishment for defraying the charge of administration exceeds one half of the revenue collected, and there is no reason for supposing it to be less in New Spain.

I have obtained a calculation of the total amount of the public revenue of Spain from America and the Philippines, which, as the reader will perceive from the two last articles, is more recent than any of the former.

Alcavalas (Excise) and Aduanas (Customs). &c. in pesos fuertes　.　-	2,500,000
Duties on gold and silver,　-　-	3,000,000
Bull of Cruzado,　-　-　-	1,000,000
Tribute of the Indians　-　-　-	2,000,000
By sale of quicksilver　-　-　-	300,000
Paper exported on the king's account, and sold in the royal warehouses　.　-	300,000
Stamped paper, tobacco, and other small duties	1,000,000
Duty on the coinage of, at the rate of one real de la Plata for each mark　-	300,000
From the trade of Acapulco, and the coasting trade from province to province　-	500,000
Assiento of negroes　-　.　-	200,000
From the trade of *Mathé*, or herb of Paraguay, formerly monopolized by the Jesuits	500,000
From other revenues formerly belonging to that order　-　-　-　-	400,000

Total　-　12,000,000

Total in Sterling money　£. 2,700,000

Deduct half, as the expence of administration, and there remains net free revenue　-　£. 1,350,000

G g 3

NOTE CXCVII. p. 297.

An author, long conversant in commercial speculation, has computed, that from the mines of New Spain alone, the king receives annually, as his fifth, the sum of two millions of our money. Harris Collect. of Voy. ii. p. 164. According to this calculation, the total produce of the mines must be ten millions Sterling; a sum so exorbitant, and so little corresponding with all accounts of the annual importation from America, that the information on which it is founded must evidently be erroneous. According to Campomanes, the total product of the American mines may be computed at thirty millions of pesos, which, at four shillings and sixpence a peso, amounts to 7,425,000l. Sterling, the king's fifth of which (if that were regularly paid) would be 1,485,000l. But from this sum must be deducted what is lost by a fraudulent withholding of the fifth due to the crown, as well as the sum necessary for defraying the expence of administration. Educ. Popular. vol. ii. p. 131. note. Both these sums are considerable.

NOTE CXCVIII. p. 297.

According to Bern. de Ulloa, all foreign goods exported from Spain to America pay duties of various kinds, amounting in all to more than 25 per cent. As most of the goods with which Spain supplies her colonies are foreign, such a tax upon a trade so extensive must yield a considerable revenue. Retablis. de Manuf. & du Commerce d'Esp. p. 150. He computes the value of goods exported annually from Spain to America, to be about two millions and a half Sterling, p. 97.

NOTE CXCIX. p. 299.

The Marquis de Serralvo, according to Gage, by a monopoly of salt, and by embarking deeply in the Manila trade as well as in that to Spain, gained annually a million of ducats. In one year he remitted a million of ducats to Spain, in order to purchase from the Condé Olivares, and his creatures, a prolongation of his government, p. 61. He was successful in his suit, and continued in office from 1624 to 1635, double the usual time.

INDEX.

H h 3

END OF THE THIRD VOLUME.

Check Out More Titles From HardPress Classics Series In this collection we are offering thousands of classic and hard to find books. This series spans a vast array of subjects – so you are bound to find something of interest to enjoy reading and learning about.

Subjects:
Architecture
Art
Biography & Autobiography
Body, Mind &Spirit
Children & Young Adult
Dramas
Education
Fiction
History
Language Arts & Disciplines
Law
Literary Collections
Music
Poetry
Psychology
Science
…and many more.

Visit us at www.hardpress.net

CPSIA information can be obtained
at www.ICGtesting.com
Printed in the USA
BVHW081813120819

555665BV00015B/1432/P